# Contents

ACADEMIC PRESS, INC.
111 Fifth Avenue, New York, New York 10003

*United Kingdom Edition published by*
ACADEMIC PRESS, INC. (LONDON) LTD.
24/28 Oval Road, London NW1 7DX

**Library of Congress Cataloging in Publication Data**

Main entry under title:

Psychobiology of stress.

    (Behavioral biology series)
    Includes bibliographies.
    1. Stress (Physiology) 2. Parachuting--Physiologi-
cal aspects. 3. Psychobiology. 4. Norway. Haeren--
Parachute troops. I. Ursin, Holger. II. Baade,
Eivind. III. Levine, Seymour. IV. Series.
[DNLM: 1. Stress, Psychological--Physiology.
2. Psychophysiology. 3. Parachuting. 4. Aviation
medicine. 5. Military medicine. 6. Psychology,
Military. 7. Hormones--Physiology. WD730 P974]
QP82.2.S8P79   612'.042      78–8119
ISBN 0–12–709250–1

PRINTED IN THE UNITED STATES OF AMERICA

# Psychobiology
# of Stress A Study of Coping Men

Edited by

## HOLGER URSIN

*Institute of Psychology*
*University of Bergen*
*Bergen, Norway*

## EIVIND BAADE

*Psychological Services of the Norwegian Armed Forces*
*Oslo, Norway*

## SEYMOUR LEVINE

*Department of Psychiatry and Behavioral Sciences*
*Stanford University School of Medicine*
*Stanford, California*

ACADEMIC PRESS
New York   San Francisco   London   1978
*A Subsidiary of Harcourt Brace Jovanovich, Publishers*

# Psychobiology
## of Stress A Study of Coping Men

# BEHAVIORAL BIOLOGY

## AN INTERNATIONAL SERIES

*Series editors*

**James L. McGaugh**

*Department of Psychobiology*
*University of California*
*Irvine, California*

**John C. Fentress**

*Department of Psychology*
*Dalhousie University*
*Halifax, Canada*

**Joseph P. Hegman**

*Department of Zoology*
*The University of Iowa*
*Iowa City, Iowa*

Holger Ursin, Eivind Baade, and Seymour Levine (Editors),Psychobiology of Stress: A Study of Coping Men

*In Preparation*

William W. Grings and Michael E. Dawson, Emotions and Bodily Responses: A Psychophysiological Approach

Enoch Callaway, Patricia Tueting, and Stephen H. Koslow (Editors), Event-Related Brain Potentials in Man

Larry L. Butcher (Editor), Cholinergic-Monoaminergic Interactions in the Brain

**Contents**

# List of Contributors

Numbers in parentheses indicate the pages on which the authors' contributions begin.

ANNA ATTERÅS (99), *Institute of Psychology, University of Bergen, Bergen, Norway*

EIVIND BAADE (125, 163), *Psychological Services of the Norwegian Armed Forces, Oslo Mil, Akershus, Oslo, Norway*

ARNOLDUS SCHYTTE BLIX (23, 41, 63, 83),* *Institute of Medical Biology, Section of Physiology, University of Tromsø, Tromsø, Norway*

JULIAN M. DAVIDSON (57), *Department of Physiology, Stanford University, Stanford, California 94305*

ROLF EIDE (99), *Institute of Psychology, University of Bergen, Bergen, Norway*

BJØRN ELLERTSEN (41, 105, 125, 163), *Institute of Psychology, University of Bergen, Bergen, Norway*

KRISTIAN HALSE (41, 125), *Psychological Services of the Norwegian Armed Forces, Oslo Mil, Akershus, Oslo, Norway*

JAN R. HANSEN (63), *Hormone Laboratory, University of Bergen School of Medicine, Bergen, Norway*

*Present address: Institute of Arctic Biology, University of Alaska, Fairbanks, Alaska 99701.

xi

TOM BACKER JOHNSEN *(35, 105, 125, 163), Institute of Psychology, University of Bergen, Bergen, Norway*

SEYMOUR LEVINE *(3, 51, 57), Department of Psychiatry and Behavioral Sciences, Stanford University School of Medicine, Stanford, California 94305*

KAARE NORUM *(75), Institute for Nutrition Research, School of Medicine, University of Oslo, Oslo, Norway*

SVEIN ROSSELAND *(23), Norwegian Army Medical Service, Trandum, Norway*

ERLA R. SMITH *(57), Department of Physiology, Stanford University, Stanford, California 94305*

PER ERIK STENHAMMER *(125), IFH-Research International A/S, P.O. Box 4375, Torshov, Oslo, Norway*

KARL F. STØA *(63), Hormone Laboratory, University of Bergen School of Medicine, Bergen, Norway*

SIGMUND B. STRØMME *(83), Laboratory of Physiology, Norwegian College of Physical Education and Sport, P.O. Box 40, Kringsjaa, Oslo, Norway*

HOLGER URSIN *(3, 23, 41, 63, 75, 83, 91, 105, 125, 163, 201), Institute of Psychology, University of Bergen, Bergen, Norway*

FRED VOLLMER *(125, 183), Institute of Psychology, University of Bergen, Bergen, Norway*

JOANNE WEINBERG *(3), Department of Psychiatry and Behavioral Sciences, Stanford University School of Medicine, Stanford, California 94305*

ELLIOT D. WEITZMAN *(91), Department of Neurology, Montefiore Hospital and Medical Center, Bronx, New York, and The Albert Einstein College of Medicine, Bronx, New York*

PER C. WIKEBY *(83),* † *Laboratory of Physiology, Norwegian College of Physical Education and Sport, P.O. Box 40, Kringsjaa, Oslo, Norway*

†Present address: Neurosurgical Department, National Hospital of Norway, University Hospital, Oslo, Norway.

# Preface

In an attempt to assess the physiological consequences to man of environmental events investigators have measured many different variables. When the environmental event is defined as being stressful, the physiological variables that are measured usually involve either some output of the pituitary–adrenal system or some function of an autonomic system. Under most circumstances a very limited number of physiological measurements are used to determine the effects of environmental perturbations, and further, the physiological measurements usually represent the effects of experience with a single event. However, when one examines the literature concerning the physiological effects of stressful events it becomes apparent that (a) there are marked individual differences, and (b) an event that appears to be stressful to an organism initially, may, upon repeated exposures, no longer elicit the same behavioral reactions or physiological responses.

The study reported in this volume uses a psychobiological approach emphasizing behavioral, neuroendocrine, and autonomic responses to a controlled, stressful situation—parachute training—and follows these responses as the individual continues to be exposed to the same environmental situation. The rationale for these studies, therefore, is that if psychoendocrine and autonomic measurements are sensitive indices of emotional responses, and if emotional responses change as a consequence of repeated experience, then these changes should also be detectable in any given individual as he gains experience with the dimensions of the stressful events.

The primary purpose of this book is to present results of an extensive study of the dynamics of the stress response in a population of healthy adult males. It is apparent that the data from these studies could also have been reported in various scientific journals. However, after much discussion it became apparent that two of the most interesting findings—relationship between psychological processes and physiological responses, and the interrelationships among physiological systems—would be obscured, if not lost, if the results were presented in a fragmented fashion.

We believe that in order to understand stress it is no longer sufficient to deal only with environmental events that activate the physiological systems which regulate stress responses. In this book we have, therefore, attempted to deal with psychological processes that ultimately inhibit the physiological responses to stress. Stress is a fact of life; contemporary man cannot eliminate it nor do we believe this would be a desirable goal. Perhaps the key to successful adaptation lies in the organism's capacity to evaluate and respond appropriately to his or her environment. Hopefully we have presented an interesting theoretical model and data of equivalent interest so that the information contained in this book is of broad interest and concern to psychologists, biologists, medical practitioners, and all others whose concern is with the ultimate well-being of man.

### Acknowledgments

The experiments described in this book were carried out at the Norwegian Army Parachute Training School. They were made possible through cooperation with the Joint Medical Services and Armed Forces of Norway and the staff of the Norwegian Army Parachute Training School itself.

In particular, we want to express our sincere gratitude to Major General A. Johnsen, Surgeon General, Joint Medical Services, Armed Forces, Norway, and Colonel J. Nærup, Surgeon General, Norwegian Army, for help on logistics and permits. We also want to thank Lieutenant Å. Roel, who served as Administration Officer during the field studies, beyond the bounds of duty.

The entire staff and every enlisted soldier of the Norwegian Army Parachute Training School supported our investigation in every possible way. We would particularly like to emphasize the outstanding patience and skill of Lieutenant Colonel T. Strand, head of the school.

We received help from many individuals during the analyses and the preparation of this volume. Laborant Aase Larsen, Institute of Psychology, University of Bergen, assisted during both the field phase and laboratory stage of the work. Major Andreas Hauge and Liv Skarstein prepared our figures, and the photographic work was done by Ragnar Jensen and Rune Haakonsen.

The staff of the University of Bergen library was very helpful and, in particular, we want to thank Jorunn Birkelund and Ester Bru Baum for their assistance.

The subject matter was discussed with many colleagues, and it is impossible to mention all of them. We will only mention two students from the Institute of Psychology, University of Bergen, Gunnar Karoliussen and Lise Næss, whose comments and analyses of the defense mechanisms were particularly useful, but we appreciate the many helpful comments of our unnamed colleagues.

We want to extend our deepest gratitude to Rosemary Gutt and Turid Mattsson, who although working on opposite sides of the ocean, somehow maintained both their and our sanity throughout the typing, retyping, reference choosing, and other tedious related tasks that are so essential for the ultimate successful completion of any book.

In light of the general topic and conclusions of this book, we would like to emphasize that there was much work involved for the authors, editors, and collaborators. But it was also a lot of fun and well worth the effort.

H. U.
E. B.
S. L.

*Part I*

# EXPERIMENT AND METHOD

# 1

# Definition of the Coping Process and Statement of the Problem[1]

SEYMOUR LEVINE, JOANNE WEINBERG,
and HOLGER URSIN

> "Courage is resistance to fear, mastery of fear, not absence of fear."
> —Mark Twain

This book is a report covering an extensive investigation of behavioral and physiological parameters following repeated exposure to a distinctly threatening situation. The purpose of the study was to examine whether mastery of fear took place, what behavioral and personality variables affected its ultimate accomplishment, and whether detectable biological changes occurred as a consequence of this mastery.

The concept of mastery of fear stated in the introductory quotation by Mark Twain is, in essence, the basis of the concept of coping. However, before we can describe the coping process we must examine and come to grips with the very basic problems that are inherent in the definition of stress. The concepts of stress and coping have both occupied key positions in psychological and physiological theorizing. These concepts are basic to individual organismic survival. It is therefore not surprising that there is a great amount of literature on the problems of coping with stress. However,

[1]S. Levine was supported by USPHS Research Scientist Award K5-MH-19936 from the National Institute of Mental Health.

3

although the concept of stress has been in extensive use for at least three decades, its definition is still elusive.

In recent years there have been attempts to resolve the issue of the primary stimuli that elicit the endocrine and autonomic responses designated as stress. In his early theorizing on stress, Selye emphasized the nonspecific quality of the stimuli that elicit these responses. Several authors have attacked this nonspecificity notion and have attempted to arrive at some resolution as to what these stimuli actually are. Mason (1975) has reevaluated the nonspecificity concept and stress theory. He pointed out that, in the initial formulation of Selye's stress theory, there was no clear "afferent limb." In the final annual report on stress that appeared in 1956, Selye himself indicated some awareness of this issue, stating that nothing was known about the nature of the mediator that ultimately released adrenocorticotropic hormone (ACTH). It should be noted that at that time the primary emphasis was on ACTH and the pituitary–adrenal system. In subsequent years many other hormones in addition to ACTH have been implicated as being responsive to stress. Among these are catecholamines, prolactin, growth hormone, and luteinizing hormone (with its subsequent effects on testosterone). In fact, some of these systems actually appear to be even more responsive to stress than ACTH. Furthermore, Mason has suggested that the primary mediator for hormonal release may be the psychological factors involved in the emotional or arousal reactions to threatening and unpleasant events in life situations. In a review of his own research, Mason pointed out that, when the psychologically threatening or arousing aspects of a situation were altered, classical stresses such as fasting and heat no longer activated the pituitary–adrenal system; in the case of heat, there was in fact a reduction in the circulating hormones. This type of evidence supports the suggestion that the apparent nonspecificity of the stimuli that activate the pituitary–adrenal system is actually due to the psychological factors underlying the situation; that is, whether the situation is in itself psychologically unpleasant or threatening. Whether this is true for other hormones released in response to stress remains to be determined.

Other work has revealed another interesting aspect of pituitary–adrenal responsiveness. It appears that the pituitary–adrenal system not only responds to classical, aversive stimulation, but also is responsive to changes in environmental contingencies involving changes in expectancies. The pituitary–adrenal system has been shown to be bidirectional in the sense that environmental changes can either rapidly elevate or rapidly suppress this system. Whether other hormonal systems are also bidirectional has not yet been demonstrated.

In a series of experiments (Coover, Goldman, & Levine, 1971) animals were trained to work for food. When they reached a stable level of performance, that is, lever pressing, an extinction procedure was initiated by eliminating the food reward. Elevations in plasma corticoids as high as those seen in response to noxious stimuli were observed. However, in a subsequent experiment, if the response was prevented by removing the lever, but food was continually delivered, there was a significant suppression of the level of circulating corticoids (Davis, Memmott, Macfadden, & Levine, 1976). In yet another experiment by Levine and Coover (1976) it was shown that when animals were chronically maintained on a food or water deprivation schedule there was a change in the circadian rhythmicity of plasma corticoids such that an elevation in the levels of circulating corticosterone occurred just prior to the feeding or watering time. When the animals were then given either food or water, or stimuli associated with food or water, such as an empty drinking tube, there was a rapid suppression of pituitary–adrenal activity. The data from these studies suggest that, when a set of predictable events is altered so that expectancies are no longer met, this change leads to activation of an arousal system that subsequently results in increased pituitary–adrenal activity and, eventually, to a new set of expectancies. Changes from predictable to unpredictable events, which thus increase ambiguity, are a sufficient condition to cause increases in pituitary–adrenal activity. An animal that has been functioning in a random, ambiguous situation does not appear to respond to a shift in predictability since it apparently has never developed expectancies within a given framework of stimulus contingencies (Levine, Goldman, & Coover, 1972). On the other hand, if expectancies are fulfilled or even if only the cues associated with reinforcement are presented, suppression of the pituitary–adrenal system occurs.

The processes producing neuroendocrine activation from changes in expectancies are best explained by a model elaborated by Sokolov (1960) to account for the general process of habituation. The pattern of habituation is well known. A subject is presented with an unexpected stimulus, and it shows an alerting or orienting reaction. The physiological components of this reaction have been well established—a general activation of the brain, cardiovascular changes, changes in the electrical resistance of the skin, and an increase in circulating adrenal corticoids. If this stimulus is repeated frequently, all of these reactions gradually diminish and eventually disappear, and the subject is said to be habituated. Sokolov's model is in essence based on a matching system in which the organism matches immediate events with a central nervous system representation of prior events. This matching process can be defined as the development of expectancies (Gray, 1975; Pribram & Melges, 1969). Thus, the habituated organism has a set of prior expectancies with which to deal with the environment, and if the environment does not contain any new contingencies the organism will no longer show physiological responses related to arousal. *Habituation* is usually defined in terms of a response to relatively neutral stimuli that initially cause arousal but are not themselves intrinsically aversive or life-threatening. Most organisms, however, live in an environment that involves repeated aversive stimulation; yet clearly organisms do not respond continually to these stimuli. This fact has led to the development of the concept of coping. *Coping* differs from habituation in that the stimuli that elicit the coping response continue to be threatening and aversive but the organism no longer responds to them; this is in contrast to the process of habituation where the stimuli themselves are relatively neutral. How, then, does an organism deal with continually threatening stimuli and suppress the responses to these stimuli?

Before any further discussion of coping can occur it seems necessary to revise the stress theory prevalent in current medical and psychological literature where stress is still defined according to the early theories of Selye (1956). We believe that much of the controversy over stress theory can be eliminated by clarification of the "afferent limb," that is, by focusing on the nature of the stimuli that provoke physiological responses, rather than by focusing primarily on the physiological responses themselves. This requires an unusual integration of physiology and psychology, disciplines that tend to be traditionally separated, and puts the emphasis on the psychological variables. However, even if we accept the hypothesis that psychological factors are the prepotent stimulators of the response to stress, we believe that there are, in fact, complicated psychological mechanisms involved in determining whether an individual does or does not respond to a specific situation. It appears that it is not just the stimuli or physical environment per se that determines the physiological response, but the individual's evaluation of these stimuli. This may be regarded as a filter or gating function. Thus, if the organism evaluates the situation as threatening and uncertain, there will be a continuing high level of activation. However, if the organism evaluates the situation as being safe and one in which he can master the probable events, the resulting physiological response will be diminished, if not absent, even though the situation itself had been extremely threatening.

## COPING

To some extent, a definition of coping is almost as elusive as a definition of stress. Coping has been inferred either by alterations in behavior or by changes in the physiological response to threatening or aversive stimulation. The concept has been used to denote all of the mechanisms utilized by an individual to meet a significant threat to his psychological stability and to enable him to function effectively (Hamburg, Hamburg, & de Goza, 1953). Most of the major theories of coping with regard to humans have concerned themselves with alterations in behavior. An individual is presumed to be coping if his behavior consists of responses to environmental factors that help him master the situation. Coping also includes the intrapsychic processes that contribute to successful adaptation to a psychological stress (Friedman, Mason, & Hamburg, 1963). The success or failure of this coping behavior may be evaluated in at least two ways:

1. A judgment can be made as to whether the behavior allows the individual to carry out certain personally or socially defined goals and to tolerate the stressful situation without disruptive anxiety or depression, regardless of whether the behavior is socially desirable.
2. Changes in internal states can be evaluated by monitoring changes in hormone levels. For example, cortisol excretion rates appear to be stable if the coping behavior is effective in protecting the individual from anxiety and depression (Friedman et al., 1963). Interestingly, both pathological and socially desirable coping patterns can effect these changes.

With regard to changes in the physiological response it is necessary to distinguish among the various mechanisms that ultimately result in a reduction in the physiological response to threatening or anxiety-producing situations. We believe that part of the problem with the coping concept has been the confusion of these different strategies. Lazarus, Averill, and Opton (1974) define coping as follows.

[Coping involves] problem-solving efforts made by an individual when the demands he faces are highly relevant to his welfare (that is, a situation of considerable jeopardy or promise) and when these demands tax his adaptive resources. Such a definition does several things: First, it emphasizes the importance of the emotional context in coping; second, it allows inclusion of both the negative or stress side of emotion as well as the positive side of potential fulfillment or gratification; third, it recognizes the overlap between problem solving and coping; and fourth, it emphasizes tasks that are not routine or automatized, that is, those in which the outcome is uncertain and in which the limits of the individual's adaptive skill are approached [pp. 250–251].

The critical aspect of the definition of Lazarus et al. within the context of this discussion is the problem-solving element; that is, an individual is faced with a reality or a threat, and coping ultimately occurs as a consequence of the individual's mastering the situation. An alternative approach to that of Lazarus et al. focuses not on adaptability or problem solving but rather on defense mechanisms that do not involve problem solving. Such defense mechanisms have also been shown to reduce arousal. However, when they do not reduce physiological arousal they cannot be considered effective coping strategies. It is this difference in the efficacy of defense mechanisms that causes much of the disagreement among investigators. If our basic hypothesis is correct, an effective cognitive defense should reduce arousal since it should alter the way an individual evaluates a threat. This should hold even if a particular defense mechanism does not represent the best possible way of coping with the threat from an objective point of view. The important thing appears to be the subjective evaluation of the situation.

In principle, defense mechanisms have been evaluated with two different scales or methods. Defensive styles may be evaluated by scales from the Minnesota Multiphasic Personality Inventory (MMPI); the scales used are the L, K, Hy–Dn (Denial of Symptoms), and R–S (Repression–Sensitization). Alternatively, one can evaluate defense mechanisms by projective techniques or interviews. These two methods have yielded different results.

Repressive and denying defenses on the MMPI scale are related to a low level of self-reported anxiety, but the physiological reactivity is high (Dykman, Reese, Galbrecht, & Thomasson, 1959; Lazarus & Alfert, 1964). This yields support for the psychoanalytic ideas of Dunbar (1954) and Alexander (1950). Dunbar states that effects that are not discharged in action tend to persist and to be followed by physiological changes (for instance, disturbed endocrine balance). By our way of thinking, the important point is whether or not the underlying conflict and the threat are reduced, and to what extent the subject evaluates his own coping strategy as being effective. If repressive and denial defenses consistently relate to high physiological reactivity, this is a signal that the underlying conflict is not reduced; therefore, these strategies are inadequate. When defense mechanisms are evaluated by projective techniques or interviews, there is also a low level of self-reported anxiety in subjects with defense mechanisms of the repressing or denial type. However, in these situations, the physiological reactivity is also low (Friedman et al., 1963; Price, Thaler, & Mason, 1957). In this case, we would suggest that the low level of physiological reactivity indicates that these strategies represent effective coping. It is obvious that these two methods of evaluation cannot measure the same phenomena (Levine & Spivack, 1964).

Weinstein, Averill, Opton, and Lazarus (1968) investigated the relationship between defensive style as evaluated by the MMPI scales and the discrepancies between self-report and autonomic indexes of "stress" resulting from observing a threatening film. They used a system developed by Byrne (1964) for classifying defense mechanisms along an axis, with "sensitizers" (or people able to express their anxieties easily) at one extreme and "repressors" (or people who deny their anxieties) at the other. They found that "repressors" showed relatively greater autonomic than self-report responses, whereas "sensitizers" tended to show the opposite pattern of response. The results were due primarily to the influence of defensive style on the self-reports. Thus, it appears that a defensive style that allows for alteration of the evaluation of a threat provides an effective strategy for coping. This subjective evaluation of threat is the important parameter; the particular defense mechanism employed is relatively unimportant.

There is still another approach to the concept of coping that has been discussed in the literature on animals. This approach examines the effects of psychological variables in stressful situations. The general procedure consists of exposing two or more animals to the same physical stressor while maintaining the subjects in different psychological states. When this is done, any difference that results from the treatment must be attributed to the psychological differences between the conditions since the physical stressor is the same. It appears that psychological factors are often more important in influencing certain outcomes than physical stimuli themselves, even if those stimuli are intense and noxious. The psychological variables that have been studied most often are those related to controllability and predictability of stress, the ability to perform appropriate responses during stress, and the previous experience of the organism in relation to these factors.

In a series of four studies, Weiss (1970) examined the effects of predictability on a variety of stress responses such as stomach ulceration, plasma corticosterone concentrations, and body weight changes. Animals receiving unpredictable shocks showed greater somatic stress reactions and more stress-induced pathology than animals receiving the same amount of predictable shock. Thus, the same physical stressor had different consequences depending on the psychological variable of predictability. Gliner (1972) also found that signaled or predictable shock was less disruptive in terms of somatic reactions to stress. In this case, rats were given a choice for predictable or unpredictable shock; animals chose predictable shock and developed fewer ulcers under this condition than animals not given this choice and receiving the same amount of shock unpredictably. Other investigators have shown this same phenomenon: When given a choice, humans, like animals, will choose signaled rather than unsignaled shock, even when no escape from shock is possible (Arabian & Desiderato, 1975; Averill, 1973; Badia & Culbertson, 1972; Badia, Culbertson, & Harsh, 1974; Lockard, 1963; Seligman, Maier, & Solomon, 1971). In fact, it has been observed that animals will choose signaled shock that is four to nine times longer and two to three times more intense than unsignaled shock (Badia, Culbertson, & Harsh, 1973; Harsh & Badia, 1975).

Two hypotheses have been proposed to account for this preference for signaled shock. The *preparatory response hypothesis* states that a warning signal provides information to subjects that permits them to make a preparatory response, either peripherally or centrally, which reduces the aversiveness of shock (Perkins, 1968). The *safety-signal hypothesis* (also called the "safe–unsafe" hypothesis) states that the effect of the signal is primarily a psychological one in that it identifies shock-free periods and thus acquires reinforcing properties (Badia & Culbertson, 1972; Badia, Culbertson, & Lewis, 1971; Badia et al., 1973; Lockard, 1963; Seligman, 1968; Seligman & Meyer, 1970). Predictable shock is thus preferred because it reliably predicts absence of shock. During shock-free periods subjects can relax their preparations for shock. Without the signal, fear is chronic and therefore more aversive. Both behavioral and physiological indexes of fear have supported this hypothesis.

In addition to the predictability of shock, the variable of escapability is another important factor. It has been observed that pretreatment of an animal with inescapable shock severely impairs learning compared to pretreatment with the same amount of escapable shock (e.g., Osborne, Mattingly, Redmon, & Osborne, 1975). A theoretical formulation known as "learned helplessness" has been devised to explain this finding. The phenomenon was first described in dogs (Maier, Seligman, & Solomon, 1969; Overmier & Seligman, 1967; Seligman & Groves, 1970). Dogs receiving inescapable shock in a Pavlovian harness were found to have severe performance deficits when later tested for escape–avoidance behavior in a shuttlebox. Most of the dogs sat passively and took the shock. Occasionally a dog would jump the barrier and escape, but would then revert to failing to escape. It was proposed that organisms exposed to inescapable and unavoidable shocks learned that shock termination was independent of their behavior. Such learning then interfered with subsequent formation of an association (or perception of a relation) between responding and shock termination even if the shocks became escapable. Furthermore, the incentive to even attempt escape in the presence of shock was also reduced. This phenomenon has since been found in humans (Seligman, 1975), in cats (Seward & Humphrey, 1967), and in rats (Baker, 1976; Looney & Cohen, 1972; Maier & Testa, 1975; Maier, Albin, & Testa, 1973; Seligman & Beagley, 1975; Seligman, Rosellini, & Kozak, 1975). Similar results have also been found using tests other than avoidance responding. For example, Osborne et al. (1975) measured classically conditioned fear and showed that animals exposed to inescapable shock showed more fear than those exposed to escapable shock. In addition, it has been found that helplessness transfers across different aversive motivational states (Rosellini & Seligman, 1975) and that an animal can become "immunized" against helplessness by exposure to escapable shock prior to exposure to inescapable shock (Seligman et al., 1975). Thus, we can summarize by stating that a psychological factor such as inescapability versus escapability of shock can change the organism's response in later tasks such that it will fail to escape and will have difficulty learning to escape even when a response accidentally occurs and is followed by shock offset.

Weiss and his co-workers found the same effects of inescapable shock on later avoidance learning but proposed an alternative hypothesis to explain the results (Glazer & Weiss, 1976a,b; Glazer, Weiss, Pohorecky, & Miller, 1975; Weiss & Glazer, 1975; Weiss, Glazer, Pohorecky, Brick, & Miller, 1975). Briefly, their explanation states that high intensity inescapable shocks do indeed produce deficits in later performance, but that these deficits are temporary and can be explained by the *"motor activation deficit hypothesis."* This hypothesis attributes the deficits to temporary depletion of norepinephrine in the brain. As a consequence of this norepinephrine depletion, animals can mediate only a limited amount of motor activity, an amount insufficient for learning and performance of the correct responses in the shuttlebox task in which they were tested. Lower levels of inescapable shock produced a long-term escape–avoidance deficit, and it was proposed that this was due to learned competing motor responses; that is, the animals learned to be inactive during shock. Under Weiss's conditions, when such animals were then tested on an avoidance task that required very little movement their performance was in fact facilitated. Whether Weiss or Seligman provides the better theoretical framework for explaining why deficits occur, there is no doubt that inescapable shock produces much more severe learning deficits than similar amounts of escapable shock.

One additional psychological variable that has a significant influence on the response to noxious stimuli is the ability to perform a coping response. Weiss (1968) observed that rats that were able to press a lever to avoid shock showed less severe physiological disturbances (e.g., weight loss, gastric lesions) than yoked controls that were not permitted to respond, even though both groups received the same amount of shock. According to Weiss (1971a,b,c), the amount of stress an animal actually experiences when exposed to noxious stimuli depends upon (a) the number of coping attempts the animal makes and (b) the amount of relevant feedback (stimuli occurring after a response and not associated with the stressor) that these coping attempts produce. As the number of coping attempts increases and/or the amount of relevant feedback decreases, the amount of stress experienced increases. Thus, in a series of studies it was demonstrated that if two groups of animals were subjected to the same amount of shock, the aversive effects of that shock were ameliorated if (a) the animal could respond, that is, avoid or escape rather than be yoked ("helpless"), and/or (b) the situation was signaled, by either a warning signal preceding shock or a feedback signal following shock.

We are still faced with the problem as to what are the criteria that define coping in an aversive situation. There has been considerable confusion concerning the best index of coping. The primary emphasis in the literature on humans has been on behavioral responses, whereas, in the animal literature, coping has been defined both in behavioral terms and in physiological terms. For the most part, the behavioral changes and physiological changes are consistent, as in the avoidance conditioning studies reported by Coover *et al.* (1973). However, there are situations in which the behavioral and physiological indexes of coping can be dissociated, and this dissociation does indeed create problems in definition. In two studies it has been shown that what might be considered inappropriate coping behavior does still lead to a reduction of the physiological response. For example, in an avoidance conditioning situation (Weinberg, 1977) in which nonlearners were compared with animals that learned, no differences in the pattern of the plasma corticoid response were observed. While nonlearning can be considered inappropriate coping *behavior,* nevertheless the same reduction in plasma corticoid levels occurred in the nonlearners as in the learners. This reduction in the physiological response can be interpreted as indicating that even though the animals did not avoid the electric shock, given the fact that they did escape and that the escape terminated the CS, there was a sufficient feedback signal to permit reduction of physiological arousal. In another study where animals were permitted only to escape but not to avoid electric shock, and no signal was given (Davis, Porter, Livingstone, Herrmann, Mac-Fadden, & Levine, 1977), a reduction in plasma corticosterone still occurred, but only after significantly more trials. Thus, when animals could make an appropriate response, even though they could not avoid the electric shock, a change in physiological arousal occurred.

In a series of studies examining the influence of brain lesions on the development of coping (Coover, Ursin, & Levine, 1974) this dissociation between behavioral and physiological indexes of coping again occurred. It was shown that rats with lesions restricted to the cingulate cortex were quite capable of learning an avoidance response, and in fact the learning curves were indistinguishable from those of normal animals. However, after their performance reached criterion, these lesioned animals did not exhibit the diminished pituitary–adrenal response to the avoidance situation to the same degree as operated controls. In addition, the normal decrease in freezing behavior during the intertrial period did not occur. The dissociation between behavior and endocrine function in this study highlights the definitional problem. If one examined only the behavior, one would have said that the animals clearly showed no deficit in their ability to cope with the avoidance learning situation. However, the absence of a change in physiological responses indicated that these animals were not coping.

Given the large body of literature that indicates that the somatic changes that occur under stress can lead to pathological states, it would appear that a reduction in the physiological response to aversive stimuli, whether or not "appropriate" behavior is also emitted at that time, would be the most relevant and adaptive change for ultimate survival. Therefore, our definition of coping is based on the ultimate reduction of the physiological arousal produced as a consequence of the novelty or threat of any given stimulus complex. In an extensive discussion of the definition of coping, the first author of this chapter suggested that "Coping is when my stomach doesn't hurt"; this is indeed a simplified version of the more formal statement just made. Thus, when the physiological responses no longer occur, even though the behavior may appear to be inappropriate, it would indicate that coping has occurred.

The data presented in the series of studies reported in this volume emphasize the physiological responses and alterations of those physiological responses as a consequence of repeated exposure to an aversive and potentially threatening situation.

## STATEMENT OF THE PROBLEM

Given the concepts of coping discussed up to this point, we undertook to determine whether we could apply an experimental model of coping derived from the animal literature to a well-defined, structured situation in humans. The animal (rat) model we used was developed by Coover et al. (1973) with a two-way shuttlebox avoidance paradigm. Animals were tested over approximately 3 weeks and the pattern of corticoid changes over time was observed. On Day 1 of training, animals made almost no avoidance responses and thus received many shocks; the levels of plasma corticosterone were significantly elevated, as would be expected. On Days 6–7 of training, most animals reached criterion (8 out of 10 correct responses) and thus received very few shocks; however, the levels of plasma corticosterone were only slightly diminished. In contrast, 10 days after reaching criterion, the levels of plasma corticosterone were significantly reduced, although the number of shocks received had not decreased any further. The drop in corticoids over the course of training was obviously not due to a decrease in the amount of shock being received and was interpreted as a physiological index of coping. In this study, as in any study of coping, there are clearly two phases: the initial fear and the gradual mastery of the task. Physiological responses reflect the processes occurring in each of these phases. In extending this model to a human situation, we therefore wanted to describe *both* the subjective experience and response to the first exposure to the fearful situation and the subjective and physiological changes occurring during the development of coping. Thus, we used both self-reports and objective psychological and physiological data to describe the changes that occurred. We wished to monitor whether the subjective experience of fear changed over time and whether physiological indicators of this fear followed any changes that occurred. Furthermore, since we were using a human population, it also appeared possible to examine whether there are psychological factors that are predictive of successful performance and successful coping and whether these psychological factors are in any way related to physiological changes. We questioned whether there are special personality types, special defense strategies, or particular physiological characteristics in those individuals who showed the best coping.

Within the context of the experimental model, there are three problem areas to be dealt with.

*1. The initial fear problem.* Somatic changes during fear have been extensively studied. Within the framework of this study, it was important to designate a situation in which fear was as realistic as possible. There was to be a real danger involved, but the situation of course had to be within ethical limits. It was also important to attempt to minimize the physical strain on the body. Very often muscle work and other physiological stresses, such as severe deprivations, interfere with the somatic changes that are activated by fear alone.

*2. The coping problem.* We wanted to observe whether changes in the physiological and psychological parameters occurred in humans given repeated exposures to a severely threatening situation. If systematic changes were demonstrable, then we could clearly extend the generality of the coping models from rats to humans; in addition, by using a multiplicity of measures, we could determine whether different physiological systems show the same kind of changes during coping.

*3. Coping strategies.* Even in the most structured situations in as primitive an animal as the rat, we are often quite surprised to find that the rat will choose strategies other than those that were designed for it and will refuse to perform according to previously established conceptions. In the human species, it seems quite obvious that with a fearful situation, regardless of how simple it is, there will still be a rich variety of coping strategies. Furthermore, these strategies will be at least in part dependent on antecedent conditions, for example, the psychological characteristics of the individual and a complex interaction among individuals in the group in which the coping skills are being developed. Since a variety of psychological tests are used to measure personality characteristics, it is possible to study how various psychological functions interact with physiological systems to produce the final individual strategy used to cope with the fear-producing situation.

To study the three problem areas we have outlined, it was important to find a fear-provoking situation that satisfied several criteria. First, we wanted fear motivation to be as "clean" as possible. Even though fear is difficult to define, and even though there are personality traits and emotions that will interact with any situation, we tried to find a situation that was as uncontaminated as possible. Second, and equally important, we wanted the individual to be able to do something about the situation. There had to be a learning of some skill involved, and this skill had to, at least in part, enable him to cope with the initial fear. Learning about the situation and the actual probabilities of the danger might also play a part in fear reduction, but active actions by the individual also had to be involved to make the situation as close to the rat model as possible. Third, we wanted a situation in which one group of individuals was followed through the entire acquisition of the coping skill. Therefore, the whole experience had to encompass a relatively short amount of time. In particular, we did not have time as experimenters to wait for a "lifelong experience." The learning phase had to involve clear-cut events ("trials") and there had to be a progressive improvement in the behavior or in the coping skill. If these conditions were met, we would be able to observe whether there is a gradual reduction in fear and the somatic concomitants to that state. Finally, we wanted an experimental design that did not involve comparisons of experienced versus inexperienced personnel; differences in selection and differences in age would be unacceptable sources of variation.

Fenz (1975) has pointed out that parachuting is an ideal situation for studying stress. It combines the intense involvement and high degree of stress usually found only in field studies with the stringent controls that can be obtained only in the laboratory. Therefore, we selected parachutist trainees in the Norwegian Army. These trainees are given the "Basic Airborne Course." The training is fairly strenuous and challenging. The first part of the training is the ground training phase, which includes learning basic jump techniques. Performance during this first phase is critical for being accepted for the second stage, which involves the airborne jumps. We decided to use the ground training phase, since in this phase we found a task that seemed to satisfy all of our criteria. The trainees go through training in a mock tower apparatus before the actual airborne jumps. This involves jumping from a 12m-high tower and sliding down a long steel wire. It is highly fear provoking for the first several jumps, both according to the school officials and according to those members of the team who tried it. It is technically a fairly easy thing to do, and the performance necessary to be accepted for further training is acquired by most men. The training period involves 14 days of training jumps, separated by days of other training. Each jump is an identifiable event, and performance gradually improves during the training phase. It is possible to study a large number of men within a short time period. A fixed number of trials may be planned ahead of time, and blood samples can be taken and the men can be followed telemetrically without any serious technical problems. All of the sources of variation in airplane jumping, such as limited numbers of subjects, difficulty in tracking the jumpers, and irregular weather conditions, are thus controlled in the mock tower training situation. A fairly large group of individuals can go through the same training program under the same conditions. This reduces the interindividual variation due to irrelevant factors and gives a better opportunity to study meaningful individual variance.

It is not surprising that the paratroop model has been used by a number of other investigators because of the characteristics stated in the preceding paragraph. Basowitz, Persky, Korchin, and Grinker (1955) performed a similar study on a population of parachute trainees. They attempted to determine how the emotional state aroused by the stress of airborne training was similar to free anxiety as evaluated by clinical observation, interview, and self-rating. They also attempted to evaluate how this particular stress affected various psychological functions, such as visual perception, memory, and intellectual control, by testing the men immediately before jumping. Since the state of the art in physiological measurements was less developed at the time Basowitz et al. conducted their study, they evaluated the physiological state primarily by determining the amount of hippuric acid excretion, which they had found previously to be elevated in patients with free anxiety. The other biochemical indexes used were also related to protein metabolism. In addition, they studied the relationships between experimental measures of stress reaction and the actual performance during training. They followed the men during the various phases of training to determine the changes in the stress reaction, and a trend in the data that we would refer to as "coping" is evident in their findings, but it was not the primary target of that investigation. The results of the Basowitz et al. study cannot be directly compared with the present study; it was carried out over a long period of time, the training period involved tasks of varying degrees of difficulty, and they did not restrict themselves to one particular coping task. However, their general finding agrees with our basic concept: Subjects who refused to jump or who were least able to cope with the training situation revealed more severe biochemical stress responses than subjects who completed training and were thus most adequate in coping with the situation. In fact, for those subjects who failed in the training, the initial level of every measure approached the levels found in individuals subjected to severe physical stresses. However, it was unclear to what extent these differences were related to differences in coping, or to differences in coping strategies. Furthermore, hippuric acid levels proved to be a very poor indicator of changes in response to stress, and no parallel with the measures in clinical patients with anxiety were found. Finally, under their conditions and with their measures, no systematic changes in the psychological indexes of stress occurred with mastery of the task.

The most extensive studies on parachutists were performed over a 15-year period by Fenz (1975) following the original reports by Epstein and Fenz (1962) and Fenz and Epstein (1962). Briefly, they studied experienced and novice sports parachutists or sky divers. They administered a word-association test and a thematic apperception test specially related to parachutist training. Autonomic activity was recorded during the word-association test, during the ride up in the aircraft, and after landing following the jump. The investigators then correlated responses with performance. A self-rating of fear was also used in some of the studies. On the basis of their findings, they formulated a set of general principles for coping behavior. They found changes in cognitive and physiological responses as a function of experience. Perhaps the most consistent and striking findings are that experienced men differ from inexperienced men with regard to the time course of their fear rating. The experienced jumper has a high fear level much earlier than the inexperienced jumper, and then fear and apprehension begin to decrease as soon as he reaches the airport and the maneuvers start. He becomes progressively calmer when he gets close to the jump itself. There is an accompanying change in physiological reactions during ascent. Furthermore, in a word-association test, there is less response to relevant words, indicating that fear is decreased with increased experience. On the other hand, for the inexperienced jumper, fear continually increases until the time of the actual jump.

Fenz (1975) has shown that both the electrodermal and psychological reaction time to stimulus words and the autonomic responses during ascent are related to good performance. Thus, there exists the possibility that the dimensions described by Fenz and Epstein in their extremely experienced jumpers may be factors that determine who is to be experienced and that, therefore, the changes they describe are not relevant for studying the development of coping. Furthermore, this type of experienced jumper differs from novice jumpers even in his heart rate response during a reaction-time task (Fenz & Jones, 1974). We feel that when experienced men, in a reaction-time task remote from parachute jumping, show both different heart rate patterning and better reaction time than novice jumpers, it is hard to accept this as an effect due to parachute experience. Rather, these findings seem to support the notion that the basic differences described by Fenz and Epstein may be due to selection factors working in their studies. The men with the particular heart rate patterns, reaction time, and physiology, as well as psychology described above, may be those who cope best with this situation. They are the ones who continue training and become experienced jumpers.

## CONCLUSION

The remainder of this volume is a comprehensive report of a study utilizing the model of parachute training as a prototype for the study of coping. There are a number of very important factors that make this study unique. First, the study was conducted within the conceptual framework of an experimental model of coping. Thus, the situation was chosen to have as many of the features of the experimental model as was possible within a naturalistic framework for humans. Second, all of the individuals who were tested were naive; thus, we could follow the course of changes in both performance and physiological measurements. Third, in the late 1960s and early 1970s, there was an enormous development in the techniques available for the appropriate measurement of multiple hormones in the blood. The availability of radioimmunoassays, both for steroid hormones and pituitary hormones, made it possible to obtain multiple measures from the same blood sample. This study utilized many of these techniques to measure several hormones at the same instant so as to be able to establish relationships between physiological measures. Finally, psychological testing was done prior to the initiation of training, and performance measures were taken during training. Thus, we hoped it would be possible to correlate the physiological measures with each other, to correlate the psychological measures with each other, and to find relationships between the physiological and psychological measures. We believe that the results of these studies make significant contributions to the understanding of the coping process.

## REFERENCES

Alexander, F. *Psychosomatic medicine*. New York: Norton, 1950.

Arabian, J. M., & Desiderato, O. Preference for signaled shock: A test of two hypotheses. *Animal Learning & Behavior*, 1975, *3*, 191–195.

Averill, J. R. Personal control over aversive stimuli and its relationship to stress. *Psychological Bulletin*, 1973, *80*, 286–303.

Badia, P., & Culbertson, S. The relative aversiveness of signalled vs. unsignalled escapable and inescapable shock. *Journal of the Experimental Analysis of Behavior*, 1972, *17*, 463–471.

Badia, P., Culbertson, S., & Harsh, J. Choice of longer or stronger signalled shock over shorter or weaker unsignalled shock. *Journal of the Experimental Analysis of Behavior*, 1973, *19*, 25–32.

Badia, P., Culbertson, S., & Harsh, J. Relative aversiveness of signaled vs. unsignaled avoidable and escapable shock situations in humans. *Journal of Comparative and Physiological Psychology*, 1974, *87*, 338–346.

Badia, P., Culbertson, S., & Lewis, P. The relative aversiveness of signalled vs. unsignalled avoidance. *Journal of the Experimental Analysis of Behavior*, 1971, *16*, 113–121.

Baker, A. G. Learned irrelevance and learned helplessness: Rats learn that stimuli, reinforcers, and responses are uncorrelated. *Journal of Experimental Psychology: Animal Behavior Processes*, 1976, *2*, 130–141.

Basowitz, H., Persky, H., Korchin, S. J., & Grinker, R. R. *Anxiety and stress. An interdisciplinary study of a life situation.* New York: McGraw-Hill, 1955.

Byrne, J. D. Repression-sensitization as a dimension of personality. In B. A. Maher (Ed.), *Progress in experimental personality research.* New York: Academic Press, 1964.

Coover, G. D., Goldman, L., & Levine, S. Plasma corticosterone increases produced by extinction of operant behavior in rats. *Physiology & Behavior, 1971, 6,* 261–263.

Coover, G. D., Ursin, H., & Levine, S. Plasma corticosterone levels during active avoidance learning in rats. *Journal of Comparative and Physiological Psychology, 1973, 82,* 170–174.

Coover, G. D., Ursin, H., & Levine, S. Corticosterone levels during avoidance learning in rats with cingulate lesions suggest an instrumental reinforcement deficit. *Journal of Comparative and Physiological Psychology,* 1974, 87, 970–977.

Davis, H., Memmott, J., Macfadden, L., & Levine, S. Pituitary-adrenal activity under different appetitive extinction procedures. *Physiology & Behavior, 1976, 17,* 687–690.

Davis, H., Porter, J. W., Livingstone, J., Herrmann, T., Macfadden, L., & Levine, S. Pituitary-adrenal activity and leverpress shock escape behavior. *Physiological Psychology, 1977, 5,* 280–284.

Dunbar, F. *Emotions and bodily changes.* (4th ed.) New York: Columbia University Press, 1954.

Dykman, R. A., Reese, W. G., Galbrecht, C. R., & Thomasson, P. J. Psychophysiological reactions to novel stimuli: Measurement, adaptation, and relationship of psychological and physiological variables in the normal human. *New York Academy of Sciences Annals,* 1959, 79, 43–107.

Epstein, S., & Fenz, W. D. Theory and experiment on the measurement of approach-avoidance conflict. *Journal of Abnormal Social Psychology, 1962, 64,* 97–112.

Fenz, W. D. Strategies for coping with stress. In I. G. Sarason & C. D. Spielberger (Eds.), *Stress and anxiety.* Vol. 2. New York: Hemisphere (Wiley), 1975.

Fenz, W. D., & Epstein, S. Measurement of approach-avoidance conflict along a stimulus dimension by a thematic apperception test. *Journal of Personality, 1962, 30,* 613–632.

Fenz, W. D., & Jones, G. B. Cardiac conditioning in a reaction time task and heart rate control during real life stress. *Journal of Psychosomatic Research, 1974, 18,* 199–203.

Friedman, S. B., Mason, J. W., & Hamburg, D. A. Urinary 17-hydroxycorticosteroid levels in parents of children with neoplastic disease: A study of chronic psychological stress. *Psychosomatic Medicine, 1963, 25,* 364–376.

Glazer, H. I., & Weiss, J. M. Long-term and transitory interference effects. *Journal of Experimental Psychology: Animal Behavior Processes, 1976, 2,* 191–201. (a)

Glazer, H. I. & Weiss, J. M. Long-term interference effect: An alternative to "learned helplessness". *Journal of Experimental Psychology: Animal Behavior Processes, 1976, 2,* 202–213. (b)

Glazer, H. I., Weiss, J. M., Pohorecky, L. A., & Miller, N. E. Monoamines as mediators of avoidance-escape behavior. *Psychosomatic Medicine, 1975, 37,* 535–543.

Gliner, J. A. Predictable vs. unpredictable shock: Preference behavior and stomach ulceration. *Physiology & Behavior, 1972, 9,* 693–698.

Gray, J. A. *Elements of a two-process theory of learning.* London: Academic Press, 1975.

Hamburg, D. A., Hamburg, B., & deGoza, S. Adaptive problems of mechanisms in severely burned patients. *Psychiatry, 1953, 16,* 1–20.

Harsh, J. & Badia, P. Choice of signalled over unsignalled shock as a function of shock intensity. *Journal of the Experimental Analysis of Behavior, 1975, 23,* 349–355.

Lazarus, R. S., & Alfert, E. Short-circuiting of threat by experimentally altering cognitive appraisal. *Journal of Abnormal Social Psychology, 1964, 69,* 195–205.

Lazarus, R. S., Averill, J. R., & Opton, E. M., Jr. The psychology of coping: Issues of research and assessment. In G. V. Coelho, D. A. Hamburg, & J. E. Adams (Eds.), *Coping and adaptation.* New York: Basic Books, 1974. Pp. 249–315.

Levine, M. & Spivack, G. *The Rorschach index of repressive style*. Springfield, Ill.: C. C. Thomas, 1964.

Levine, S., & Coover, G. D. Environmental control of suppression of the pituitary-adrenal system. *Physiology & Behavior*, 1976, *17*, 35–37.

Levine, S., Goldman, L., & Coover, G. D. Expectancy and the pituitary-adrenal system. In R. Porter & J. Knight (Eds.), *Physiology, emotion & psychosomatic illness* (Ciba Foundation Symposium 8). Amsterdam: Elsevier, 1972. Pp. 281–296.

Lockard, J. S. Choice of a warning signal or no warning signal in an unavoidable shock situation. *Journal of Comparative and Physiological Psychology*, 1963, *56*, 526–530.

Looney, T. A. & Cohen, P. S. Retardation of jump-up escape responding in rats pretreated with different frequencies of noncontingent electric shock. *Journal of Comparative and Physiological Psychology*, 1972, *78*, 317–322.

Maier, S. F., Albin, R. W., & Testa, T. J. Failure to learn to escape in rats previously exposed to inescapable shock depends on nature of escape response. *Journal of Comparative and Physiological Psychology*, 1973, *85*, 581–592.

Maier, S. F., Seligman, M., & Solomon, R. Pavlovian fear conditioning and learned helplessness: Effects on escape and avoidance behavior of a) the CS-US contingency and b) the independence of the US and voluntary responding. In B. A. Campbell & R. M. Church (Eds.), *Punishment and aversive behavior*. New York: Appleton-Century-Crofts, 1969.

Maier, S. F., & Testa, T. J. Failure to learn to escape by rats previously exposed to inescapable shock is partly produced by associative interference. *Journal of Comparative and Physiological Psychology*, 1975, *88*, 554–564.

Mason, J. W. A historical view of the stress field, Part 2. *Journal of Human Stress*, 1975, *1*, 22–36.

Osborne, F. H., Mattingly, B. A., Redmon, W. K., & Osborne, J. S. Factors affecting the measurement of classically conditioned fear in rats following exposure to escapable versus inescapable signaled shock. *Journal of Experimental Psychology: Animal Behavior Processes*, 1975, *1*, 364–373.

Overmier, J. B., & Seligman, M.E.P. Effects of inescapable shock upon subsequent escape and avoidance responding. *Journal of Comparative and Physiological Psychology*, 1967, *63*, 28–33.

Perkins, C. C., Jr. An analysis of the concept of reinforcement. *Psychological Review*, 1968, *75*, 155–172.

Pribram, K. H., & Melges, F. T. Psychophysiological basis of emotion. *Handbook of Clinical Neurology*, 1969, *3*, 316–342.

Price, D. B., Thaler, M., & Mason, J. W. Preoperative emotional states and adrenal cortical activity; studies on cardiac and pulmonary surgery patients. *Archives of Neurology and Psychiatry*, 1957, *77*, 646–656.

Rosellini, R. A., & Seligman, M.E.P. Frustration and learned helplessness. *Journal of Experimental Psychology: Animal Behavior Processes*, 1975, *104*, 149–157.

Seligman, M.E.P. Chronic fear produced by unpredictable electric shock. *Journal of Comparative and Physiological Psychology*, 1968, *66*, 402–411.

Seligman, M.E.P. *Helplessness: On depression, development and death*. San Francisco: Freeman, 1975.

Seligman, M.E.P., & Beagley, G. Learned helplessness in the rat. *Journal of Comparative and Physiological Psychology*, 1975, *88*, 534–541.

Seligman, M.E.P., & Groves, D. P. Nontransient learned helplessness. *Psychonomic Science*, 1970, *19*, 191–192.

Seligman, M.E.P., Maier, S. F., & Solomon, R. L. Unpredictable and uncontrollable aversive events. In F. R. Brush (Ed.), *Aversive conditioning and learning*. New York: Academic Press, 1971.

Seligman, M.E.P., & Meyer, B. Chronic fear and ulcers in rats as a function of the unpredictability of safety. *Journal of Comparative and Physiological Psychology*, 1970, *73*, 202–207.

Seligman, M.E.P., Rosellini, R. A., & Kozak, M. J. Learned helplessness in the rat: Time course, immunization, and reversibility. *Journal of Comparative and Physiological Psychology*, 1975, *88*, 542–547.

Selye, H. *Stress*. Montreal: Acta, Inc., 1956.

Seward, J., & Humphrey, G. L. Avoidance learning as a function of pretraining in the cat. *Journal of Comparative and Physiological Psychology*, 1967, *63*, 338–341.

Sokolov, E. N. *The central nervous system and behavior*. Transactions of the Third Conference, Josiah Macy Foundation, New York, 1960.

Weinberg, J. Modulation of the deleterious effects of preshock by shock-induced fighting in rats or fighting is its own reward! Doctoral dissertation, Stanford University, 1977.

Weinberg, J., & Levine, S. Early handling influences on behavioral and physiological responses during active avoidance. *Developmental Psychobiology*, 1977, *10*, 161–169.

Weinstein, J., Averill, J. R., Opton, E. M., Jr., & Lazarus, R. S. Defensive style and discrepancy between self-report and physiological indexes of stress. *Journal of Personality and Social Psychology*, 1968, *10*, 406–413.

Weiss, J. M. Effects of coping responses on stress. *Journal of Comparative and Physiological Psychology*, 1968, *65*, 251–260.

Weiss, J. M. Somatic effects of predictable and unpredictable shock. *Psychosomatic Medicine*, 1970, *32*, 397–408.

Weiss, J. M. Effects of coping behavior in different warning signal conditions on stress pathology in rats. *Journal of Comparative and Physiological Psychology*, 1971, *77*, 1–13. (a)

Weiss, J. M. Effects of punishing the coping response (conflict) on stress pathology in rats. *Journal of Comparative and Physiological Psychology*, 1971, 77, 14–21. (b)

Weiss, J. M. Effects of coping behavior with and without a feedback signal on stress pathology in rats. *Journal of Comparative and Physiological Psychology*, 1971, *77*, 22–30. (c)

Weiss, J. M., & Glazer, H. I. Effects of acute exposure to stressors on subsequent avoidance-escape behavior. *Psychosomatic Medicine*, 1975, *37*, 499–521.

Weiss, J. M., Glazer, H. I., Pohorecky, L. A., Brick, J., & Miller, N. E. Effects of chronic exposure to stressors on avoidance-escape behavior and on brain norepinephrine. *Psychosomatic Medicine*, 1975, *37*, 522–534.

# 2

# Subjects and the Methods Used in the Field Phase of the Experiment

HOLGER URSIN, ARNOLDUS SCHYTTE BLIX,
and SVEIN ROSSELAND

## SUBJECTS

This book is based on an investigation of the 72 men who were evaluated for the annual training course in the Norwegian Army Parachute School in 1974 and the 44 men who were accepted for further training. Their mean age was 20.1 years, ranging from 19 to 23 years; 68 were regular soldiers, and 4 were sergeants. Their general ability level, educational background, and general psychological characteristics are discussed in Chapter 13.

## SELECTION

At the age of 18, all Norwegian men are subject to serve in the military for 12 months—in the Army, Air Force, or Navy. Men serving in the Army go through an initial basic recruit training at recruit centers lasting for 8–10 weeks, after which they are sent to regular units. Intake takes place four times a year; a relatively large contingent is received by the training centers in July. The Norwegian Army Parachute School is advertised at all main training centers in July. On the average, 200 apply for parachute training

23

PSYCHOBIOLOGY OF STRESS:
A Study of Coping Men

each year. About 80 are accepted for evaluation, and in general they proceed to the school after approximately 4 weeks of basic training. Applicants must be of good general physical health, their medical classification must be good, and they should also have a "good general intelligence." There are no particular demands for previous training.

No special benefits are promised, and there is no extra pay, but there is prestige involved in obtaining the particular red beret and the parachutist wing emblem, at least among those that apply for such training.

Admission to the school is based on applications from volunteers. Instructors from the parachute school visit the main basic training centers around the country and evaluate the applicants. Each applicant is interviewed by an instructor, and based on an evaluation of motivation, abilities, and general fitness a total of 80 is accepted.

Our investigation took place in 1974, in August and September (see Table 2.1). After arrival, the first couple of days were used for basic investigations, and the men were tested physiologically and psychologically. Immediately after their arrival on the first morning, before the personnel of the school had introduced themselves and any samples had been taken, we gave an orientation to all men. A brief outline of the experiment was given. It was made clear that psychological and medical tests would be used and that the medical tests would include blood sampling and collection of urine samples. A brief outline of the aim of the investigation was given. We emphasized that the investigation would elucidate the physiological effects on the body of coping with potentially dangerous occupations. Attention was directed toward the strain and the jumping, and very little was said about the coping aspect and nothing was said about expected results. It was also made clear that participation in this experiment was completely voluntary and that all results obtained from the experimental parts of our investigations would be

**TABLE 2.1**
**Time Course**

| August | 8 | Arrival | N = 72 |
|---|---|---|---|
| | 9 | Physiology, psychology | |
| | 10 | Basal blood sample, physiology, psychology | |
| | 11 | Sunday—military exercises | |
| | 12 | Jump Day 1 | N = 57 |
| | 12–21 | "Hell Week" | |
| | 22 | Jump Day 2 (start mock tower training period) | N = 44 |
| | 27 | Jump Day 5 | |
| September | 9 | Jump Day 11 | |
| | 10 | Last day in mock tower training period | |
| | 15 | Start airplane jump period | |

treated confidentially. Any questions they had would be answered. Very few raised their voice for questions and all agreed to volunteer. We cannot exclude, of course, that their unanimous willingness to cooperate was based, at least in some cases, on the misconception that their future in the school depended on their collaboration. We tried to make it quite clear that their acceptance for further training was in no way contingent on whether or not they participated in the investigation or on the results we obtained.


## TIME COURSE

A total of 72 men arrived at the Parachutist Training Center on Thursday, August 8, 1974, for further evaluation.

a. *Arrival day.* Thursday, August 8, was used only for registration, room allocation, and allotment of equipment.

b. *Basal days.* August 9 and 10 were used for general psychological and medical tests. The psychological tests are described in detail in Chapter 13. These tests attempted to evaluate the resources and strategies used in threatening situations and the motivation and interests of each man. The medical tests included an ordinary medical examination by the medical officer of the unit and a basic or reference experiment for our heart rate measurement, for which oxygen uptake and heart rate were measured during various work loads (see Chapter 9). The medical tests also included blood samples and urine samples collected before any training took place ("basal sample"). These samples gave us the basal or reference values for all of the physiological indicators we followed during the course of this study.

c. *Sunday, August 11.* The men were not given any rest on Sunday; they had various types of exercise and training. The most strenuous exercise was to run 5000 m with field pack and rifle. This took place before lunch. A field maneuver took place in the evening. The men were then sent to bed at 2300–2400 hr (11–12 PM). They got nothing to drink from lunch until the next morning, but were not disturbed in any other way during that night.

d. *Jump Day 1.* The next morning, Monday, August 12, the men were awakened at 0600 hr as usual. Water was now available ad libitum. A restricted breakfast (see Testing Day Routine) was served around 0630 hr. From then on the standard routine for tower training was followed with a few exceptions, except that on this first day of jumping each man made only one jump. The strap length between the trolley wire and the parachute belt was also longer on Jump Day 1, allowing for a longer fall (2.3 m) than during the regular training (1.6 m). No instructions were given before this first jump, giving the men a maximal uncertainty about the situation.

e.  *Hell Week.* The training period between Jump Day 1 and the mock tower training period (starting with Jump Day 2) has been referred to as "Hell Week." The men had been prepared for this, and they knew that the purpose of this period was to test their "willpower." They were disturbed during the nights and the maneuvers were quite exhausting, but the orders were not meant to be completely meaningless or humiliating in any sense.

f.  *Mock tower training.* During the mock tower training period, we took various samples from the men three times: August 22 (Jump Day 2), August 27 (Jump Day 5), and September 9 (Jump Day 11). After our last sample days, the men had two more jump days before their last and final jump from the tower. On this last jump day, they had to have a certain number of accepted jumps from the tower to proceed to the parachute training, and they also had to perform at least one acceptable jump on this last day ("examination jump"). On each of the sample days, Jump Days 1, 2, 5, and 11, blood and urine samples were collected. Blood samples were obtained after the first training jump on each of the sample days (post-jump samples). No pre-jump samples were collected; it was felt that blood sampling procedures before the jump might interfere with the psychological stress of jumping. For urine samples this point was of no importance. Urine samples were collected before the jump procedure took place; this constituted the pre-jump sample. A second, post-jump sample was collected 2 hr later.

g.  *Jumps from airplanes.* After the mock tower training period, the men proceeded to the jumps from airplanes. During this period we did not make any systematic observations, but one of us (S. Rosseland) followed the men throughout the whole course. During the jumps from airplanes, the performance of all men was observed by the instructors, and our evaluation of the performance during this period was based on the notes from the instructors. We also recorded the heart rate of four men during jumps from an airplane. The military psychologists also followed the men and their performance during this period.

## TESTING DAY ROUTINE

During the investigation, as on ordinary days, the reveille was blown at 0600 hr. The men dressed in their regular field uniforms, but also carried identification numbers on chests and backs. The markers were the same as those used for athletic competitions and made it easy to identify each man at a distance (for instance, in the air when sliding down the wire).

Breakfast was served at the ordinary hour, 0630–0730. On test days, the breakfast was standardized; all men at three open sandwiches, one with fresh tomatoes, one with Norwegian Brown cheese, and one with jam. They drank .5 liter of skimmed milk on Jump Days 1 and 11; for the two other days, ordinary milk was given since skimmed milk was unavailable. Coffee, tea, Cokes, and smoking were not allowed. The men followed these and all instructions very carefully, even if they found this breakfast less substantial than their usual breakfast.

At 0700 hr, all men emptied their urinary bladders. Officers and members of the research team reminded the men of the procedures during this early morning hour and, again, the instructions were carried out very conscientiously. At 0730 hr they had their regular morning formation. They then marched at ease to the training tower area, a 10-min walk, arriving just before 0800 hr. The parachute belts were distributed and strapped on. The tower training itself started between 0800 and 0830 hr on blood sampling days and was finished at 1126, 1036, 0946, and 0947 hr, respectively. Before the jumps, at 0800 hr, and after most of the men had jumped once, at 1000 hr all of the men urinated in cartons that carried each man's number.

## MOCK TOWER APPARATUS TRAINING PROCEDURE

The mock tower apparatus is used to assist in training basic jump techniques and important points in the performance of parachute jumps. It also serves to familiarize the aspirant with opening the reserve parachute, and parachute malfunctions may be simulated.

The tower is 12 m high and consists of five platforms with a staircase between each (Figure 2.1). Four trainees were placed on each platform. When the four men on the top platform had jumped, the four on Platform 4 moved up to the top platform, the four on Platform 3 moved to Platform 4, and so on. There were four men on each platform at all times, except on the top platform from which the jumping took place.

At the bottom of the tower, the parachute belts strapped on each soldier were controlled by the instructing officer. The soldiers were dressed in their full field equipment except for weapon, the same as for regular jumps. On the top platform, the suspension belts and packs were fixed to a hook on the trolley. The man asked for permission to jump. As soon as the order had been given, he stepped out from the platform and fell down until the rope to the trolley was tightened; the trolley then ran down the long wire. They jumped with their backs toward the end of the wire. The tower there-

**Figure 2.1.** Schematic drawing of the mock tower training apparatus.

fore appeared to move away from him in the same way as the airplane would disappear from his view if he were jumping from a real aircraft. The men on the top platform were standing with their backs to the movements down the wire and moved backward whenever a man had jumped out. The movements followed a standard routine to imitate the stepwise movements they were supposed to perform in the aircraft.

In the beginning, very little was demanded from their performance during their sliding down. As they proceeded in the course they were to take the correct X-position and count loudly to 4 sec by saying "1000, 2000," etc. After 4 sec they were approximately halfway down the wire, and at this point they crossed their arms to imitate the pulling of the rip cord. Both arms were to go back to the X-position, without loss of stability, and they counted another 4 sec. At this point they had reached the end of the wire, and they loosened the straps from the harnesses, climbed down a rope ladder, and ran back to the instruction officer for the critique of the jump. After having received this critique, they lined up for another jump at the bottom of the tower. The total distance between the end of the wire and the tower is 70 m (Figure 2.2).

The same standard procedure was followed during our sample days, except for the blood sample taken immediately after the jump. This took place in a large tent from a Light Field Hospital Unit. The men ran directly from the rope ladder into this tent, had their blood sample taken, filled in a fear rating score (see the following), and ran to the instruction officer for the critique of their jump.

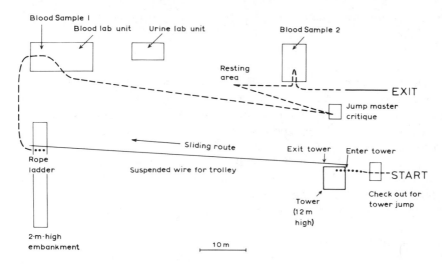

**Figure 2.2.** Map of the mock tower area.

After having received this critique, they rested for 20 min in a particular location close to the tower. During this period, we attempted a calm and relaxed atmosphere, and it was clear that during this time they were our responsibility and that the Army officers were not supposed to interfere with them. The men were sitting down and relaxing. Several team members were close to them during this time, and we avoided all talk about blood sampling and other stressful topics. During this time, a clinical psychologist interviewed as many men as he could cover for relaxed and nonprovoking conversations on Jump Day 1. The second blood sample was obtained 20 min after the first. This sample was taken in a smaller tent by a second blood sampling team. After the first blood sample, each man carried a card with the time of his first blood sample, and the men also made sure that this timing was kept. Watches were synchronized before blood sampling started. After the second blood sample had been obtained, the men returned to the tower training or other military activities.

At the bottom of the tower the men filled in a self-rating schedule for fear. Another was filled in on Platform 4, immediately before they entered the top platform. The third and last self-rating of fear was taken immediately after the jump and the blood sample.

A tape recorder was placed close to the instruction officer and his critique of each jump was recorded.

The last man in each group of four carried telemetry equipment for monitoring heart rate. At the top platform, oxygen uptake was measured from this last man. The heart rate was monitored during the stay on the top platform and during the jump itself.

Climbing the stairs to the top platform increased the pulse and respiration, at least in some team members. Care was taken to perform the initial filling of the tower during morning hours slowly and gradually. Thus, the first men that jumped each day also had a waiting period in the tower on each platform. At the bottom of the tower the equipment was inspected, and each man demonstrated the procedure during the jump. This consisted of moving in the correct way on a small platform, stopping at a simulated door, and jumping through this door holding the correct positions for the correct time. The time was marked by again counting loudly "1000, 2000," etc. After "4000" each man imitated exactly how the rip cord is pulled and then counted for 4 sec more. When all four men in one team had been controlled they entered the low platform, and the men moved slowly upwards in the tower until the tower was completely filled. It took 10–15 min to fill the tower in this way. This meant that the first four men to jump had approximately the same conditions in the tower as the rest of the group.

Except for the straps from the trolley to the harness being longer on Jump Day 1, the whole procedure was similar throughout the training period. More skills were expected during the later stages in training, but there were no abrupt changes in the criteria. More details on performance and errors are given in Chapter 4.

## BLOOD SAMPLING

Blood samples were taken between 0800 and 1100 hr. Care was taken to collect the blood samples as quickly as possible. The men were never kept waiting in front of a blood sampler. The time was taken when a man entered the blood sampling tent or office. The sampling time was never allowed to go beyond 2 min; most samples were collected in less than 45 sec. A standard procedure was followed: A rubber tube was secured around the arm to increase venous pressure, and an automatic vacuum container (Venoject) was used (these tubes are sterile and contain heparin). A total of 10 ml of blood was taken in each sample. The Venoject tube was clearly marked with the sample number and the man's number and was immediately transferred to the centrifuge. After centrifuging, the plasma was distributed to six small containers and immediately frozen. The samples were kept frozen during transportation to the participating laboratories and until analysis.

The "basal sample" was collected Saturday, August 10, between 0830 and 0930 hr. The men had collected their first urine specimens at 0800 hr and were gathered in front of the hospital and medical office building. They were waiting for the "examination" in a relaxed atmosphere. The weather was cool, with an occasional light drizzle (see "Weather Conditions"). No one complained of freezing or any discomfort. The atmosphere was relaxed. The resting pulse among men was between 50 and 72. The men were sitting down and resting during the waiting period. Four men at a time were followed into the laboratory building by the project leader through two sets of doors. As soon as they had entered the main hall, they were immediately taken care of by four different blood samplers, two nurses and two medical doctors, one man per blood sampler. After the blood sample was taken, the men left the building through the other end and could not be observed by those who still waited. When all samples had been taken, another four men were followed in, in the same quiet way.

Two "post-jumping blood samples" were taken after the jumps. One sample was taken immediately after the jump (Sample 1); the second sample was taken 20 min later (Sample 2). As soon as the men had climbed down the rope ladder they ran to the entrance of the large laboratory tent. A technician followed each man to a blood sampler. The number was checked and the proper tube was filled with 10 ml of blood, again following the standard routine for obtaining venous samples. Most samples were obtained in less than 1 min after the man arrived in the laboratory tent. The men then left this tent after having filled out their fear score. After the first jump they went directly to the waiting area; after the other jump they went to the instruction officer for their critique and then to the waiting area. Each man carried a note stating the clock time of the first sample and the time for the next sample, 20 min later. The men helped in controlling that this time was kept accurately.

In the second blood sampling tent, two other blood samplers were present. A technician helped in sending the right man to the free blood sampler at the correct time. After the second blood sample, the man walked back to the base of the tower for further jumps or for other military activities.

The field laboratory with centrifuge and deep freezer was located in the same large tent in which the first blood sample was obtained. One experienced laboratory technician with the help of two nurses took care of the centrifuging and the pipetting. During the first jump, the whole laboratory procedure lasted from 0800 to 1500 hr before all samples had been placed in the freezer. For the other tower training jumps all samples were in the freezer before 1200 or 1300 hr.

Four hundred and thirty-eight blood samples were obtained in total; 67 samples were obtained from the basal level, 57 from Jump Day 1. From the tower training days the numbers varied between 42 and 44 each day. A few of the samples were too small to allow all analyses to be performed, but this was not found to influence the group data. Missing data were treated statistically by a method described in the next chapter ("Data Analysis," Chapter 3).

## ATTRITIONS FROM THE SCHOOL

A total of 15 men were dismissed or resigned from the school before the first jump, and another 13 after this jump (see Table 2.2). For all of these men psychological testing and basal sampling had been obtained. Often more than one reason was given for attrition. Some were dismissed by the medical officer; the reasons given by the medical officers included use of spectacles and physical incapabilities that they judged to be unfavorable in parachutist training. "Physical incapacity" was a reason given by the school; most often this consisted of an inability to run 5000 m with pack within the allotted time (24 min).

Two men resigned voluntarily during the weekend before the first jump, and there were also two slight physical traumas during this weekend that led to dismissal.

During the strenuous period following the first jump ("Hell Week") another 13 men were dismissed or resigned voluntarily. A man was often advised by the instructor if his chances of going through the course were judged to be slim. The medical officer also collaborated with the men and the instructors; some of his exclusions may not have been purely medical, but could at least in part represent a "face saving." He also tended to give medical assistance and avoid exclusions if the man wanted very strongly to go through the training in spite of minor medical problems, most often muscle and joint trouble after slight traumas. These men were helped with medication against muscle pain.

**TABLE 2.2**
**Reasons for Attrition** [a]

| | |
|---|---|
| Physical incapacity | 10 |
| Psychologically unfit | 2 |
| Poor performance | 2 |
| Medical advice | 7 |
| Physical advice | 6 |
| Voluntary withdrawal | 8 |
| Exhausted | 2 |

[a] Twenty-eight men. More than one reason given for several men.

## MEDICATION

Records were kept for all drugs dispensed by the medical officer of the school. This doctor also interviewed each subject and asked specifically for psychotropic or other drugs that might have been used. This was judged to be important since such drugs might have influenced or interfered with measurement of several of the physiological indicators we used (see, for instance, Radó, Simon, Jahos, Takó, & Nagy, 1974). Such drugs might also have influenced the psychological tests. However, no such drug use was recorded. Two men received chlorzoxazone (Paraflex) to relax their muscles; another 11 men received phenylbutazone (Artrizin) to prevent inflammation. Both drugs were given during the experimental period for short durations only. No other drugs were used. Most men were vaccinated against diphtheria and tetanus on August 30 and against typhoid fever on September 2.

## WEATHER CONDITIONS

The weather conditions did not vary much between jump days and were not a source of any additional strain on the men. The temperature varied between 9.3 and 14.9°C at the time of sampling, according to the weather records from the neighboring air field. There was almost no wind on any of the days and no rain at the time of sampling. Humidity varied between 80 and 100%, and air pressure was normal.

## REFERENCE

Radó, J. P., Simon, T., Jahos, E., Takó, J., & Nagy, O. Interference of psychotropic drugs with cortisol determinations. *Hormone and Metabolic Research*, 1974, 6, 530–531.

# 3

# Data Analysis

TOM BACKER JOHNSEN

The purpose of the present chapter is to describe in detail the more general aspects of the different analyses that generated the results discussed in the other chapters. The main topics are a description of the data matrix, the procedure used to handle the missing observations, and the computational methods.

## COMPUTER PROGRAMS

The computer programs employed in the analysis were all part of a general-purpose program library developed at the Department of Psychometrics, Institute of Psychology, University of Bergen. This program library is described by Johnsen (1976). From this program library (called MULVRP, *Multivariate Programs*) a rather small number of programs were employed. The methods included the following and are described under "The Data Matrix."

a.  A general program for data management that includes the strategy employed for "plugging" the data matrix to reduce the number of missing observations.

35

PSYCHOBIOLOGY OF STRESS:
A Study of Coping Men

    b.   A program for the computation of correlation matrices and another program for factor analysis.

    c.   Multiple regression.

    d.   A simple program for one-way analysis of variance (ANOVA) for the testing of simple group differences.

## THE DATA MATRIX

The data matrix used in the computations consisted essentially of three groups of variables: (a) a set of values for the plasma levels of five different variables (each with a base level) plus four pairs of values representing the two post-jump measurements during the course and the urine levels of catecholamines (Chapter 2); (b) a set of test results from a number of psychological tests (described in Chapter 13); and (c) a set of performance ratings for the jumps at different stages during the course (Chapter 4).

The total sample included 72 subjects, and this data matrix was divided into two subgroups: the "accepted men," who completed the whole course ($N = 44$), and the "dismissed men," who withdrew from the course after the first few jumps in the mock tower ($N = 28$). Obviously, there are many missing observations in the data matrix. Most of these occur in the group of dismissed men, simply because the observations could not be made. However, in the group of accepted men, any missing observations will have more serious consequences. When an index is computed (for instance, the "fall" and "rise" indexes used in Chapter 14), the result must be regarded as invalid if one or more of the observations involved in the computations are missing. Therefore, if the data matrix contains a large number of missing observations, the number of valid values for the indexes may be reduced to an unacceptable level. This will be particularly relevant for the urine samples where the number of missing observations was relatively high, since not all men produced a specimen at all sample points. There are also missing values for the hormones based on blood samples, albeit for different reasons. Consequently, the number of missing values in the original data matrix must be reduced as much as possible.

### Treatment of Missing Observations

There are several methods suggested in the literature for "plugging" the data matrices. The simplest is to replace the missing observations in the matrix with the arithmetic mean of the valid observations on the same variable. However, this strategy also has several disadvantages. The variances for the variables (after the plugging has been performed) will be reduced, and the same will happen to the correlations (covariances) between the variables.

To obtain a better estimate of the "true" covariance matrix corresponding to the original observations, a "plugging strategy" based on the prediction of values for the missing observations through multiple regression may be used. We have followed a procedure proposed by Frane (1976), which is more expensive from a computational point of view. The method involves the following steps.

1.  The data matrix is divided into blocks of variables, consisting of all observations of one hormone. In the prediction of the missing observations, only the variables within this block are used, because this avoids introducing spurious correlations between hormones by the prediction of values from all of the valid observations in the data matrix. The next steps are then carried out on each block as a separate unit.

2.  Locate one missing observation in the block and test the other observations for the same subject to see which are valid and could be used to predict the missing observation. In terms of multiple regression, the missing observation is the criterion variable and the other valid observations in the same vector are the predictors. If the number of predictors is greater than or equal to 2, the next steps are performed; otherwise a new missing observation is located.

3.  Scan the remaining cases in the data matrix and locate the subjects for whom the observations for the criterion variable and the predictors are all valid. Use these vectors to compute a covariance matrix for the set of variables and for the means and standard deviations for each variable.

4.  Use the covariance matrix, the means, and the standard deviations to compute raw score regression weights for the predictors in the standard manner (see, for instance, Kerlinger & Pedhazur, 1973, Chapter 4).

5.  The raw score weights are then used on the valid observations of the subject to whom the original missing observation belonged in the computation of a value to replace the observation.

6.  Store the value and return to Step 2.

It should be noted that the computed values are based only on the valid observations within each block and that the computed values are ignored until the process is completed. The effect of the procedure is that the means in the new data matrix will be slightly different from the corresponding means in the original matrix, but only to the extent that the means of the valid observations used in the regression equation are different from the sample means. The standard deviations in the new data matrix will be lower than the original values, dependent on the multiple correlations between the variables within each block. The main advantages of this approach are that the covariance matrix corresponding to the new data matrix will not be substantially different from the original and that the values used in the "plugging" process should be more meaningful than the variable means.

The basic assumption for the procedure is that the occurrence of missing observations is essentially a random process; therefore, the method was used only on the 44 subjects who completed all jumps, since this group was fairly homogeneous in other respects.

## METHODS OF ANALYSIS

All results concerning accepted men reported in the other chapters are based on the plugged data matrix (where the plugging has been limited to the hormonal data from the "accepted men"). The remainder of the data matrix is used without modifications.

To use as much as possible of the information in the data matrix, the methods used in the computations implied "missing data" computations with no restrictions other than those imposed by the mathematical restrictions inherent in the methods.

*Univariate distributions.*    All means, standard deviations, and variances reported in the other chapters are based on the total number of valid observations for the subsample of units being discussed at the moment.

*Correlations.*    The correlations reported in the text are all normal Pearson product–moment correlations, each computed on all of the subjects within the sample (or subsample) for which both of the observations on the two variables are valid. This may of course mean that the different correlations reported in the text will in some cases be based on a smaller number of cases than are included in the subsample being discussed at the moment. In principle, this will also mean that each correlation reported under the different analyses may represent somewhat different *populations,* which will then have consequences for the generalization of the reported results.

*Factor analysis.*    Each of these analyses was based on a correlation matrix where each correlation was computed in the manner described directly above. Thus, the correlation matrix is based on a maximum number of valid observations (after "plugging") in the subsample under consideration.

As to the factoring part of the analysis, a principal components method was employed, that is, without any prior transformation of the correlation matrix with respect to diagonal or off-diagonal values. The reason for this is obvious: The objective is primarily descriptive and no specific assumptions about the underlying structure of the variables are needed.

It should be stressed that factor analyses are purely descriptive in nature and are only introduced to offer some help in the analysis of these complex matrices. The interpretation, therefore, must be cautious. There are several reasons for this. Some of the variables involved had skewed distributions. The correlations describe rectilinear relations only, where it would be reasonable to assume that there were strong curvilinear components in the relations. Also, some of the $N$ values on which the correlations were based were very low in relation to the total number of variables in each analysis. A principal components analysis was used without any modifications of the correlation matrix with commonality estimates, etc.

To determine the number of factors to be retained in the factor analyses, the so-called Kaiser criterion (Kaiser, 1960) was used. This criterion is based on retaining the factors with eigenvalues larger than 1.0. This rule was not used in a strict sense, especially because of the need for comparing results from different subsamples of the data matrix, where there were small variations in the number of factors to be retained according to the criterion.

To simplify the interpretation of the factor matrices, the pattern matrices were rotated by a conventional varimax procedure (Kaiser, 1959) using only the factors determined by the criterion above.

*Multiple regression.*    The results from the multiple regression analyses are based on the same types of correlation matrices as those employed in the factor analysis. In any tests of significance the degrees of freedom were adjusted accordingly.

*Group differences.*    The differences between groups were computed with a standard ANOVA program resulting in an $F$ test for testing the significance of the difference. Since there were two groups in most of these tests, the $t$ values reported are the square roots of the $F$ values.

## REFERENCES

Frane, J. W. Some simple procedures for handling missing data in multivariate analysis. *Psychometrika*, 1976, *41*(3).

Johnsen, T. B. *Introduction to the MULVRP Programs; users guide.* Report No. 4, Department of Psychometrics, Institute of Psychology, University of Bergen, 1976.

Kaiser, H. F. Computer programs for Varimax rotation in factor analysis. *Educational and Psychological Measurement,* 1959, *19,* 413–420.

Kaiser, H. F. The application of electronic computers to factor analysis. *Educational and Psychological Measurement,* 1960, *20,* 141–151.

Kerlinger, F. N., & Pedhazur, E. J. *Multiple regression in behavioral research.* New York: Holt, Rinehart & Winston, 1973.

# 4

# Development of Performance and Fear Experience

KRISTIAN HALSE, ARNOLDUS SCHYTTE BLIX,
BJØRN ELLERTSEN, and HOLGER URSIN

We discussed the animal model of stress and coping in Chapter 1. Coping appears to be a crucial dimension for reduction of fear and the corresponding physiological responses. In this chapter we will discuss the relationship between fear and performance in an experimental situation.

Several factors may be expected to elicit fear in the mock tower. First, there is the height and the jump itself. Furthermore, the soldiers were aware that if their performance was bad during this task, they would not be allowed to jump from the airplane. Poor performance in the mock tower might suggest to the man that he did not know how to handle the real jump from the aircraft, which indeed might lead to disaster. These factors therefore contributed to a close relationship between performance in the mock tower and the soldier's fear in this situation.

According to our model, we expected to see a gradual improvement in performance in the tower training situation and a corresponding decrease in subjectively experienced fear. If this were the case, it would be safe to conclude that we have a situation analogous to the animal model. Our next step was to test whether we would obtain the physiological changes that we predicted from our rat studies. In the following sections we will first report the results of the subjective fear rating and of the performance in the mock

41

PSYCHOBIOLOGY OF STRESS:
A Study of Coping Men

tower as evaluated by the instructors and then we will discuss whether we achieved the experimental situation we attempted.

## METHOD

All men were asked to fill in a self-rating of fear before and after the jump. The soldiers had been instructed in the use of this form and had also filled in such a form before the first jump. This instruction took place immediately after the Defense Mechanism Test (DMT, see Chapter 13), on August 9 and 10. The form asked them to describe specifically how they felt (see Table 4.1). During the instruction session, it was stressed that experience told us that most people were frightened when they are going to jump from the tower, even if the tower training itself is not dangerous. We told them that there was no reason to feel ashamed of any fear or anxiety in this situation. We also stressed that it was the level or degree of their sensation that was important, not the quality of their experience. The exact words used were not important—the phenomenon we were trying to measure could be called restlessness, nervousness, unquiet feelings, etc. Again, we emphasized that what they answered on this question had nothing to do with the selection for further training.

A short repetition of how to use the form was given just before the tower training started on the tower training sample days (August 12, 22, and 27). It

**TABLE 4.1**
**Subjective Fear Rating**

|  | Person nr.: |
|---|---|
| I feel - - - - - | |
| Very frightened/anxious | 10<br>9 |
| Clearly frightened/anxious | 8<br>7 |
| A little frightened/anxious | 6<br>5 |
| Possibly a little frightened/anxious | 4<br>3 |
| Absolutely quiet/no anxiety | 2<br>1 |

was also necessary to give this instruction on the very last sample day (September 9), due to the relatively long delay since the previous sample day.

The first form to be filled in on every sample day was on Platform 1 at the bottom of the tower. The second form was filled in on Platform 4, the last platform before the top platform from which the jumps took place. The soldiers later told us that their fear level was much higher on the top platform, but it was impossible to have the men fill in a form on that platform for practical reasons.

Finally, they filled in the same form just after the blood sample had been taken. To fill in this form, it was necessary to have a technician helping each man, since many were still busy pressing the cotton against their arms after the venous blood sampling. We also tried to have research staff or other trusted personnel close to the other two scoring locations.

The forms were available at each scoring location and each soldier marked with an X the cell indicating the level of fear he felt most appropriate to himself at that time. The paper was marked with his number, folded, and put into a cardboard box, very much like an ordinary voting procedure. Care was taken to make this scoring as discreet and individual as possible, and they were specifically asked not to peek over each other's shoulders and not to discuss the fear level. Even so, we observed that there was conversation between the men on the platforms where the self-rating took place. We did not have any strict control of whether or not communication on the self-rating system really took place. Subjective fear scores were obtained from most men who jumped from the tower. For comparison with performance, only scores from the 44 accepted men were used. However, we also obtained fear scores from the 13 men from the dismissed/quit group that participated in the first jump from the tower (Jump Day 1). This material is not included in the figures or calculations and will only be dealt with briefly in this chapter.

### Evaluation of Tower Jumps (K1)

The material for performance during tower training is only available for the 44 men who went through the whole training period in the mock tower. The performance on Jump Day 1 was not scored at all. For the 44 men there are also subjective fear scores on all sample days in the mock tower training period.

The instructors kept records of the jump, and the first set of data derives from a simple coding of the number of acceptable jumps for each training day. Each jump was coded as accepted or not accepted. We simply summed the number of accepted jumps for each man. The group performance is evident from Figure 4.1. This number constitutes our score for tower perfor-

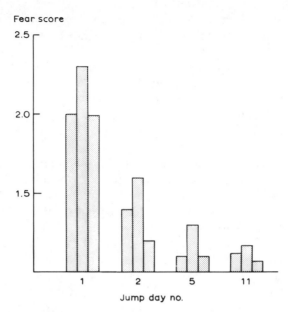

**Figure 4.1.** Self-rating of fear of men who went through tower training. The three columns for jump represent the average scores at the bottom of the tower, those just before jumping (the second highest platform), and those just after the jump. On the first day some of the soldiers reported what they felt during the jump, and the resulting confused scores were excluded.

mance, which will be referred to as K1. (K2 is the performance score for jumps from airplanes; see Chapter 13.) As training proceeded a few more criteria were added in the evaluation of each jump. The acceptance level for a jump, therefore, was changed as training proceeded. A tape recorder was placed close to the instructor giving the evaluation of each jump. Each soldier identified himself with his number and name, and the instructor then gave his critique.

## RESULTS

### Self-Rating of Fear

There was a clear tendency for the soldiers to report higher levels of fear on the highest platform. Figure 4.1 illustrates this on each sample day.

The statistical distribution of fear ratings was very skewed due to the fact that only the lower fear ratings were used by the soldiers. Nonparametric statistics were therefore used in the analyses. The tendency for the fear

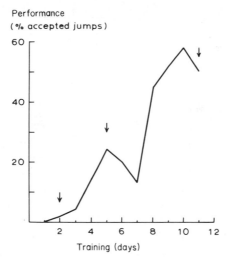

Performance
(% accepted jumps)

Training (days)

**Figure 4.2.** Performance in the mock tower for each jump day, with percentage of accepted jumps for the whole group. The arrows indicate sampling days.

ratings to be highest on the top of the platform was only significant on Jump Day 1 (Friedman two-way analysis of variance, $\chi^2 (2) = 6.07, p < .05$). The difference between the fear rating on top of the platform and the two other ratings gradually decreased as training proceeded.

There was also a gradual reduction in the fear levels reported, as can be seen from Figure 4.1. This reduction was statistically significant for the level of fear reported on the top platform (Friedman two-way analysis of variance, $\chi^2 (3) = 25.50, p < .001$).

## Performance

Figure 4.2 illustrates the performance scores on the different jump days. As can be seen from this figure, there is a clear increment over time. The number of accepted jumps increased over time, in spite of the fact that the demands on the performance also increased. Since the acceptance criterion changed over time, no statistical treatment of these data was performed.

## Dismissed Men

The subjective fear scores tended to be higher in the 13 men dismissed after Jump Day 1 and before the mock tower training period, but this tendency was not significant. This group showed a particular relationship between their fear level and the hormone responses. We will return to this issue in Chapter 14.

## DISCUSSION

The data on performance indicate that there was a clear training effect over time in the mock tower training period. The soldiers familiarized themselves with the various elementary jump techniques and the different types of errors that can occur during sky diving. The soldiers learned basic jump techniques, simulated parachute malfunctions, and familiarized themselves with the activation of the reserve parachute. During this learning period there was also a gradual reduction in the subjective fear level. There was a gradual increment in the soldier's trust in becoming a parachutist and in his abilities to master not only the mock tower training, but also the real jumps. There were, of course, many motivational factors involved in this, and we will discuss these questions in Chapters 13–16. In this chapter we are concerned only with satisfying our basic conditions: a gradual improvement in performance and a gradual reduction in subjective fear experience. The effectiveness and usefulness of self-rating of fear have been stressed by Basowitz, Persky, Korchin, and Grinker (1955, p. 82). Relatively moderate levels were reported during the mock tower training period in their study, as was the case with our soldiers. The Basowitz et al. ratings were taken before the actual training took place, and the level before an event is not necessarily predictive of what the fear will be at the crucial point. We found that there was a clear increment in self-rating of fear from the bottom to the top of the training tower. The time relationship is complex and may depend on experience or on personality characteristics related to who is going to be a good jumper (Fenz & Jones, 1972; see Chapter 1 for a discussion).

In conclusion, we seem to have a satisfactory experimental situation. We seem to have found a type of situation that makes it possible to test whether the animal model (Coover, Ursin, & Levine, 1973) is predictive for humans in similar situations. The men appeared to modify their behavior in a dangerous situation, they gradually learned to do the right things, and they also gradually learned that this particular situation was not dangerous to them. They gradually developed an expectancy of safely getting back down to the ground.

Therefore, we hypothesize that physiological parameters should show the same gradual decrement over time. We expect all physiological indicators of activation that are at work to show the same gradual decrease evident in the reports of subjective fear. In the following chapters, we will test this hypothesis for each of the physiological parameters that were measured.

## REFERENCES

Basowitz, H., Persky, H., Korchin, S. J., & Grinker, R. R. *Anxiety and stress. An interdisciplinary study of a life situation.* New York: McGraw-Hill (Blakiston Division), 1955.

Coover, G. D., Ursin, H., & Levine, S. Plasma-corticosterone levels during active avoidance learning in rats. *Journal of Comparative Physiological Psychology,* 1973, *82,* 170–174.

Fenz, W. D., & Jones, G. B. Individual differences in physiological arousal and performance in sport parachutists. *Psychosomatic Medicine,* 1972, *34,* 1–8.

*Part II*

# PHYSIOLOGY

# 5

# Cortisol Changes Following Repeated Experiences with Parachute Training[1]

SEYMOUR LEVINE

It has become increasingly apparent that neuroendocrine integration involves a multiplicity of responses to environmental change (Mason, 1975a). However, in attempting to assess the effects of psychological variables, the single most widely studied physiological parameter has been the activity of the pituitary–adrenal system. The history of the research in this area has been plagued by many problems, including the definition of stress (Levine, Goldman, & Coover, 1972; Mason, 1975b), the particular measurement used to indicate activity of the pituitary–adrenal system, and lack of control for the variety of variables with the potential to affect this system, including diet, drugs, circadian rhythms, and individual differences. In spite of these difficulties, however, it is obvious that the pituitary–adrenal system is extremely sensitive to changes in psychosocial situations.

In general, the evidence indicates that many presumably diverse stimuli can elicit marked elevations in pituitary–adrenal activity. There has been evidence (Allen, Allen, Greer, & Jacobs, 1973) indicating that certain variables can also produce suppression or inhibition of pituitary–adrenal

[1]Supported by Research Grant NICH&HD 02881 from the National Institutes of Health and USPHS Research Scientist Award K5-MH-19936 from the National Institute of Mental Health.

51

PSYCHOBIOLOGY OF STRESS:
A Study of Coping Men

activity (Davis, Memmott, Macfadden, & Levine, 1976; Goldman, Coover, & Levine, 1973; Levine & Coover, 1976; Levine *et al.*, 1972). At first glance the diversity of stimuli capable of eliciting a pituitary–adrenal response appears to support Selye's (1956) notion of "nonspecificity." However, it has been pointed out by Mason (1975b, p. 25) that although "emotional arousal is certainly one of the most ubiquitous or relatively 'nonspecific' reactions common to a great diversity of situations," it is distinctly possible that instead of the hormonal responses "being elicited by a great diversity of stimuli, . . . the hormonal responses are being elicited largely by a single stimulus or stimulus class common to a great diversity of situations, namely, the ubiquitous factors which elicit emotional arousal."

Activation of the pituitary–adrenal system by affective disturbances is no longer surprising or illuminating. What is surprising is that there has been relatively little attention paid to the mechanisms by which organisms modulate and inhibit the pituitary–adrenal response to a variety of both acute and chronic stimuli that can generally be defined as stressful. In both animals and man there appear to be mechanisms by which organisms process and evaluate stimuli and by which organisms minimize the emotional impact of those stimuli and thus inhibit the normally occurring increased activity of the pituitary–adrenal system.

In Chapter 1, we defined coping in part as that process by which organisms actively utilize environmental information to reduce the physiological response to existing environmental challenge. The design of the present experiment was motivated by a series of studies by Coover, Ursin, and Levine (1973) using an animal model of coping, with change in pituitary–adrenal activity during the process of active avoidance conditioning as the major indicator of coping. In the present studies we attempted to replicate, in a human situation, those conditions in which coping could be demonstrated in normal human subjects. The requirements of the design, based on the animal model, demanded two features: *(a)* that the organism have the capacity to improve his performance during repeated exposures to the same task and *(b)* that the characteristics of the task remain constant so that if physiologic changes were to occur they would be a function of the subject's reaction to that task and not of the changes in the task itself. Thus, this experiment asks the questions: How does the pituitary–adrenal system respond when men are faced with repeated but discrete exposures to fear-eliciting stimuli? How does the pattern of change in excretion of plasma cortisol relate to patterns of other hormonal changes occurring at the same time? The need for such an endocrine profile has been stressed by workers like Mason. Mason (1975b) states that "the picture emerging so far, from our study on *multihormonal patterns,* in fact, is one suggesting that such patterns are organized in a rather *specific* or *selective* manner, depending upon the particular stimulus under study, and probably in relation to the complex *interdependencies* in hormonal actions at the metabolic level [p. 27]." Although the present report focuses primarily on the measurements of plasma cortisol, this is the first of a series of chapters on several hormonal responses to the same stimuli in the same men. Ultimately we hope to demonstrate that there are indeed such profiles of endocrine response to the same stimulus conditions and that these profiles are idiosyncratic. Furthermore, although there are general patterns of responsiveness, there are also unique patterns that account for a large portion of the variance that we call individual differences.

## METHODS

The general methods used in this study are described in Chapter 2, which discusses in detail the overall methodology. Briefly, blood samples were obtained prior to exposure to the tower (basal samples), immediately following the first jump, and immediately following selected subsequent jumps from the tower. On all of these occasions, in addition to the immediate blood sample, a second blood sample was taken 20 min after the subject had reached the ground. All plasma samples were assayed in duplicate by the competitive protein-binding method of Murphy (1967). A human plasma pool was obtained from Stanford Clinical Laboratories and duplicate 0.1-ml aliquots were precipitated with ethanol and run with each assay for quality control. The globulin-binding source was .3% rat female morning plasma that had been previously absorbed on charcoal to reduce endogenous steroids (Westphal, 1971, p. 193). Tritiated hydrocortisone was obtained from New England Nuclear Corp. Dextran-coated charcoal was used to separate bound from free steroid, and the charcoal supernatants were decanted into 10 ml of Bray's solution and counted in a liquid scintillation counter. For 23 assays, the within-assay coefficient of variation for the control pool was 4.7% and the between-assay coefficient of variation for the control pool was 9.2%.

## RESULTS

Separate one-way analyses of variance were performed on the immediate post-jump sample and on the 20-min post-jump sample. The Days factor was treated as a repeated measure. The results of the analysis of variance (Bruning & Kintz, 1968) of the cortisol values obtained immediately after the jumps showed a highly significant change over Days ($F(3,126) = 47.8$, $p$

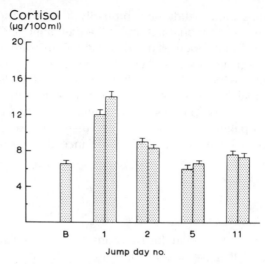

**Figure 5.1.** Plasma levels of cortisol. B, basal level. For each jump day two samples were obtained, one immediately after the jump and one 20 min later. The vertical line on the top of each bar indicates the standard error.

< .01; see Figure 5.1). The major source of this effect was the marked elevation seen in plasma cortisol values following the first jump. The $t$ tests for correlated samples showed that there was a significant fall from the first post-jump sample to the second post-jump sample ($p$ = .002). Furthermore, there was a significant fall from the second sample to the third sample ($p$ = .002). It should be noted, however, that although these differences are statistically significant, the absolute magnitude of change from the second to the third jump sample is relatively small compared to the magnitude of change seen following the first jump, in relationship both to basal levels prior to the jump and to subsequent values obtained after jump. The analysis of variance for the cortisol values obtained 20 min after the jump showed essentially the same pattern ($F(3,105)$ = 57.9, $p$ < .01). Again, there was a highly statistically significant change over Days and there was a significant fall from day to day until the third sample day, when the levels seemed to plateau. There was no further reduction, as was the case with samples obtained immediately after the jump.

## DISCUSSION

There now exists a large body of evidence that unequivocally demonstrates the sensitivity and lability of the pituitary–adrenal system in response to a wide variety of stimuli that can be generally classified as psychogenic.

The primary emphasis of much of this research on the pituitary–adrenal system has been on attempting to find some physiological correlate of emotion. Therefore, the major studies have examined the activation of the pituitary–adrenal system. It is now very clear, both in the animal literature and in human studies, that there also exists a process by which there is an active suppression of the adrenocortical response. In animals, the data indicate that factors such as control and feedback are important in the eventual reduction of the pituitary–adrenal response to repeatedly stressful stimuli.

In humans, although there have been no systematic experimental reports until this present experiment, there have been studies that have inferred that coping mechanisms can affect the adrenocortical response to stress. The primary focus of those studies, however, was on taking a naturally occurring life stress such as threat of surgery and noting that there are marked individual differences in the response to these events. The argument has been made that when there is little or no elevation in circulating corticoids the individual is coping. It is apparent that the term "coping" has a wide variety of interpretations and that, therefore, its use in various contexts has required constant definition and redefinition.

We believe that the definition of coping in terms of problem solving and the utilization of information is clearly exemplified in the experimental model that we have established in this study. In the present experiment, although there were individual differences in response to the initial tower jump, there was a striking consistency in the elevations of plasma cortisol among all men. The uniformity of this response can be a function of the fact that the stimulus was complex and included both fear and novelty since these individuals were totally inexperienced with this situation. Furthermore, since this was a training situation, there was a high degree of peer pressure to perform even though there was a high fear component in relationship to the potential danger of the tower. What is impressive about these results is not the uniformity of the elevation but the marked drop as a consequence of only one experience with the tower. Thus, coping mechanisms appeared to develop very rapidly in this human population and the ability to utilize the information about this situation, even after one exposure, was very apparent.

Both aspects of the coping model presented by Weiss (1968, 1971) can be inferred from this situation: (a) appropriate responses, that is, the subject, after the first experience, had already improved his performance in relationship to the task; (b) feedback, and perhaps this is even more important, because the subject had gone through the experience, which, although potentially dangerous and threatening, had no bad consequences and, thus, the maximum amount of feedback about the absence of danger in a potentially threatening situation was quickly obvious.

This experiment was in part generated by an animal model in which reductions in pituitary–adrenal activity, while still exposed to the stressful situation, were interpreted as coping. Although the process appears to be very similar in humans, the major difference appears to be in the rapidity with which humans can process information and utilize this information to show rapid adjustments to the situation. Although plasma cortisol levels were slightly elevated in the second jump, this elevation was nowhere comparable to that seen following the first jump; thus, we can assume that by the second jump, following just one exposure, the subjects had indeed processed the information about this situation and were successfully coping.

## REFERENCES

Allen, J. P., Allen, C. F., Greer, M. A., & Jacobs, J. J. Stress-induced secretion of ACTH. In A. Brodish & E. S. Redgate (Eds)., *Brain-pituitary-adrenal interrelationships.* Basel: S. Karger, 1973. Pp. 99–127.

Bruning, J. L., & Kintz, B. L. *Computational handbook of statistics.* Glenview, Ill.: Scott, Foresman and Company, 1968.

Coover, G. D., Ursin, H., & Levine, S. Plasma corticosterone levels during active avoidance learning in rats. *Journal of Comparative and Physiological Psychology, 1973, 82,* 170–174.

Davis, H., Memmott, J., Macfadden, L., & Levine, S. Pituitary-adrenal activity under different appetitive extinction procedures. *Physiology & Behavior, 1976, 17,* 687–690.

Goldman, L., Coover, G. D., & Levine, S. Bidirectional effects of reinforcement shifts on pituitary adrenal activity. *Physiology & Behavior, 1973, 10,* 209–214.

Levine, S., & Coover, G. D. Environmental control of suppression of the pituitary-adrenal system. *Physiology & Behavior, 1976, 17,* 35–37.

Levine, S., Goldman, L., & Coover, G. D. Expectancy and the pituitary-adrenal system. In R. Porter & J. Knight (Eds.), *Physiology, emotion and psychosomatic illness.* Amsterdam: Elsevier, 1972. Pp. 281–296.

Mason, J. W. Emotion as reflected in patterns of endocrine integration. In L. Levi (Ed.), *Emotions—their parameters and measurement.* New York: Raven Press, 1975. Pp. 143–181. (a)

Mason, J. W. A historical view of the stress field, part 2. *Journal of Human Stress, 1975, 1,* 22–36. (b)

Murphy, B.E.P. Some studies of the protein-binding of steroids and their application to the routine micro and ultramicro measurement of various steroids in body fluids by competitive protein-binding radioassay. *Journal of Clinical Endocrinology, 1967, 27,* 973–990.

Selye, H. *Stress.* Montreal: Acta, Inc., 1956.

Weiss, J. M. Effects of coping responses on stress. *Journal of Comparative and Physiological Psychology, 1968, 65,* 251–260.

Weiss, J. M. Effects of coping behavior in different warning signal conditions on stress pathology in rats. *Journal of Comparative and Physiological Psychology, 1971, 77,* 1–13.

Westphal, U. Steroid-protein interactions. In F. Gross, A. Labhart, T. Mann, L. T. Samuels, & J. Zander (Eds.), *Monographs on endocrinology,* Vol. 4. Berlin: Springer-Verlag, 1971.

# 6

# Testosterone

JULIAN M. DAVIDSON, ERLA R. SMITH,
and SEYMOUR LEVINE

It has long been known that chronic exposure of animals to stress can inhibit reproductive function (Baker, 1952; Selye, 1939), and similar indications can be found in the clinical literature (Sturgis, 1962). With the introduction of reliable methods for assaying gonadotropins in blood, it was established that various traumatic environmental conditions are associated with suppression of gonadotropins, particularly luteinizing hormone (LH) (Negro-Vilar, Orias, & McCann, 1973). On the other hand, recent findings have also shown that *acute* stress can stimulate the release of these pituitary hormones (Ajika, Kalra, Fawcett, Krulich, & McCann, 1972), just as in the classical case of adrenocorticotropic hormone (ACTH). The relationship between the early excitatory and later inhibitory phases, the mechanisms involved, and the possible adaptive value of these reactions are still little understood.

Testosterone, the major secretory product of the mammalian testes, is the specific concern of this chapter. The suppressive effects of stressful conditions on testosterone secretion have been well documented in the rat (Bardin & Peterson, 1967; Bliss, Frischat, & Samuels, 1972) as well as in other

[1]J. M. Davidson's research was supported by NASA Contract 9-14716. S. Levine's research was supported by NICHHD-02281 and Research Scientist Award K5-MH-19936.

57

PSYCHOBIOLOGY OF STRESS:
A Study of Coping Men

animal species, including primates (Mason, Kenion, & Collins, 1968; Rose, Gordon, & Bernstein, 1972). The many different noxious stimuli used in these studies include electric shock, prolonged swimming, anesthesia, avoidance conditioning, surgery, and fasting. In humans, testosterone suppression has also been reported in such traumatic situations as surgery (Carstensen, Amer, Wide, & Amer, 1973), intense military training (Kreuz, Rose, & Jennings, 1972), and severe exercise (Vermeulen, 1973). However, the testosterone response to acute stress of purely psychogenic origin has not been elucidated in humans.

How do circulating testosterone levels respond when men are faced with repeated exposure to a fear-evoking situation and how does the course of change in testosterone secretion relate to that of the classical glucocorticoid "stress hormones"? This chapter addresses these questions.

## METHODS

Analyses of testosterone were performed on blood samples obtained (a) in the basal state; (b) immediately after the first, second, fifth, and eleventh training jumps; and (c) 20 min after these jumps. Eliminating missing samples, 38–42 of the parachutists were represented in the final analyses.

Plasma testosterone was assayed by radioimmunoassay according to the method of Frankel, Mock, Wright, and Kamel (1975) with minor modifications. An androgen-specific antiserum (supplied by B. Caldwell) was used, and an organic extraction of testosterone from plasma was the only purification step. The antiserum cross-reacts with dihydrotestosterone and the $5\alpha$-androstan–$3\alpha$ and $3\beta$, $17\beta$-diols to the extent of about 47%. Chromatography to separate these steriods did not, however, materially increase the accuracy of testosterone measurements, due to the low blood levels of the interfering androgens and the losses involved in the additional processing (Falvo & Nalbandov, 1974; Damassa, 1976).

The statistical analysis was performed by analysis of variance by subjects (Bruning & Kintz, 1968) followed by t tests for correlated means for comparisons between individual samples.

## RESULTS

The ANOVA treatment by subjects (Bruning & Kintz, 1968) of plasma testosterone levels in samples obtained immediately after the jump showed a significant change over Days ($F(3,129) = 113.5, p < .001$, two tailed). The t test for correlated samples showed that there was a significant fall below the basal level on the first jump and a significant increment from the first to the

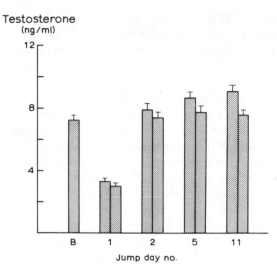

**Figure 6.1.**   Plasma testosterone levels.

second jump (see Figure 6.1). There was a significant increase above the basal level on the fifth jump, and this increment was also evident on the eleventh ($p < .001$).

The ANOVA analysis for the blood samples obtained 20 min after the jump showed a similar picture during the first part of the experiment. Again, there was a significant fall in plasma testosterone after the first jump below basal levels, and the values returned to slightly above the basal level following the second jump. The decrement in the 20-min sample over that obtained immediately after the second jump was not significant. Following the fifth and eleventh jumps, however, the values dropped significantly from the first to the second samples ($p < .001$), and the second samples were not significantly different from those obtained on the basal day.

The pattern of response thus manifested three separate elements of importance: *(a)* a profound drop in testosterone level after the first jump; *(b)* elevated levels immediately after all subsequent jumps, with gradual increments from jump to jump; and *(c)* declining levels during each 20-min post-jump period.

## DISCUSSION

Though physical stresses are well known to depress circulating testosterone levels, these data show that marked supression can also be caused by conditions where the independent variable is purely psychogenic—fear-provoking situations. This response disappeared after the second exposure to the stress, 1 week later, presumably because much less fear was experienced at that time. On the other hand, the small but significant rise over basal levels found on subsequent exposures indicated that testosterone was still responding in the later jumps, albeit in the opposite direction.

Since it was not possible to identify when apprehension was first felt by the subjects, the time course of this response cannot be accurately determined. Nevertheless, the data can be plausibly interepreted by reference to the clinical and animal literature on effects of stress on testosterone levels. Studies in humans and experimental animals show that testosterone suppression is a response with a relatively slow time course (hours to days) and that it is found following relatively severe stresses. Experimental studies in rats show that mild and severe stresses can acutely (within a very few minutes) elevate blood levels of the hormones of the pituitary–testicular axis. Thus, for instance, a 15-min rotation in an animal centrifuge elevated plasma LH in male rats, whereas a 4-hr exposure to this stress suppressed both LH and testosterone (Gray, Smith, Damassa, Ehrenkranz, & Davidson, 1977). We have also found marked elevations of plasma testosterone 15 and 30 min after the stresses of restraint and cardiac puncture (under ether anesthesia) in the squirrel monkey (Coe, Mendoza, Smith, Davidson, & Levine, unpublished data).

Thus, it seems likely that the testosterone suppression on the first jump was in response to severe apprehension felt throughout that morning—as indicated by the very high urinary epinephrine levels at 8 a.m. and the self-reported fear level. On later jumps, it seemed reasonable to assume that, although the subjects were not as stressed earlier in the day, the apprehension they experienced immediately before the jump was reflected in a transient rise in plasma testosterone, which disappeared by 20 min after jumping. Whether this was followed by a phase of testosterone suppression is of course not known.

Conflicting views are presented in the literature as to the mechanisms by which stress reduces testosterone levels. A variety of studies have reported that there is no change in follicle-stimulating hormone and LH secretion following surgical stress, despite suppression of the level of androgen (Aono, Kurachi, Mizutani, Hamanaka, Vozumi, Nakasimi, Koshiyama, & Matsumoto, 1972; Carstensen et al., 1973; Monden, Koshiyama, Tanaka, Mizutani, Aono, Hamanaka, Vozumi, & Matsumoto, 1972). The major hormone involved in control of testosterone production is LH, and it is often difficult to substantiate decreases in this hormone below the normal level in males because of assay sensitivity problems coupled with the variability resulting, in part, from the pulsatile secretion of LH. We have clearly demonstrated, however, that LH is suppressed under conditions where rats were subjected to different stresses that reduced plasma testosterone (Gray et al., 1977 and unpublished data). A study on men utilizing continuous sampling and sophisticated statistical analysis clearly demonstrated the close relationship between suppression of testosterone and LH levels following surgery (Ellis, Evans, Phillips, Murray, Jacobs, James, & Dudley, 1976).

Selye's (1939) original concept of the relationship between the effects of stress on ACTH and on gonadotropins was that, when the pituitary is driven to markedly increase ACTH secretion, a shift in secretory capacity occurs such that reduction of the secretion of other hormones necessarily follows. It is now clear, however, that such a mechanism is not compatible with the biphasic gonadotropic response to stress, since gonadotropins and ACTH are elevated simultaneously during the acute poststress phase.

In this study, the elevation in plasma cortisol and its recovery coincided with the suppression of plasma testosterone and its return to the base level. This suggests that the pituitary–adrenocortical activation, which is most rapid, may be responsible for the pituitary–testicular suppression. A plausible mechanism exists for such an effect: Elevated corticosteroids can depress the pituitary–gonadal axis, presumably by acting on the hypothalamo–pituitary unit to inhibit gonadotropin secretion (Kirchner, Lipsett, & Collins, 1965; Smith, Johnson, Weick, Levine, & Davidson, 1971). However, it seems that the adrenals are not necessary for the testicular effect in rats, since the suppression of testosterone by subcutaneous implantation of a gauze sponge was not prevented by adrenalectomy (Gray et al., 1977). Although such experimental data are not available on man, the lack of an individual correlation between cortisol and testosterone levels on any given jump (see Chapter 12) indeed suggests that the pattern of response of the two hormones over successive exposures to the stress represents independent correlated events rather than causally interrelated events.

## REFERENCES

Ajika, K., Kalra, S. P., Fawcett, C. P., Krulich, L., & McCann, S. M. The effect of stress and Nembutal on plasma levels of gonadotropins and prolactin in ovariectomized rats. *Endocrinology*, 1972, *90*, 707–715.

Aono, T., Kurachi, K., Mizutani, S., Hamanaka, Y., Vozumi, T., Nakasimi, A., Koshiyama, K., & Matsumoto, K. Influence of major surgical stress on plasma levels of testosterone, luteinizing hormone and follicle-stimulating hormone in male patients. *Journal of Clinical Endocrinology and Metabolism*, 1972, *35*, 535–542.

Baker, B. L. A comparison of the histological changes induced by experimental hypoadrenocorticalism inanition. *Recent Progress in Hormone Research*, 1952, *7*, 331.

Bardin, C. W., & Peterson, R. E. Studies of androgen production by the rat: Testosterone and androstenedione content of blood. *Endocrinology*, 1967, *80*, 38–44.

Bliss, E. L., Frischat, A., & Samuels, L. Brain and testicular function. *Life Sciences*, 1972, *2*, 231–238.

Bruning, J. L., and Kintz, B. L. *Computational Handbook of Statistics.* Glenview, Ill.: Scott, Foresman & Co., 1968.

Carstensen, H., Amer, I., Wide, L., & Amer, B. Plasma testosterone, LH and FSH during the first 24 hours after surgical operations. *Journal of Steroid Biochemistry,* 1973, *4,* 605–611.

Damassa, D. A. A quantitative analysis of the physiological and behavioral roles of testosterone in male reproductive function. Ph. D. thesis, Stanford University, 1976.

Ellis, B. W., Evans, P. F., Phillips, P. D., Murray, M. A. F., Jacobs, H. S., James, V. H. T., & Dudley, H. A. F. Effects of surgery on plasma testosterone, luteinizing hormone and follicle-stimulating hormone: A comparison of pre- and postoperative patterns of secretion. *Journal of Endocrinology,* 1976, *69,* 25p (abstract).

Falvo, R. E., & Nalbandov, A. V. Radioimmunoassay of peripheral plasma testosterone in males from eight species using a specific antibody without chromatography. *Endocrinology,* 1974, *95,* 1466–1468.

Frankel, A. I., Mock, E. J., Wright, W. W., & Kamel, F. Characterization and physiological validation of a radioimmunoassay for plasma testosterone in the male rat. *Steroids,* 1975, *25,* 73–98.

Gray, G. D., Smith, E. R., Damassa, D. A., Ehrenkranz, J. R. L., & Davidson, J. M. Chronic suppression of pituitary-testicular function by stress in rats. *Federation Proceedings,* 1977, *36,* 322 (abstract).

Kirchner, M. A., Lipsett, M. B., & Collins, D. R. Plasma ketosteroids and testosterone in man: A study of the pituitary testicular axis. *Journal of Clinical Investigation,* 1965, *44,* 657.

Kreuz, L. E., Rose, R. M., & Jennings, J. R. Suppression of plasma testosterone levels and psychological stress. *Archives of General Psychiatry,* 1972, *26,* 479–482.

Mason, J. W., Kenion, C. C., & Collins, D. R. Urinary testosterone response to 72-hr avoidance sessions in the monkey. *Psychosomatic Medicine,* 1968, *30,* 721–732.

Monden, Y., Koshiyama, K., Tanaka, H., Mizutani, S., Aono, T., Hamanaka, Y., Vozumi, T., & Matsumoto, K. Influence of major surgical stress on plasma testosterone, plasma LH and urinary steroids. *Acta Endocrinologica,* 1972, *69,* 542–552.

Negro-Vilar, A., Orias, R., & McCann, S. M. Evidence for a pituitary site of action for the acute inhibition of LH release by estrogen in the rat. *Endocrinology,* 1973, *92,* 1680–1684.

Rose, R. M., Gordon, T. P., & Bernstein, I. S. Plasma testosterone levels in the male rhesus: Influences of sexual and social stimuli. *Science,* 1972, *178,* 643–645.

Selye, H. The effect of adaptation to various damaging agents on the female sex organs in the rat. *Endocrinology,* 1939, *25,* 615.

Smith, E. R., Johnson, J., Weick, R. F., Levine, S., & Davidson, J. M. Inhibition of the reproductive system in immature rats by intracerebral implantation of cortisol. *Neuroendocrinology,* 1971, *8,* 94–106.

Sturgis, S. H. *The Gynecologic patients.* New York: Grune & Stratton, 1962.

Vermeulen, A. Testosterone in plasma: A physio-pathological study. *Verhandelingen van de Koninklijke Vlaamse Academie voor Geneeskunde van Belgie,* 1973, *35,* 95–180.

# 7

# Urinary Levels of Epinephrine and Norepinephrine in Parachutist Trainees

JAN R. HANSEN, KARL F. STØA,
ARNOLDUS SCHYTTE BLIX, and HOLGER URSIN

Catecholamines, released locally from the sympathetic nerve terminals and systemically from the adrenal medulla, are mediators of many of the bodily changes that occur in states of arousal and fear and in defense situations (Cannon, 1932; Euler & Hellner, 1952). The catecholamines released in excess of the local capacity for reuptake and metabolism (Iversen, 1967) occur in the circulation and appear eventually in the urine together with their metabolites.

All arousal or "stress-producing" stimuli seem to increase the circulation levels of catecholamines, as also indicated by the increased urine levels. This has been reported for situations ranging from laughter and fear to changes in work schedules (Levi, 1972). Physical stress in itself may also influence these hormones (Sonka, Kopecka, Parlova, Zbirkova, & Stas, 1974). Even so, the possibility of a specificity in this endocrine response has been a matter of great interest (Ax, 1953; Elmadjian, 1959; Elmadjian, Hope, & Lamson, 1957; Schachter, 1957).

Very little is known about the relationship between the catecholamines and coping. The possibility of such a relationship has long been an important issue in the debate on "stress" and health. For instance, Charvat, Dell, and Folkow (1964) suggested that an increase in adrenergic activity which

63

PSYCHOBIOLOGY OF STRESS:
A Study of Coping Men

was not followed by an increase in muscle activity could be nonadaptive and thus lead to pathological changes in the cardiovascular system. Repeated cardiovascular "drives" may contribute to a gradual development of essential hypertension, at least in genetically predisposed men, as is the case in rats (Folkow, 1975).

There is one particular reason for using indicators from urine samples rather than blood sampling: The sampling procedure itself is a minor stressor. We found it to be of interest to use at least one biochemical indicator of activation that did not involve blood sampling. On the other hand, not all men were able to produce urinary specimens on command under our field conditions. We have found this to be a source of some systematic variation (Chapters 12 and 13).

Methods are now available for analyzing epinephrine and norepinephrine and their metabolites in blood and urine with a high degree of specificity (Passon & Peuler, 1973). This chapter examines the relationships between a strict fear state that does not contain aggressive components or heavy work loads and the urine levels of epinephrine and norepinephrine.

## MATERIALS AND METHODS

### Sampling of Urine

All participants collected their samples in carefully labeled containers (unused 1-liter milk cartons) at the times indicated, and they all followed the same strict routine. After a breakfast that was a controlled diet including .5 liter of milk (skimmed on Days 1 and 12; whole milk all other days) but omitting coffee, tea, cola, and other soft drinks, all men emptied their bladders at 0700 hr; this urine was discarded. One hour later (0800 hr), at the base of the mock training tower on jump days or in front of the Medical Center on the basal day, each bladder was again emptied as completely as possible, and this collected urine represented the pre-jump sample.

For basal levels, sampled on August 10, this was the only sample obtained on that day. During the tower training days, a second, 2-hr sample was obtained at 1000 hr. All training procedures were stopped when the sample was due, and everyone urinated at the same time, regardless of their location in the tower or in the field.

The men were clearly instructed about the necessity of emptying the bladder completely each time, and they were told not to urinate except in the carton during the test period and, in fact, had little opportunity to break this rule.

The urinary samples were immediately brought to a field laboratory, where all samples were transferred to plastic bottles and acidified to pH2–3 with small quantities of concentrated sulfuric acid before freezing in a deep freezer. Further transportation was carried out in containers with dry ice. The samples were stored at $-20°C$ until analysis. All samples from one man were analyzed in the same run to avoid interassay variation.

A total of 381 samples was collected. As noted above, not all men were able to produce a specimen every time. Protocols were kept over which samples were not obtained so as not to confuse these with possible losses during analysis (see Chapter 12). Full sets of data (at least 8 of the 9 possible samples) were obtained only from 22 of the 44 men. In addition to the losses during the field experiment, some samples were also lost in the laboratory procedure.

## Assay for Urinary Norepinephrine and Epinephrine

A radiometric method originally devised by Engelman, Portnoy, and Lovenberg (1968) and modified by Passon and Peuler (1973) was used for the determination of urinary levels of catecholamines. The method is highly specific and sensitive enough to estimate normal amonts of both epineph- rine and norepinephrine even in plasma. The assay is based on the conver- sion of epinephrine and norepinephrine to their corresponding [$^3$H] metanephrines by the enzyme catechol O-methyltransferase (COMT), with $S$-[$^3$H] adenosylmethionine ([$^3$H]SAM) serving as the methyl donor. After separation of the metanephrines by thin-layer chromatography, conversion to vanillin with $NaIO_4$, and a number of extractions, the final vanillin extract is then measured by liquid scintillation counting.

Preliminary experiments showed that assays directly in acidified urine resulted in considerable errors, with values apparently varying inversely with concentration of urine. Extracts were therefore routinely made prior to the radiometric assay. The procedure used was a slight modification of published methods (Robinson & Watts, 1965; Viktora, Baukal, & Wolff, 1968), and the main steps may be summarized as follows. The pH of the urine was adjusted to 8.3–8.5 with NaOH. Catecholamines were absorbed to acid-washed $Al_2O_3$. After subsequent washings with distilled water, the catecholamines were extracted with acetic acid.

Rat liver catechol O-methyltransferase was isolated as described by Axel- rod and Tomchick (1958) with the modifications proposed by Passon and Peuler (1973).

Extracts corresponding to 100 $\mu$l of urine were adjusted to pH 8.2 with .2 M Tris·Cl buffer and processed according to Passon and Peuler (1973) as follows.

Epinephrine and norepinephrine were converted to metanephrine (MN) and normetanephrine (NMN) by incubation for 60 min at 37°C in a mixture containing, in addition to the urine extracts, SAM, [$^3$H] SAM, reduced glutathione, MgCl$_2$, and COMT. The reaction was stopped by adding borate buffer, pH 11.0. Unlabeled MN and NMN were also added.

MN and NMN were extracted into toluene:isoamyl alcohol (3:2) by shaking. After centrifugation, the organic phase was transferred to another tube and taken to dryness by heating under a stream of air. The residue was dissolved in ethanol, streaked on a silica gel plate, and developed for 3 hr in isopropanol:$n$-butanol:H$_2$O:formic acid (60:20:19:1). After air-drying, the bands corresponding to MN and NMN were scrapted off, having been located under uv light. MN and NMN were eluted from the silica gel by shaking with 4 N NH$_4$OH and H$_2$O. MN and NMN were converted to vanillin by incubating the eluate with NalO$_4$ at 37°C for 10 min. The eluate was then acidified with 10 N acetic acid and the vanillin was extracted into toluene. Another extraction into 2 N NH$_4$OH was followed by lowering the pH with acetic acid once more and then extracting into toluene. Liquifluor was added to this final toluene extract, which was counted in a Packard 3330 liquid scintillation counter. Calculation was based on standards of epinephrine and norepinephrine carried through the whole assay. Blanks were subtracted from both standards and samples. Creatinine was determined according to the method of Slot (1965), modified for urine, and expressed as micrograms in the total volume of urine collected for each sample for each individual.

## RESULTS

### Creatinine

The creatinine values obtained for the 0800- and 1000-hr samples showed little individual variation, and these data thus indicated that each individual had produced samples representative of the total urine production at the respective sampling intervals. Values for catecholamines were therefore expressed as micrograms per microgram of creatinine in each of the individual samples. All ANOVA tests and data on the changes over time derive from the 22 men with full sample series. Additional data from the men who did not go through the whole training period will not be dealt with in this chapter, but are used in the factor analyses and the correlation studies reported in Chapters 13–16.

### Epinephrine

The mean values of epinephrine in the urine collected in the course of the study are given in Figure 7.1.

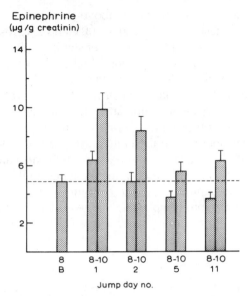

**Figure 7.1.** Urinary levels of epinephrine before (0800 hr) and after (1000 hr) the jump from the mock tower training apparatus. The vertical line on the top of each bar indicates the standard error of the mean. B, basal level obtained at 0800 hr. The broken horizontal line illustrates that the 0800 hr levels (pre-jump) gradually drop below the level obtained on the basal day.

Pre-jump values of epinephrine reached a maximum on the first day of jumping ($p < .01$, $t$ test for correlated samples) and declined significantly with time for each of the following pre-jump periods (cf. Figure 7.1). An ANOVA treatment by subjects (Bruning & Kinz, 1968) of the results from the urinary samples obtained at 0800 hr on jump days showed a significant change over Days ($F(3,63) = 11.3$, $p < .001$, two tailed). It should be noted that epinephrine was lower during the pre-jump period on the last 2 test days (Jumps 5 and 11, Figure 7.1) than on the basal day ($p < .01$), thus indicating that the adrenomedullary discharge during the second morning in camp was significantly above that recorded when the participants had been exposed to the camp program for nearly a month.

Post-jump values of epinephrine were significantly higher than the pre-jump values throughout the experiment ($p < .001$ for all days, $t$ tests). Analogous to that observed for the pre-jump values, a significant decline in the post-jump values of epinephrine was also observed with Time in Training ($F(3,63) = 13.34$, $p < .001$, ANOVA).

It should be noted that there was no significant difference between the post-jump levels of epinephrine obtained on the first and second jump days.

Both of these values were significantly above those obtained in the post-jump samples for the last 2 test days ($p < .001$ and $.01$, respectively). The values from Jump Days 5 and 11 did not differ significantly, even though the values on Jump Day 11 were significantly higher than the basal value ($p < .05$), which was not the case for Jump Day 5.

These data show that the situation occurring between 0800 and 1000 hr on each of the jump days clearly stimulated the adrenal medulla to release epinephrine, which was found in the urine within the end of this period.

There was a clear decrease in the epinephrine response to the situation, which was particularly clear for the pre-jump (0800-hr) values. There was also a clear reduction in the absolute values reached in the post-jump samples, but there was a significant response in this system even in the well-trained men. Since the pre-jump value decreased over time, we cannot determine whether the post-jump increase itself was decreasing.

## Norepinephrine

The mean values of norepinephrine in the urinary samples are shown in Figure 7.2.

Pre-jump values of norepinephrine rose above the basal value only on Jump Day 1. The ANOVA analysis showed a clear change over Days ($F(3, 63) = 19.1, p < .001$), but this was probably due to the value before the first jump, which was the highest value obtained and the only value significantly higher than the basal level ($p < .001$, $t$ test for correlated samples). No other pre-jump value differed from the basal value or from the other pre-jump values. This was in remarkable contrast to the epinephrine findings. In the late jumps, pre-jump levels of epinephrine reached a level below the basal level; this did not happen for norepinephrine. Norepinephrine reached its peak value on the pre-jump sample Jump Day 1; epinephrine pre-jump values were also highest at that time, but for epinephrine there was a further increment after the jump.

The 1000-hr post-jump norepinephrine values were higher than the basal values for both Jump Day 1 ($p < .001$) and Jump Day 2 ($p < .01$), as well as for Jump Day 11 ($p. < .05$). Again, there was a clear decline with training. The change for these values was significant over Days ($F(3,63) = 11.8, p < .001$, ANOVA). The decline from Day 1 was clear, and so was the decline from Jump Day 2 to Jump Day 5 ($p. < .05$), which was not significantly different from the basal level. The value on Day 11 was not different from that on Day 5, but was significantly higher than the basal level ($p < .05$). The increase from the pre-jump values was not as evident as for epinephrine. It should be noted that, unlike the values for epinephrine, there was no signifi-

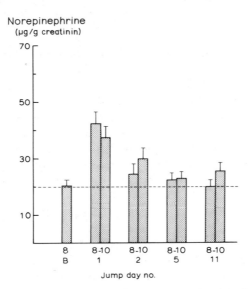

**Figure 7.2.** Urinary levels of norepinephrine before (0800 hr) and after (1000 hr) the jump from the mock tower training apparatus. The vertical line on the top of each bar indicates the standard error of the mean. B, basal level obtained at 0800 hr. The broken horizontal line illustrates that the 0800 hr levels (pre-jump) do not drop below the level obtained on the basal day.

cant rise from the pre-jump values on Day 1 or Day 5. The 0800-hr pre-jump value was very high for Day 1, and there was no further increase at 1000 hr; on the contrary, there was a tendency for a decrease to occur. For Day 2, there was an increase from the 0800-hr pre-jump value ($P < .01$). On Jump Day 5, there was no significant difference from the basal value or from the 0800-hr pre-jump value, but there was an increase on Jump Day 11 ($p < .001$).

The rationale behind our design was to have the 1000-hr sample as a post-jump ("stress") sample after the men had jumped. This schedule worked out except for the first day, when only 24 of the 57 men had actually jumped at 1000 hr and only 8 of those gave a full sample series (see Figures 7.1 and 7.2).

This gave us the opportunity to evaluate how much of the "stress" evident in the sample on Jump Day 1 was due to the jump itself. There was no statistical difference between the epinephrine or norepinephrine levels found at 1000 hr in those eight men who had jumped compared with the rest of the full sample material ($t\ (20) = 1.33$ and $0.81$, respectively).

## DISCUSSION

Due to its sensitivity and specificity, the method used for the catecholamine determination allowed a better differentiation between epinephrine and norepinephrine in urine samples than had been possible previously. The uniformity of the creatinine values indicated that the sampling procedure had been adequate and that the men had emptied their bladders satisfactorily. The levels of norepinephrine and epinephrine excretion observed for the reference sample were within the range reported in other studies, and the creatinine values were also in good agreement between individuals. It is therefore reasonable to assume that the methods employed and the sampling procedure used were satisfactory for our purpose.

The urinary samples seemed to yield a representative picture of the internal state of an individual, since both arousal and coping effects were evident and they were similar in certain aspects to those derived from the blood samples. This nontraumatic sample procedure has great advantages, as pointed out by Levi (1972). However, because there were slight differences between those men who were able to produce urinary specimens under the field conditions and those who were not, we shall return to this point in the discussion of the psychology factor analyses (Chapter 13).

Both amines were excreted in our situation, which involves a minimum of physical activity. Secretion of both catecholamines responded to the psychological situation in principle like the other hormones, and in principle according to our basic hypothesis. There was a clear and significant rise in both catecholamine hormones on Jump Day 1, paralleling the relatively high level of subjective fear. As performance improved and the subjective fear was reduced or eliminated, the release of both amines was reduced. Again, for both amines, it was not the external situation or the physical demand but the subjective evaluation of the situation that determined the internal state. For this important psychological and physiological dimension, both amines reacted in much the same way.

However, there were some clear differences between the two amines. Norepinephrine secretion reached the highest level before the first jump, and there was no further significant increase in the post-jump sample taken at 1000 hr. Only eight of the men had jumped at that time. For the second jump, the jump itself made a significant difference. However, no such increase was evident on Jump Day 5. On Day 11 there was again a significant increase from the pre-jump to the post-jump sample.

The fluctuation in pattern of epinephrine excretion was different from that of norepinephrine excretion. There was a significant increase from the pre-jump to the post-jump sample on all days.

We found that the epinephrine response was surprisingly stable. Every time the man performed his jump, this hormone showed an increment. The additional heart rate response (see Chapter 9) also showed stability; there was no significant change over time. We conclude that, even in fairly experienced jumpers, there remains a short-lasting sympathetic activation at the time of the crucial behavior, the jump. This reaction has many similarities to the defense reaction (Folkow & Neil, 1971). We will refer to such short-lasting activations as *phasic* activation. During the preparation of this chapter, a report from Froberg, Karlsson, Levi, and Lidberg (1975) appeared. They found that in men kept awake and constantly stressed there was a clear circadian rhythm in the epinephrine level, with a significant increment in the early morning hours. Since we did not investigate this possibility in our material, a circadian morning increment must be considered an alternative explanation to our findings for that hormone. However, we still hold that there is a "phasic" activation, evident at least from our heart rate data (Chapter 9). In addition, the epinephrine increase correlates with psychological factors and other physiological indicators of activation.

Bloom, Euler, and Frankenhaeuser (1963) found no "habituation" to the stress of parachute jumping in their comparison of a number of officers and trainees or between the first and the sixth jump from airplanes. We agree that, for epinephrine, there is a persistent increase even in coping men, but there is a significant decline in the total level reached.

Norepinephrine responded to the apprehension experienced by the men before their first jump and occurred in response to a subjective fear even at the bottom of the tower on Jump Day 1. This hormone, therefore, appears to be involved in a longer-lasting activation. We will refer to such long-lasting activation as *tonic* activation. This tonic activation is influenced by the coping effect.

There was also a tonic component in the epinephrine response. As coping developed and subjective fear was reduced, the 0800-hr values of epinephrine were significantly reduced to values lower than the "basal" value. This was not evident for norepinephrine. The release of these two amines, therefore, differed in their sensitivities to the apprehension before the jump; pre-jump levels of epinephrine were clearly related to fear, whereas the norepinephrine response perhaps was influenced by a less well-defined challenge to the coping potential of the individual. In the men who quit after the first jump, there was a very significant correlation between fear score and norepinephrine level. This may be a "fear of failure" component, and Chapter 14 deals with why no such relationship was found among the accepted men.

It has long been known that the central nervous system is capable of selective activation of epinephrine- and norepinephrine-producing cells in the adrenal gland (Folkow & von Euler, 1954). Most of the norepinephrine in the urine seems to be derived from the adrenergic nerve endings, which always "spill over" a fraction of the transmitter to the blood and, ultimately, a fraction of this substance appears in the urine. It has been postulated that the two catecholamines are selectively released in different emotional states, but no clear story has been revealed as yet.

Obrist (1976) suggested that what he referred to as "active coping" with fear precipitated an epinephrine-like effect on the cardiovascular system and that "passive coping" evoked norepinephrine-like effects. Experimental evidence for this position comes mainly from Frankenhaeuser and her group. She held that epinephrine is involved in the active coping behavior of healthy individuals, not only in fight and flight situations, but also when individuals cope with the stressors of everyday life (Frankenhaeuser & Johansson, 1975). The ability of children (Johansson, Frankenhaeuser, & Magnusson, 1973) and adults (Frankenhaeuser, Nordheden, Myrsten, & Post, 1971) to cope with the environment correlated with the epinephrine output. The results were less consistent for norepinephrine. The norepinephrine issue may be confused if the tasks involve muscular use, since muscular exercise itself may increase the amount of norepinephrine that escapes to the bloodstream (Folkow, Häggendahl, & Lisander, 1967).

Obrist related his activity/passivity dimension to different emotional states such as aggression and fear. We found no support for a differentiation along this axis. In our situation, where fear must be assumed to be dominating without or with very little aggression, both catecholamines responded. Epinephrine seemed to be involved in "active coping," as suggested by Obrist. We suggest that norepinephrine is related to types of apprehension, which may be what Obrist referred to as "passive coping." The relationship between the catecholamines and specific psychological variables will be discussed in more detail in Chapter 14.

In conclusion, the jump itself gave an epinephrine response in addition to a norepinephrine response that was built up during the anticipatory period in the tower. The norepinephrine response, which is both neural and humoral, expressed a general activation of the sympathetic nervous system, with vasoconstriction and increased blood pressure, but with moderate or no increase in heart frequency, probably because of a vagal compensation. The epinephrine response, which has primarily a metabolic effect, was related to the defense alarm reaction released in response to the jump. Immediately before the jump, and as part of the defense alarm response, vagal inhibition of the heart was withdrawn. This revealed the sympathetic bias on the heart.

Tonic and phasic activations differed with regard to the coping effect. The apprehensive aspects of the catecholamine response were reduced with coping, which was evident from the decreases in norepinephrine, the pre-jump levels of epinephrine, and the other blood variables. The "defense-alarm response" was not strongly influenced by coping; it continued to occur even in fairly experienced men.

## ACKNOWLEDGMENTS

The authors are grateful to Karen Helle, University of Bergen, and Bjørn Folkow, University of Gothenberg, for valuable discussions.

## REFERENCES

Ax, A. F. The physiological differentiation between fear and anger in humans. *Psychosomatic Medicine,* 1953, *15,* 433–442.

Axelrod, J., & Tomchick, R. Enzymatic O-methylation of epinephrine and other catechols. *Journal of Biological Chemistry,* 1958, *233,* 702–705.

Bloom, G., Euler, U.S. von, & Frankenhaeuser, M. Catecholamine excretion and personality traits in paratroop trainees. *Acta Physiologica Scandinavica,* 1963, *58,* 77–89.

Bruning, J. L., & Kinz, B. L. *Computational handbook of statistics.* Glenview, Ill.: Scott, Foresman & Co., 1968.

Cannon, J. *The wisdom of the body.* New York: Norton, 1932.

Charvat, J., Dell, P., & Folkow, B. Mental factors and cardiovascular disorder. *Cardiologia,* 1964, *44,* 124–141.

Elmadjian, F. Excretion and metabolism of epinephrine. *Pharmacological Review,* 1959, *11,* 409–415.

Elmadjian, F., Hope, J. M., & Lamson, E. T. Excretion of epinephrine and norepinephrine in various emotional states. *Journal of Clinical Endocrinology and Metabolism,* 1957, *17,* 608–620.

Engelman, K., Portnoy, B., & Lovenberg, W. A sensitive and specific double-isotope derivative method for the determination of catecholamines in biological specimens. *American Journal of Medical Science,* 1968, *255,* 259–268.

Euler, U.S.von, & Hellner, S. Noradrenalin excretion in muscular work. *Acta Physiologica Scandinavica,* 1952, *26,* 183–191.

Folkow, B. Central neurohormonal mechanisms in spontaneously hypertensive rats compared with human essential hypertension. *Clinical Science and Molecular Medicine,* 1975, *48,* 205s–214s.

Folkow, B., & Euler, U.S.von. Selective activation of noradrenaline and adrenaline producing cells in the cat's adrenal gland by hypothalamic stimulation. *Circulation Research,* 1954, *2,* 191–195.

Folkow, B., Häggendal, J., & Lisander, B. Extent of release and elimination of noradrenaline at peripheral adrenergic nerve terminals. *Acta Physiologica Scandinavica,* 1967, *suppl. 307,* 1–38.

Folkow, B., & Neil, E. *Circulation,* New York; Oxford University Press, 1971.

Frankenhaeuser, M., & Johansson, G. Behaviour and catecholamines in children. In L. Levi (Ed.), *Society, stress and disease*. London: Oxford University Press, 1975 Pp. 118–126.
Frankenhaeuser, M., Nordheden, B., Myrsten, A.-L., & Post, B. Psychophysiological reactions to understimulation and overstimulation. *Acta Psychologica*, 1971, *35*, 298–308.
Frøberg, J.E., Karlsson, C.-G., Levi, L., & Lidberg, L. Psychobiological circadian rhythms during a 72-hour vigil. *Försvarsmedicin*, 1975, *11*, 192–201.
Iversen, L. L. *The uptake and storage of noradrenaline in sympathetic nerves*. Cambridge: Cambridge University Press, 1967.
Johansson, G., Frankenhaeuser, M., & Magnusson, D. Catecholamine output in school children as related to performance and adjustment. *Scandinavian Journal of Psychology*, 1973, *14*, 20–28.
Levi, L. Stress and distress in response to psychosocial stimuli. *International Series of Monographs in Experimental Psychology*, 1972, No. 17.
Obrist, P. A. The cardiovascular-behavioral interaction—as it appears today (Presidential address, 1975). *Psychophysiology*, 1976, *13*, 95–107.
Passon, P. G., & Peuler, J. D. A simplified radiometric assay for plasma norepinephrine and epinephrine. *Analytical Biochemistry*, 1973, *51*, 618–631.
Robinson, R. L., & Watts, D. T. An automated trihydroxyindole procedure for the differential analysis of catecholamines. *Clinical Chemistry*, 1965, *11*, 986–997.
Schachter, J. Pain, fear and anger in hypertensives and normotensives. A psychophysiological study. *Psychosomatic Medicine*, 1957, *19*, 17–29.
Slot, C. Plasma creatinine determination. A new and specific Jaffe reaction method. *Scandinavian Journal of Clinical and Laboratory Investigation*, 1965, *17*, 381–387.
Šonka, J., Kopecká, J., Pavlová, A., Žbirkova, A., & Staś, J. Effects of diet and exercise on catecholamine excretion. *Hormone and Metabolic Research*, 1974, *6*, 532.
Viktora, J. K., Baukal, A., & Wolff, F. W. New automated fluorometric methods for estimation of small amounts of adrenaline and noradrenaline. *Analytical Biochemstry*, 1968, *23*, 513–528.

# 8

# Fatty Acid Mobilization[1]

## KAARE NORUM and HOLGER URSIN

Fatty acids are important in mammals both as an energy store and as important components in complex lipids necessary for the structural and functional integrity of biological membranes (Scow & Chernick, 1970). The fatty acids are stored in adipose tissue as triglyceride. They may be mobilized and released into the blood plasma as free fatty acids (Jeanrenaud, 1965). The free fatty acids may be mobilized by fasting and by activity in the sympathetic nervous system. There are complex interactions with hormones like insulin, glucocorticoids, growth hormone, and various hypophysial peptides (Scow & Chernick, 1970).

The sympathetic nervous system seems to be the primary stimulator of fatty acid mobilization when there is a sudden demand for energy, as in exercise or exposure to cold (Carlson, 1965). It also seems to be the sympathetic nervous system that is responsible for the increase in serum levels of

[1]The analysis of plasma fatty acids was supported by grants to K. Norum from Anders Jahre Foundation and the Norwegian Research Council for Science and the Humanities.

75

PSYCHOBIOLOGY OF STRESS:
A Study of Coping Men

fatty acids following a frightening or stressful situation (Bogdonoff & Nichols, 1965).

There may be a direct effect of norepinephrine on fat cells even if the means by which norepinephrine could pass from the adrenergic fiber to the fat cell have not been determined (Scow & Chernick, 1970). It is also possible that the sympathetic nervous system affects fatty acid mobilization by altering the blood flow through adipose tissue (Scow & Chernick, 1970). Sympathetic nerve stimulation and intra-arterial infusions of norepinephrine in dogs release free fatty acids and glycerol from subcutaneous fat (Fredholm & Rosell, 1968) and omental fat (Ballard & Rosell, 1971). Both routes are antagonized selectively by β-blocking drugs; the type of β receptor has not been established, but the lipolysis is mediated via a lipase that is activated by cyclic AMP (Robinson, Butcher, & Sutherland, 1971).

From a physiological point of view, it is to be expected that free fatty acids will increase during states where there is an increased plasma level of catecholamines or increased activity in the sympathetic nervous system. It has been shown that free fatty acids increase in man during fear (Cardon & Gordon, 1959). As pointed out by Bogdonoff and Nichols (1965), the increase in free fatty acids is not specific to fear, but accompanies quite different emotional states and other psychological situations. Bogdonoff, Estes, Harlan, Trout, and Kirshner (1960) pointed out that free fatty acids increased in all types of acute central nervous system arousals. Increased levels of free fatty acids have been observed to follow sexual arousal (Gustafson, Winokur, & Reichlin, 1963), verbal learning tasks (Powell, Eisdorfer, & Bogdonoff, 1964), and various social interactions connected with establishment of leadership roles (Bogdonoff, Back, Klein, Estes, & Nichols, 1962). Physical exercise was believed to be an important cause of free fatty acid release. Friedberg, Harlan, Trout, and Estes (1960) showed that acute exercise itself lowered plasma free fatty acids, followed by a significant rise immediately after the exercise. Bogdonoff and Nichols (1965) reported that even the suggestion of heavy muscular exercise was enough to increase the free fatty acids during hypnosis. The conclusion must be that psychological activation and central nervous system arousal are enough to release free fatty acids.

To our knowledge, the effect of coping and fear reduction on stress-induced elevations in plasma levels of fatty acids has not been studied previously. Since subjectively experienced fear showed a decrease after the acquisition of coping, it was to be expected that the free fatty acids would drop, even when the individual was in the same stimulus or "stress" situation. However, some vigilance and attention were definitely involved in the jump procedure, even in the coping individual, and some residual activation was to be expected.

## METHODS

Following blood sampling after the jump (see Chapter 2), the samples were frozen immediately and transported on dry ice to the laboratory. Samples were kept frozen until analysis. Triplicate aliquots of 50 $\mu$l from each plasma sample were taken for free fatty acid analysis. The plasma samples were extracted, and the heptane phase was washed with .05% $H_2SO_4$ by the procedure of Trout, Estes, and Friedberg (1960). Aliquots of the washed heptane phase were transferred to small glass-stoppered tubes, and 2 ml of rhodamine 6-G dye (George T. Gurr, Ltd., London) was added to each tube (Anderson & McCarty, 1972). After 15 min at room temperature, the absorbancies of the samples at 515 nm were determined in a Beckman DB spectrophotometer. Palmitic acid (Sigma No. P-0500) dissolved in heptane was used as the standard.

## RESULTS

An ANOVA treatment by subjects (Bruning & Kinz, 1968) of the blood samples obtained immediately after the jump showed a significant change over Days ($F(3, 129) = 138.8, p < .001$). Only the first jump produced a high level, and this level was significantly higher than all other values

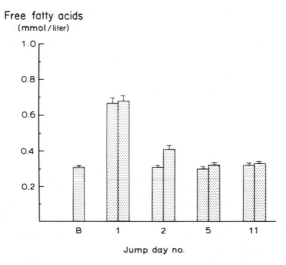

**Figure 8.1.** Plasma levels of free fatty acids. B, basal level. For each jump day two samples were obtained, one immediately after the jump and one 20 min later. The vertical line on the top of each bar indicates the standard deviation of the mean.

($p$ < .001 for all comparisons). The levels following the other jumps did not differ significantly from each other or from the basal value. For the blood samples obtained 20 min after the jump, there was again a significant change over Days ($F(3, 93) = 56.9, p < .001$). Here the first jump was significantly higher than all other jumps ($p < .001$) for all three comparisons. The values following the second jump were also higher than the two following jumps ($p < .001$) and higher than the basal value ($p < .001$). In other words, there was a fall in the post-jump values from the first jump to the second and from the second to the third. Then an asymptotic value was reached that did not differ from the basal value.


## DISCUSSION

The plasma levels of free fatty acids followed the predictions; there was a significant decrease with increased experience.

Psychological activation leads to a very fast increment of free fatty acids. This increase has been observed 10 to 15 min after activation (Bogdonoff & Nicholas, 1965) and there was also a very rapid turnover—95% of the injected palmitic acid was removed from the plasma in 10 min. There was not much difference in the two plasma samples we collected, one immediately after the jump and one 20 min later. The second sample, therefore, seemed to be more resistant to the reduction due to decreased fear and increased coping. This was probably due to the slow increase in fatty acids and that the experience increasing the fatty acids above all was connected with the jump itself. This was fairly evident from the heart rate data (see Chapter 9). Even though the heart rate did not indicate any change over time due to experience, it showed that the peak of arousal was when the man jumped from the tower. The reduction due to fear reduction was first evident in the arousal that took place *before* the jump, which influenced the free fatty acids in the sample taken immediately after the jump. The fear reduction appeared at a later stage for the arousal due to the jump and the period immediately after the jump, which influenced the blood sample taken 20 min after the jump.

It seems clear that the increase in free fatty acids was not related to any physical exercise. The amount of work involved in climbing down from the wire was very minimal indeed and did not influence the first sample.

The free fatty acids decreased to a level that was in the same region as the "basal" value. This was not a complete resting value; the men were wide awake and were probably apprehensive because blood samples were to be taken. We tried to avoid a stressful situation, but it should be made clear that we did not obtain absolute resting values.

Since free fatty acids increase rapidly, it is difficult to obtain basal values even in a hospital situation. The stress values we obtained correspond to the "normal" levels given by Carlson and Wadstrøm (1958), who caution against comparing experimental values to "normal" values because the plasma levels of fatty acids are so variable. One main source of such a variation is psychological stress, for instance, the blood sampling itself. Bogdonoff and Nichols (1965) have found that just showing the needle is enough to increase the plasma level of fatty acids. From our data it should be safe to conclude that it was not the external situation or stimulus situation itself that was the decisive factor, but individual and experience-dependent factors such as expectancy, mastery, and coping with the specific situation.

A complete reduction of free fatty acid release is not to be expected in dealing with subjects performing potentially dangerous tasks or performing at peak levels. Using competitive racing driving, Taggart and Carruthers (1971) found a significant increment in free fatty acids, triglycerides, and cholesterol following a race.

The relationship between stress and coronary heart disease has been discussed frequently. It has been suggested that people with "behavior pattern type A" have an increased risk of myocardial infarction (Friedman & Rosenman, 1959). A relationship between life style, personality factors, or other behavior factors and cardiovascular disease may be explained by an acute or chronic adrenergic overdrive. Carlson (1970) has pointed out that all of the environmental factors suggested to carry risks for developing atherosclerosis lead to an increase in the blood plasma level of free fatty acids. Therefore, it is possible that the increase in plasma free fatty acids may be a factor in the relationship between the environment and heart disease. The increase in free fatty acids may lead to an acute increment in blood platelet aggregation and to disturbances in heart muscle metabolism leading to rhythm abnormalities (Oliver, 1974). A continuous elevation in plasma free fatty acid level will lead to increased production of triglycerides in the liver and, therefore, to an increased output of lipoproteins from the liver. This could, in the long run, lead to an increased concentration of plasma cholesterol, a well-known factor contributing to coronary heart disease (Westlund & Nicolaysen, 1972).

The sensitivity of the plasma levels of free fatty acids to psychological factors should be taken into account when therapeutic and prophylactic enterprises are evaluated. It is not sufficient to consider the "stress" of the blood sampling procedure itself, because it is the total situation of the patient that is important. In particular, we want to warn against the possiblity of self-fulfilling prophecies in this field. Patients who follow certain guidelines with great care may show the desired reduction of plasma free fatty acids or cholesterol, not only because of the diet or other interventions, but because they have confidence in the therapeutic or prophylactic procedure. They are confident that their levels will be low, and this confidence may in itself produce low levels of the indicators. On the other hand, individuals who believe that they have high levels may actually have high levels because of this fear. Patients who are concerned about and show fear of heart trouble may have high levels because of this fear, and this factor may interfere with conclusions based on correlation studies of the relationship between plasma lipids and heart disease.

## REFERENCES

Andersen, M. M., & McCarty, R. E. Rapid and sensitive assay for free fatty acids using Thodamine 6 G. *Analytical Biochemistry*, 1972, *45*, 260–270.

Ballard, K., & Rosell, S. Adrenergic neurohumoral influences on circuation and lipolysis in canine omental adipose tissue. *Circulation Research*. 1971, *28*, 389–396.

Bogdonoff, M. D., Back, K. W., Klein, R. F., Estes, E. H. Jr., & Nichols, C. The physiologic response to conformity pressure in man. *Annals of Internal Medicine*, 1962, *57*, 389–397.

Bogdonoff, M. D., Estes, E. H. Jr., Harlan, W. R., Trout, D. L., & Kirshner, N. Metabolic and cardiovascular changes during a state of acute central nervous system arousal. *Journal of Clinical Endocrinology and Metabolism*, 1960, *20*, 1333–1340.

Bogdonoff, M. D., & Nichols, C. R. Psychogenic effects on lipid mobilization. In A. E. Renold, & G. F. Cahill Jr. (Eds.), *Handbook of physiology, section 5, adipose tissue*. Washington D.C.: American Physiological Society, 1965. Pp. 613–616.

Bruning, J. L., & Kinz, B. L. *Computational handbook of statistics*. Glenview, Ill.: Scott, Foresman, & Co., 1968.

Cardon, P. V., Jr., & Gordon, R. S., Jr. Rapid increase of plasma unesterified fatty acids in man during fear. *Journal of Psychosomatic Research*, 1959, *4*, 5–9.

Carlson, L. A. Inhibition of the mobilization of free fatty acids from adipose tissue. Physiological aspects of the mechanisms for the inhibition of mobilization of FFA from adipose tissue. *Annals of the New York Academy of Sciences*, 1965, *131*, 119–142.

Carlson, L. A. Pharmacologic control of free fatty acid mobilization and plasma triglyceride transport. In R. J. Jones (Ed.), *Atherosclerosis. Proceedings of the second international symposium*. Berlin: Springer, 1970. Pp. 516–521.

Carlson, L. A., & Wadstrøm, L. B. A colorometric method of determining unesterified fatty acids in plasma. *Scandinavian Journal of Clinical and Laboratory Investigation*, 1958, *10*, 407–414.

Fredholm, B., & Rosell, S. Effects of adrenergic blocking agents on lipid mobilization from canine subcutaneous adipose tissue after symathetic nerve stimulation. *Journal of Pharmacology and Experimental Therapeutics*, 1968, *159*, 1–7.

Friedberg, S. J., Harlan, W. R., Jr., Trout, D. L., & Estes, E. H., Jr. The effect of exercise on the concentration and turnover of plasma nonesterified fatty acids. *Journal of Clinical Investigation*, 1960, *39*, 215–220.

Friedman, M., & Rosenman, R. H. Association of specific overt behaviour pattern with blood and cardiovascular findings. *Journal of American Medical Association*, 1959, *169*, 1286–1296.

Gustafson, J. E., Winokur, G., & Reichlin, S. The effect of psychic-sexual stimulation on urinary and serum acid phosphatase and plasma nonesterified fatty acids. *Psychosomatic Medicine,* 1963, *25,* 101–105.

Jeanrenaud, B. Lipid components of adipose tissue. In *Handbook of physiology.* Washington, D.C.: American Physiological Society, 1965. Pp. 169–177.

Oliver, M. F. Free fatty acid and the ischaemic myocardium. *Advances in Cardiology,* 1974, *12,* 84–93.

Powell, A. H., Jr., Eisdorfer C., & Bogdonoff, M. D. Physiologic response patterns observed in a learning task. *Archives of General Psychiatry,* 1964, *10,* 192–195.

Robinson, G. A., Butcher, R. W., & Sutherland, E. W. *Cyclic AMP.* New York: Academic Press, 1971.

Scow, R. O., & Chernick, S. S. Mobilization, transport and utilization of free fatty acids. In M. Florkin & E. H. Stotz (Eds.), *Comprehensive chemistry,* Vol. 18. Amsterdam: Elsevier, 1970. Pp. 19–49.

Taggart, P., & Carruthers, M. Endogenous hyperlipidaemia induced by emotional stress of racing driving. *Lancet, 1,* 1971, 363–366.

Trout, D. L., Estes, E. H., & Friedberg, S. J. Titration of free fatty acids of plasma, a study of current methods and a new modification. *Journal of Lipid Research,* 1960, *1,* 199–202.

Westlund, K., & Nicholaysen, R. Ten year mortality and morbidity related to serum cholesterol. *Scandinavian Journal of Clinical and Laboratory Investigation,* 1972, *30* (suppl. 127), 1–24.

# 9

# Additional Heart Rate

SIGMUND B. STRØMME, PER C. WIKEBY,
ARNOLDUS SCHYTTE BLIX, and HOLGER URSIN

In a previous report Blix, Strømme, and Ursin (1974) presented a case for the usefulness of "additional heart rate" as an indicator of psychological activation. This concept is based on the fact that a fairly linear relationship exists between oxygen uptake and heart rate under aerobic (steady-state) conditions (e.g., Åstrand, 1960). Consequently, if in any situation heart rate exceeds the value predicted from the actual oxygen consumption of the subject, then the additional heart rate is likely to be due to some kind of psychological activation. Simultaneously measuring heart rate and oxygen uptake when the parachute trainee approached the edge of the upper mock tower platform enabled us to calculate his "additional heart rate" (Figure 9.1). This additional heart rate value might be a valid indicator of even very transient psychological activation, which might not appear in the endocrine measurements.

## SUBJECTS AND METHODS

### Subjects

The investigation was carried out at the Norwegian Army Parachute Training School. From a group of 44 men who were accepted for the mock tower

83

PSYCHOBIOLOGY OF STRESS:
A Study of Coping Men

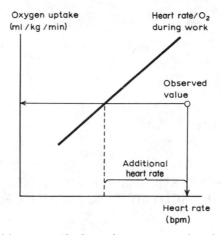

**Figure 9.1.** Additional heart rate. The heavy line represents the relationship between heart rate and oxygen uptake during muscular work. The additional heart rate is the difference between the heart rate corresponding to the oxygen uptake measured and the real heart rate measured in a "stressful" situation.

training (see Chapter 2), 13 were randomly chosen for participation in this particular investigation.

## Measurements of Heart Rate and Oxygen Consumption

The normal relationship between heart rate and oxygen consumption during pure physical work load was obtained for each subject in a camp laboratory. This was done twice, once during the test days before the first jump and again after the last jump from the tower. The subjects were tested at rest, in standing postures, and during moderate work loads (300, 600, and 900 kpm) on a bicycle ergometer. Oxygen uptake was calculated after analysis of expiratory air using a Beckman E 2 oxygen analyzer and a Beckman IR 215A carbon dioxide analyzer. These instruments were frequently calibrated using a Scholander .5-cc gas analyzer (Scholander, 1947). Heart rate was obtained telemetrically employing thoracic leads to a Medinik telemetry unit connected to a Siemens Model 14 mingograph.

During the jump training from the mock tower (Jump Days 1, 2, 5, and 11), the measurements were, in principle, carried out in the same way as during the laboratory tests. The telemetric transmitter and electrodes were placed on the subjects at the base of the tower. When the men reached the top platform clips were placed over their noses and they breathed through mouthpieces connected to large Douglas bags. During the tower training period our subjects were always No. 4 in their group, and the recording was therefore done while they waited for their turn. The sampling lasted for 4 min and was terminated at the moment when the trainee threw himself out from the tower. Heart rate was recorded during the gas collection and the jump itself. The collected air was metered through a gasometer, and the composition of every gas sample was analyzed in duplicate by use of a Scholander .5-cc gas analyzer (Scholander, 1947).

## Calculations

The "additional heart rate" for each individual was calculated on the basis of the relationship obtained between heart rate and oxygen uptake for each subject during the laboratory test, as described previously by Blix et al. (1974) (Figure 9.1). The heart rate was counted for 10-sec periods. The values obtained 280, 160, 40, and 10 sec before and 10 sec after the jump are presented. We assumed constant oxygen uptake throughout the recording period and during the jump itself.

## Additional Observations

For four of the the men, heart rate was recorded during jumps from the aircraft using the telemetry unit described under "Measurements of Heart Rate and Oxygen Consumption."

## RESULTS

For all test days, there was a clear "additional heart rate," but only immediately before the jump. Almost no additional heart rate could be detected as late as 280 sec before the jump, not even on the first day (Figure 9.2). Just before the jump, as well as just after it, a rather large increase in additional heart rate (40 and 60 bpm, respectively) was observed.

There was a significant interaction between Jump Days and Sample Points within each day on a two-way ANOVA ($F(12, 144) = 2.8, p < .01$). However, it was not possible to pinpoint this difference to any particular plot point with $t$ tests. This indicates that, although there was a significant effect of the repeated sessions, this effect was quite modest. The data in Figure 9.2 suggest that there may be a more "discriminated" response with increasing number of trials, that is, the response may be more connected to the jump at later trials. Since this was not confirmed by our statistical analysis, it will not be dealt with further.

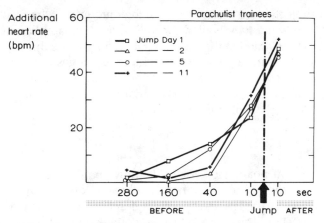

**Figure 9.2.** Additional heart rate measured before and after jumps.

## Additional Observations

The heart rates found in the four men monitored during jumps from the aircraft are given in Table 9.1. There were no dramatic increments in the heart rate above what was found in the tower, even though the absolute rates tended to be higher in three of the four men during the jump from the aircraft.

## DISCUSSION

The heart rate response in the men followed a very characteristic pattern. At the beginning of recording, at the top platform, there was no "additional

**TABLE 9.1**
**Comparison of Heart Rates in Tower and Parachute Jumps in Four Men**

| | Heart rate | | | | | |
|---|---|---|---|---|---|---|
| | Tower jump day | | | | Parachute jump | |
| Subject no. | 1 | 2 | 6 | 12 | Exit aircraft | Chute opened |
| 1 | 153 | 154 | 148 | 162 | 162 | |
| 2 | 112 | 117 | 119 | 125 | 140 | 122 |
| 3 | 161 | 150 | 170 | 147 | 178 | 167 |
| 4 | 116 | 129 | 126 | 139 | 180 | 153 |

heart rate." As the men approached the jump, there was a clear and significant increase in heart rate, to a value high above that predicted from their oxygen uptake. We refer to this increment as "additional heart rate." We interpreted this type of tachycardia as an indicator of psychological activation, since there was no increase in oxygen uptake.

The psychophysiological mechanisms involved in this cardiac response must differ from those involved in the regulation of the hormones measured in the same men, where the coping effect is very pronounced. For all hormones measured there was a clear reduction from Jump Day 1. This was not the case with the cardiac response. Quite the contrary, this response was very stable throughout the whole training period. In previous work on air pilots, we found a significant additional heart rate during landings and takeoffs even in very experienced pilots (Blix et al., 1974), and Smith (1967) also found heart rate acceleration during every landing and takeoff in experienced pilots.

There is another exception from the plasticity and sensitivity to the coping effect in other physiological changes recorded in these men. Even though epinephrine total levels showed the expected fall from Jump 1 to later jumps, there was a significant increase in epinephrine levels during all jumps when pre- and post-jump values were compared (Chapter 7). Since no pre-jump values were obtained for the blood variables, we cannot exclude that there was a short-lasting activation influencing all hormones. We should discriminate between such fast- and short-lasting "phasic" activation, evident in our heart rate data, from the long-lasting "tonic" activation influencing the maximum level of circulating hormones, blood glucose, and free fatty acids. Coping, as we have defined it, is identified by a diminishing tonic component (see also Chapter 7 for a discussion). Even in coping individuals, there appeared to be a short-lasting or "phasic" activation during the coping act. This phasic component consists of tachycardia without increased oxygen uptake (additional heart rate) and at least an increase in the level of epinephrine. For testosterone, the data suggest that there was a short-lasting increase (Chapter 6), which was evident only after the late jumps when there was no suppression effect, at least at the time blood samples were obtained. We do not know whether other hormones are sensitive to this short-lasting activation.

The physiological mechanisms involved in the phasic activation seem to be quite similar to the "defense reaction" used in cardiovascular physiology, for instance, by Folkow and co-workers (see Folkow & Neil, 1971). The men had a high sympathetic tone, even before they started climbing the tower, at least on Jump Day 1. This was evident from the high levels of norepinephrine in the pre-jump samples obtained on the first jump day. Since their heart rates were not increased initially at the top of the tower, in spite of their high levels of norepinephrine even before they started climbing, we must assume an increment in vagal tone in combination with vasoconstriction and hypertension. Immediately before the jump, this vagal tone was withdrawn, and the suppressed tachycardia became evident. There was also an increment in epinephrine, as was seen in our urinary samples, but this was probably not the reason for the increment in heart rate.

The heart rate acceleration during tower jumps was very pronounced. There was no increase or only a moderate increase when the men jumped from the aircraft for the first time. This finding indicates that the mock tower situation was a valid method.

The relatively low heart rate at the beginning of the recording on the top platform could represent an orienting response deceleration (Lacey, 1967), for instance, due to the nose clip or other procedural interventions. This seems unlikely since there was no evidence of any habituation from day to day. Unfortunately, we were not able to record from the lower platforms, due to limited radio channel capacity.

When subjects are uncertain about the nature and the timing of a stressor, they respond with heart rate acceleration up to the time of the occurrence of the stressor. Deceleration is only seen when there is previous experience with the stressor and when the stressor has a predictable onset (Deane, 1961; Elliott, 1966; Lacey, 1967). The lack of heart rate acceleration before the parachutist jump in a study by Fenz and Epstein (see Dronsejko, 1972) may have been an effect of overtraining. We saw no evidence of any such change in heart rate acceleration, even when all other physiological indicators suggested that coping developed very rapidly. We also saw no evidence of any deceleration in the experienced pilots we observed during landings or takeoffs in our previous study of additional heart rate (Blix et al., 1974).

## REFERENCES

Åstrand, I. Aerobic work capacity in men and women with special reference to age. *Acta Physiologica Scandinavica*, 1960, 49 (suppl. 169).

Blix, A. S., Strømme, S. B., & Ursin, H. Additional heart rate—an indicator of psychological activation. *Aerospace Medicine* 1974, 45, 1219–1222.

Deane, G. E. Human heart rate responses during experimentally induced anxiety. *Journal of Experimental Psychology*, 1961, 61, 489–493.

Dronsejko, K. Effects of CS-duration and instructional set on cardiac anticipatory responses to stress in field dependent and independent subjects. *Psychophysiology*, 1972, 9, 1–13.

Elliott, R. Effects of uncertainty about the nature and advent of a noxious stimulus (shock) upon heart rate. *Journal of Personality & Social Psychology*, 1966, 3, 353–357.

Folkow, B., & Neil, E. *Circulation.* New York: Oxford University Press, 1971.

Lacey, J. I. Somatic response patterning and stress: Some revisions of activation theory. In M. H. Appley and R. Trumbull (Eds.), *Psychological stress: Issues in research.* New York: Appleton-Century-Crofts, 1967. Pp. 14–42.

Scholander, P. F., Analyzer for accurate estimation of respiratory gases in one-half cubic centimeter samples. *Journal of Biological Chemistry,* 1947, *167,* 235–250.

Smith, R. Heart rate of pilots flying aircraft on scheduled airline routes. *Aerospace Medicine,* 1967, *38,* 1117–1119.

# 10

# Growth Hormone

ELLIOT D. WEITZMAN and HOLGER URSIN

There are several reasons for studying growth hormone (GH) when the internal state of a coping individual is to be evaluated. GH has been shown to increase under conditions of acute pain, fear, or other anxiety-provoking situations (Williams, 1974). In this regard, GH responds in a manner similar to that of the adrenocorticotropic–cortisol system and the catecholamines. In addition, GH has a unique feature compared with the other hypothalamic–pituitary-controlled hormones, in. that its plasma concentration is usually zero, or very near zero, and therefore a behaviorally evoked stimulus gives a clear, sharp, separate secretory response (Weitzman, 1976). Since a GH secretory response can also be induced by rapid change in the plasma concentration of certain amino acids, circulating blood factors might also induce a GH response under certain circumstances (Lucke, Hoffken, & Morgner, 1974). It has been shown that the central nervous system is the probable major control site for the release of GH through inhibitory and stimulatory hypothalamic–pituitary releasing polypeptide hormones.

There is no evidence that, under chronic "stress" or prolonged anxiety states lasting for hours, there is sustained secretion of GH (Sachar, 1975). Under normal, relaxed, comfortable conditions, GH secretion is clearly se-

91

PSYCHOBIOLOGY OF STRESS:
A Study of Coping Men

creted in an episodic manner consisting of short-lasting or "phasic" stimulus–response patterns with no evidence that secretion is sustained for any prolonged time period (Weitzman, 1975). Only under pathological states, such as with pituitary tumors, is there a continuous sustained secretion as indicated by a persistent nonzero GH level (Sassin, Hellman, & Weitzman, 1974). This sustained GH concentration leads to pathology, gigantism in children, and acromegaly in adults and the various somatic and metabolic complications related to it.

The adaptive value of this pattern of episodic acute secretion is not known. GH influences blood glucose and liver enzymes (Abrams, Grumbach, & Kaplan, 1971; Williams, 1974) and is part of a complicated anabolic metabolic activating system. Hower, GH does not appear to be necessary for sustained well-being in adults. After hypophysectomy it has not been necessary to replace GH (Williams, 1974), as is the case for other pituitary hormones. However, if it is not replaced in children, hypopituitary dwarfism results (Gardner, 1969).

## METHOD

Nine blood samples were obtained in total from each of the 44 men who went through the whole training period: one "basal" sample and two samples after each of four different jumps. The first sample was obtained immediately after the first jump; the second sample was obtained 20 min later after a resting period. Further details about the method are given in Chapter 2. The samples were frozen immediately and kept frozen until analysis.

Plasma GH concentrations were determined in duplicate by standard radioimmunoassay techniques using charcoal–dextran separation of bound from free hormone with an $^{125}$I-labeled GH tracer. The assay is sensitive to plasma GH concentrations of .5 ng/ml and greater. To minimize the effect of interassay variability, all samples from a subject were determined in the same assay run and all subjects were included in consecutive assays using the same tracer preparation, standards, and antibody.

## RESULTS

The growth hormone concentration data show the same general picture as cortisol, catecholamines, free fatty acids, and the inverted pattern of testosterone. There was a significant increment in concentration from baseline to the post-jump condition. In addition, the response values decreased with subsequent jumps and improvement in training (Figure 10.1).

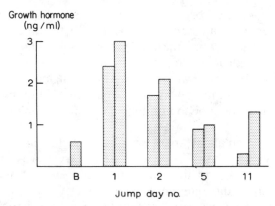

**Figure 10.1.** Plasma concentrations of growth hormone. B, basal level. For each jump day two samples were obtained, one immediately after the jump and one 20 min later.

The data clearly show that the basal value of GH was zero or near zero; therefore, the increase was very clear. The decrease was also very clear, and the last jumps did not produce significant elevations. The generated data showed a skewed distribution, and a Friedman analysis of variance (two way) was used. This analysis confirmed that there was a significant effect as a function of time. The data for the sample obtained immediately after the jumps showed $\chi^2 = 17.0, p < .001$. The analysis for the values obtained 20 min after the jump also showed a significant effect related to training ($\chi^2 = 14.3, p < .005$).

A Wilcoxon comparison between the different jumps and basal levels also showed that the basal concentration was significantly different from both values obtained on Jump Day 1. The second value obtained on Jump Day 2 was also significantly different from basal concentration. The first value obtained on Jump Day 1 was significantly different from all other values except for the second values on Jump Days 1 and 2. The second value obtained on Jump Day 1 was also significantly higher than all other values, except for the first value on Jump Day 1 and the second value on Jump Day 2.

The sequence of values obtained immediately after each jump indicated that the decrease from Jump Day 1 to Jump Day 2 was only borderline significant ($p = .06$). The slight decrease from Jump Day 5 to Jump Day 11 was not significant.

Essentially the same pattern emerged for the second sample, obtained 20 min after the jump. The decrease from Jump Day 1 to Jump Day 2 was not significant, but the decrease from Jump Day 2 to Jump Day 5 was significant ($p < .02$). However, there was a significant increase from Jump Day 5 to Jump Day 11 ($p < .005$) for this second value. This was possibly related to the relatively long period between Jump Days 5 and 11 or the impending "examination jump," but it occurred only after the waiting period and after the critique from the jump master. The increment of the value in this sample taken immediately after the jump to the second value was highly significant ($p < .001$). Several other physiological indicators suggested a moderate increase from Jump Day 5 to Jump Day 11, but this increase was not as significant as the growth hormone and was not limited to the second sample.

For each experimental day, there was a suggested increment from the first to the second value. The difference on Jump Day 1 was only borderline significant ($p < .054$) and the values for Jump Days 2 and 5 were not significant, whereas the difference on Jump Day 11 was significant ($p < .001$). This again suggests that growth hormone has a somewhat longer response than many of the other indicators and that, instead of the rest period after the jump leading to a decrease, there was an increment in the concentration of this hormone. Since there is a rapid half-life of approximately 20 min for GH, this subsequent continued increment indicates that considerable hormone continued to be secreted even though the acute psychophysiological event had been terminated (see Williams, 1974).

The individual variation was considerable, but there seemed to be some systematic variation in addition to the effect of coping behavior and quitting versus remaining in the course. If one compares soldiers with high values after the first training jump with those who had low values after the same jump, the high responders remain high responders throughout the training course. There was a total of 10 subjects who had high values (>5 ng/ml) and 13 with low values (<1 ng/ml). The mean concentration of GH in the subsequent three jumps was 2.12 ng/ml for the high value group, compared with only .44 ng/ml in the low value group.

This supports the concept that, if a soldier demonstrates a high value in the early pre-jump training period, then there is a higher probability that he will continue to show higher values in the course of training. If he shows very low values in the early jump training situation he will continue to have low values in the later jump situation. Several soldiers consistently had very high values throughout the entire training program. Their medical records were checked, and there were no indications of any pathology.

It is evident that there was a tendency for an increment in GH concentration from the first sample to the second sample every day. During this 20 min, the men were to relax with nothing else to do except wait for the second blood sample. Immediately after the first sample was obtained, and after they had filled in the questionnaire about their present fear state, they ran to the jump master for his comments about their jumps. For the first jump (48 men), 28 showed an increase and 20 did not show an increase for

Sample 1. The increase was substantial in 10 men (<3 ng/m1). There were also 10 additional responders on the second sample. Some who responded on the first sample had reached zero again on Sample 2. For the last jump day, there was also a clear tendency toward an increment after the jump. Eleven had an increase in GH concentration, 8 responded only on the second sample, and 3 decreased GH concentration.

On the "basal" day it was found that the samples obtained from the last nine men were consistently higher than those obtained first on that day, and, although the time difference was only 1 or 2 hr, it is nevertheless possible that the nine men in the last group had a longer time to anticipate the venipuncture for the blood sample. It is also possible that the relaxed atmosphere before blood sampling could have led some of the men waiting the longest to take a brief nap, which again could produce an increment in GH (Weitzman, 1975). Comparison with other hormones did not demonstrate that other systems had a similar pattern.

## DISCUSSION

In spite of considerable individual differences, there were clear GH responses shown for the post-jump blood samples. The general finding is, again, a gradual decrement in hormonal response parallel to the reduction in subjectively experienced fear and a gradually improved performance.

Feldman and Brown (1976) have shown that, in monkeys, plasma concentrations of GH increase in response to electric shock and shaping to avoid shock. Monkeys that had been trained and were able to avoid the shock, however, did not show any evidence of GH activation. They obtained the same results for cortisol, in agreement with the data from the rat (Coover, Ursin, & Levine, 1973). Their data also suggest a higher threshold for the GH response; the response occurred only after some conditioning had taken place.

There was a very clear increment in GH evident in the first sample, obtained immediately after the jump, and in the second sample, obtained 20 min later. The increment observed in the first sample must be assumed to be due to the jump itself and the anticipation of jumping. For the second sample, there may be an additional contribution because of concern about drawing the next blood sample. Since immediately after the first blood sample was obtained the men were exposed to the jump master's critique, as well as possible comments made by their peers, it is possible that this also contributed to increments in the second sample. Only on the last 2 sample days were there questions from the soldiers about the sampling procedure itself, for example, how many samples were going to be obtained. We had the distinct impression that at the earlier jump the men were far too excited to pay attention to the blood sampling procedure.

GH may, therefore, be a good indicator of physical or emotional activation in situations requiring performance of the subject (Miyabo, Asato, & Mizushima, 1977; Miyabo, Hisada, Asato, Mizushima, & Ueno, 1976; Noel, Suh, Stone, & Frantz, 1972). In this respect, GH may be an indicator comparable to cortisol, or catecholamines. In addition, it showed a gradual decrement due to coping behavior, as did the other indicators. Therefore, GH may be an equally good indicator for the accompanying internal state, as compared to conventionally used indicators. Clearly, more studies are needed using GH concentrations in plasma as a measure of coping capabilities and individual personality differences for situations that demand emotional and physical performance. The fact that the concentration of GH is essentially zero under conditions of quiet wakefulness makes this psychoendocrine system a potentially ideal one for such a purpose, because it avoids the question of "initial values."

## REFERENCES

Abrams, R. L., Grumbach, M. M., & Kaplan, S. L. The effect of administration of human growth hormone on the plasma growth hormone, cortisol, glucose, and free fatty acid respone to insulin: Evidence for growth hormone autoregulation in man. *journal of Clinical Investigation*, 1971, *50*, 940–950.

Coover, G. D., Ursin, H., & Levine, S. Corticosterone and avoidance in rats with basolateral amygdala lesions. *Journal of Comparative and Physiological Psychology*, 1973, *85*, 111–122.

Feldman, J. & Brown, G. M. Endocrine responses to electric shock and avoidance conditioning in the rhesus monkey: Cortisol and growth hormone. *Psychoneuroendocrinology*, 1976, *1*, 231–242.

Gardner, L. (Ed.). *Endocrine and genetic disease of childhood*. Philadelphia: Saunders, 1969.

Lucke, C., Hoffken, B., & Morgner, K. D. L-dopa induced GH secretion. Comparison with isulin tolerance test, arginine infusion and sleep induced GH secretion. *Acta Endocrinologica* (Kbh), 1974, *77*, 241–249.

Miyabo, S., Asato, T., & Mizushima, N. Prolactin and growth hormone responses to psychological stress in normal and neurotic subjects. *Journal of Clinical Endocrinology and Metabolism*, 1977, *44*, 947–951.

Miyabo, S., Hisada, T., Asato, T., Mizushima, N., & Ueno, K. Growth hormone and cortisol responses to psychological stress: Comparison of normal and neurotic subjects. *Journal of Clinical Endocrinology and Metabolism*, 1976, *42*, 1158–1162.

Noel, G. L., Suh, H. K., Stone, J. G., & Frantz, A. G. Human prolactin and growth hormone release during surgery and other conditions of stress. *Journal of Clinical Endocrinology and Metabolism*, 1972, *35*, 840–851.

Sachar, E. J. Neuroendocrine abnormalities in depressive illness. In E. J. Sachar (Ed.), *Topics in psychoendocrinology*. New York: Grune and Stratton, 1975. Pp. 135–156.

Sassin, J. F., Hellman, L., & Weitzman, E. D. Twenty-four hour growth hormone and cortisol secretion in acromegaly. *Transactions of the American Neurological Association,* 1974, *99,* 244–245.

Weitzman, E. D. Neuroendocrine pattern of secretion during the sleep-wake cycle of man. *Progress in Brain Research,* 1975, *42,* 93–102.

Weitzman, E. D. Circadian Rhythms and episodic hormone secretion in man. *Annual Review of Medicine,* 1976, *27,* 225–243.

Williams, R. H. *Textbook of endocrinology* (5th ed.). Philadelphia: Saunders, 1974.

# 11

# Blood Glucose

## ROLF EIDE and ANNA ATTERÅS

The nervous system is entirely dependent on glucose for fuel. Severe hypoglycemia in man gives rise to symptoms of disturbed nervous functions such as tremor, tachycardia, visual disturbance, and ultimately the loss of consciousness (Williams, 1968). Moderate hypoglycemia leads to some disturbances in nervous and psychological functioning (Eide & Atterås, 1974; Jarosz, 1970). It would thus be of adaptive value to the organism for the level of blood glucose to increase according to the demands of the nervous system in situations of stress. Glucose is also of great importance to muscular activity, although muscles can use other sources of energy. Cannon, Shohl, and Wright (1911) demonstrated glucosuria in cats under stress. Glucose mobilization was considered a part of the energy mobilization syndrome, preparing the organism for fight or flight (Cannon, 1929).

Little research has been done on the role of blood glucose in man under stress. In diabetic patients, emotional stress increases circulating glucose (Mirsky, 1948), which may explain the importance of emotional factors in patients with diabetes mellitus. Simpson, Cox, and Rothschild (1974) found that noise stress impaired performance on a pursuit rotor task and that glucose preloading of the subjects attenuated the performance. This change in performance was accompanied by a reduction in the high blood glucose level caused by preloading. Baumann, Ziprian, Gödicke, Hartrodt,

99

PSYCHOBIOLOGY OF STRESS:
A Study of Coping Men

Naumann, and Laüter (1973) found an increase in blood glucose in hypertensive patients given timed mental arithmetic problems. O'Hanlon and Horvath (1973) found a significant increase in blood glucose in subjects during a vigilance test compared with a resting condition. This increase was also found in the control group, who viewed neutral slides in the test period.

That there is not a simple and linear relationship between stress and blood glucose level is evident from the studies of Jarosz (1970), who found increased, decreased, and unchanged blood glucose levels in neurotics told they were to receive lumbar punctures. There have also been reports suggesting that acute fear increases glucose level, whereas chronic, substained conflict decreases blood glucose and increases the danger of ketosis in diabetic patients (Gitelson & Tiberin, 1952; Linko, 1950).

Paradoxical findings regarding the blood glucose level during stress may be related to the complex homeostatic regulation of blood glucose. Briefly, the sugar-reducing effects of insulin are opposed by the action of glucagon, catecholamines, glucocorticosteroids, and growth hormone (Williams, 1968). Superimposed on this regulatory mechanism are food intake and glucose metabolism, each of which changes blood glucose substantially (Eide & Atterås, 1974).

As shown by O'Hanlon and Horvath (1973), there seems to be a feedback loop between blood sugar level and the catecolamine-regulating centers in the hypothalamus. Low levels of glucose trigger activity in those centers, resulting in an increased release of epinephrine and norepinephrine. After some delay, hepatic glycogenolysis is increased and blood glucose rises; in turn, this induces a reduction in catecholamine release. In the basal state, O'Hanlon and Horvath found significant negative correlations between blood glucose and both catecholamines. During stress, insignificant correlations were found. This shows that predictions of blood glucose during stress are difficult to make and are probably dependent on time factors.

In the present study an increase was predicted in both catecholamines and glucocorticosteroids during parachute jump training and that this increase would be reduced as a function of repeated exposure. We further predicted that blood glucose would follow the same pattern and that the severity of the acute stress would tend to override a negative feedback of glucose on catecholamines so that glucose would be positively correlated to catecholamines as well as to cortisol.

## METHODS

For the general setup and procedure of the investigation see Chapters 2–4. Samples for glucose analysis were drawn from the same blood used for all other analyses. For glucose analysis, the Mercotest (o-toluidine method) and a Linsin 3 photometer were used.

## RESULTS

There was a significant increase in blood glucose level from the basal condition to the jump situation. This increase was significant ($p < .001$) for all jumps (Figure 11.1).

An ANOVA treatment by subjects of the blood samples obtained immediately after the jump showed a significant change in blood glucose level over Days ($F(3,123) = 21.1, p < .001$). There was no difference between the first and second sample day and then a significant decrease was evident from Sample Day 2 to Sample Day 3 ($p < .001$). From the third to the last sample day, there was again an increase, which was significant at the .001 level. However, the first jump and the second sample day produced the highest levels obtained, and the differences between these 2 days and the last sample were significant at the .001 and .01 levels, respectively.

For the blood sample taken 20 min after the jump, there was a significant change over Days ($F(3,99) = 7.33, p < .001$, ANOVA). The same pattern

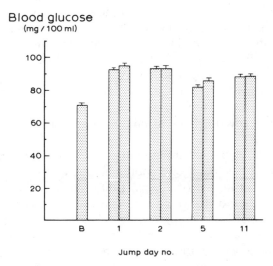

**Figure 11.1.** Levels of blood glucose. B, basal level. For each jump day two samples were obtained, one immediately after the jump and one 20 min later. The vertical line on the top of each bar indicates the standard error.

was evident from the *t* tests for this second sample. There was no significant difference between the plasma level following the first jump and the first day in the training period, which corresponded to the second sample day; however, there was a significant decrease on Sample Day 3 ($p < .001$). Again, there was a tendency toward a slight increase in blood glucose for the last jump; this did not reach significance when compared with Sample Days 2 and 3. The values for the last jump were still significantly lower than those for the first jump ($p < .05$).

## DISCUSSION

As predicted, blood glucose clearly increased in the stress situations compared to the basal value, and this increase tended to be reduced as a function of training. Unexpectedly, we found a slight increase in glucose on the last sample day. This might have been due to some apprehension in the subjects due to the approaching final jump examination.

It will be evident from Chapter 12 that blood glucose shows some relationship to both cortisol and catecholamines, but at different levels of stress: It is correlated with catecholamines at the highest level and with cortisol at lower levels. This may be explained on the basis that these hormones affect glucose in different ways: cortisol by stimulating gluconeogenesis and the catecholamines by enhancing glucogenolysis. It follows that the effect of catecholamines on blood glucose is more direct and has a shorter time lag. Exactly how this accounts for the fact that catecholamines are related to glucose at high stress levels and to cortisol at lower levels remains unclear. It is also possible that glucose is related to catecholamines only at the highest stress level because the negative feedback of glucose on the hypothalamus is ineffective at this level. The correlation of blood glucose with plasma testosterone observed on the first jump day cannot be readily explained, and we shall abstain from any speculations on this relationship because it may be spurious.

The positive correlation of growth hormone with blood glucose may be explained on the basis that growth hormone antagonizes the blood sugar-lowering capacity of insulin (Williams, 1968). The fact that glucose correlates highest with the growth hormone level in the blood sample 20 min later makes this interpretation doubtful, and the relationship of glucose to growth hormone remains unclear in this investigation. Since two powerful agents influencing blood glucose, insulin and glucagon, were not measured in this investigation, we cannot completely explain the mechanism of glucose regulation during stress.

## REFERENCES

Baumann, R., Ziprian, H., Gödicke, W., Hartrodt, W., Naumann, E., and Läuter, J. The influence of acute psychic stress situations on biochemical and vegetative parameters of essential hypertensives at the early stage of the disease. *Psychotherapy and Psychosomatics,* 1973, *22,* 131–140.

Cannon, W. B. *Bodily changes in pain, hunger, fear and rage.* New York: Appleton, 1929.

Cannon, W. B., Shohl, A. T., and Wright, W. S. Emotional glycosuria. *American Journal of Physiology,* 1911–12, *29,* 280–287.

Eide, R., & Atterås, A. The influence of normal variations in blood glucose level on psychophysiological reactivity, emotional state and reasoning ability. *Reports from the Institute of Psychology, University of Bergen,* No. 6, 1974.

Gitelson, S., & Tiberin, P. Effect of emotional stress on the blood pyruvic acid level. *Acta Endocrinologica,* 1952, *11,* 345–350.

Jarosz, M. Emotional stress and blood glucose level. The effects of hypoglycemia on mental functions. *Studia Psychologiczne,* 1970, *10,* 155–163.

Linko, E. Lactic acid response to muscular exercise in neurocirculatory asthenia. *Annales Medicinal Internal Fennial,* 1950, *39,* 161–176.

Mirsky, I. A. Emotional factors in the patient with Diabetes Mellitus. *Bulletin of the Menninger Clinic,* 1948, *12,* 187–194.

O'Hanlon, J. F., & Horvath, S. M. Interrelationships among performance, circulating concentrations of adrenaline, noradrenaline, glucose, and the free fatty acids in men performing a monitoring task. *Psychophysiology,* 1973, *10,* 251–259.

Simpson, G. C., Cox, T., & Rothschild, D. R. The effects of noise stress on blood glucose level and skilled performance. *Ergonomics,* 1974, *17,* 481–487.

Williams, R. H. Hypoglycemia and hypoglycemoses. In R. H. Williams (Ed.), *Textbook of endocrinology* (4th ed.) Philadelphia: W. B. Saunders, 1968. Pp. 803–847.

# 12

# Relationship between the Hormonal Responses to Activation and Coping

BJØRN ELLERTSEN, TOM BACKER JOHNSEN,
and HOLGER URSIN

All of the physiological variables monitored demonstrated a signficant high level when the fear level was high. Upon repeated exposure, all variables, except heart rate, followed the pattern that we have referred to as the "coping effect." In a situation with repeated exposures to a threatening situation, coping can be said to have taken place when there is a reduced physiological response to the threat (Chapter 1). Most physiological processes seem to be involved in the response to psychological threats through the "activation" process (Malmo, 1966). This is true for autonomically innervated organs, studied in the classical psychophysiological experiments, and it also seems to be true for a wide variety of endocrine processes (see Chapter 16). Therefore, one might expect that it would suffice to follow only one of these hormones or somatic processes, using this as an indicator of the internal state.

However, it is well known that the conventional indicators of activation from the autonomic nervous system show a very low degree of intercorrelation. Lacey (1950) has pointed to the remarkable lack of internal consistency between the various autonomic response systems; humans seem to have individual response patterns in the autonomic nervous system. This may have a genetic background, but since these functions are subject both to

PSYCHOBIOLOGY OF STRESS:
A Study of Coping Men

classical and to instrumental conditioning (Birk, 1973), individualization in human response patterns is to be expected, also from a learning point of view. However, hormone systems seem to be less readily subject to selective classical or instrumental control, and, in particular, there is no evidence of discriminative control. At least there is no available evidence of response-specific conditioning of any one hormone, that is, conditioning of one hormone without affecting other hormones or autonomic response systems. Using multiple hormonal indicators in this study, we had the opportunity to investigate the covariance and relationship between the various hormonal responses during the various levels of activation obtained. We hoped to be able to avoid at least the learning sources, which may produce individualization in the responses studied in classical psychophysiology, and thereby get a closer examination of the "activation" concept.

Because we followed activation over time, from basal level to a high level of activation and then to a gradual reduction back to basal levels, we should be able to observe differences in intercorrelations between the indicators depending on the activation level. The whole physiology matrix was therefore examined for correlations and factor patterns (see Chapter 3 for an explanation of the statistical methods). According to some previous experiments, group variability in response patterns increases during psychological activation (Lazarus & Eriksen, 1952; Grinker, 1953; Krause, 1961; Martin, 1961). Frazier, Weil-Malherbe, and Lipscomb (1969) found that, at least for catecholamines, there was more synchrony or coupling under stress conditions than under normal or resting conditions.

## MATERIALS AND METHODS

The physiological data obtained on the basal day and after each jump were analyzed using several mathematical tests, correlations, factor analyses, and $t$ tests. The relationship between the various samples should be clarified first. On each jump day, there were four sets of data. At 0800 hr, before any men had jumped, we obtained the first urine analysis, referred to as Sample 1 for urine analysis. This sample gave the pre-jump epinephrine and norepinephrine values. At 1000 hr, after most of the men had jumped (except for Jump Day 1), we obtained our second urine sample, which again yielded epinephrine and norepinephrine values, referred to as post-jump urine samples for each day. Immediately after each jump we obtained the first blood sample, and a second blood sample was obtained 20 min later. These two sets of blood samples yielded values for blood glucose, cortisol, free fatty acids, testosterone, and growth hormone. Both blood samples were post-jump samples.

For the analyses that are reported, we compared all post-jump values for all variables with all others. One should caution against some of the comparisons, particularly for the comparisons of levels obtained from blood samples with those obtained from urine samples. On the other hand, special attention would be warranted if the analyses revealed consistent relations. The most conservative analyses are those that are within one set of blood samples only, for instance, comparisons of plasma levels in the samples obtained 20 min after the jump.

We also used "stress" samples, 1000-hr urine values and blood samples (either immediately after the jump or 20 min later), or the mean of these two blood samples. There were differences in the time courses for the various hormones. Both rise time and half-life varied for the plasma variables and we obtained only two sampling points. Growth hormone was a very rapid indicator, with a short half-life. The other variables were slower and reached their peaks of activity either just before or just after the time of the second sample. For the urine value, we collected a specimen that represented the total sum of activation over a 2-hr period, where the jump is believed to represent only the peak value.

All longitudinal comparisons were restricted to the men who continued throughout the whole training period ($N = 44$). Some comparisons were also made between accepted men and dismissed men; in these cases, of course, we only used data to which both accepted and dismissed men contributed.

## CONSTRUCTED VARIABLES

In addition to the ordinary data matrix, we also constructed a set of variables to test more directly for the activating and "coping" effects on each hormone. Since we were particularly interested in the activation found initially and in the subsequent decrease in activation, we constructed several "rise" and "fall" indexes. All rise indexes were calculated as increases from the basal value, the value obtained before the training started. Three such indexes were constructed; the difference or increase from the basal value to the first sample obtained after the first jump (Rise Index 1), the difference between the basal value and the second value obtained after the first jump (Rise Index 2), and the difference between the basal value and the arithmetic mean of the two samples obtained after the first jump (Rise Index 3). We also calculated the difference between Samples 1 and 2 on the first jump day. As is evident from the previous chapters, for most hormones and other indicators the maximum change was found on the day of the first jump. Corresponding indexes were also calculated for the urine values of epinephrine and norepinephrine. It should be remembered that the difference between the basal value and the first urine value is a difference between values before any jumps had taken place. An 0800-hr urine value higher than the basal value for epinephrine or norepinephrine points to an anticipatory effect on the day of the first jump.

When the arousal evaluation was based on differences between basal level and the level obtained before the day of maximum change, we hoped to reduce any systematic variation due to "high responders" and "low responders," men with a constitutional high or low level of each hormone.

The fall indexes were calculated for the postulated coping effect. Three such indexes were calculated. "Fall Index 1" was based on the "first" samples, that is, the samples obtained immediately after the jump. The index is the difference between the first sample obtained on Jump Day 1 and the arithmetic means of the first samples obtained on Jump Days 5 and 11. "Fall Index 2" was based on the "second" samples, which were obtained 20 min after the jump. The index is the difference between the second sample on Jump Day 1 and the arithmetic means of the second samples obtained on Jump Days 5 and 11. The "Total Fall Index" was based on the difference between the arithmetic mean for the two samples obtained on Jump Day 1 and the arithmetic mean of the samples obtained on Jump Days 5 and 11.

We also calculated the differences between the two samples obtained on each day, for evaluation of hormones with a slow rise time or perhaps a short half-life, producing marked differences between the two blood samples. This may illustrate the possible effects related to the jump itself and the period after the jump. For the epinephrine and norepinephrine values, these differences point to differences between baseline or "tonic" arousal and arousal that was due to the jump itself, which we have referred to as "phasic arousal" (Chapter 7).

All data obtained were analyzed for correlations with the different performance criteria: whether or not the men got accepted for further training, the performance in the mock tower training period, and, finally, the performance in the jumps from the airplane. We will also compare all physiology data and all indexes with the subjective fear level reported in the tower. Finally, we will also look for differences between those men who did produce urinary specimens and those who did not.

## RESULTS AND DISCUSSION

### Longitudinal Studies (N = 44): Correlation Matrices

This matrix is a complex one, consisting of nine repeated measurements for all hormones. For jump days there were two blood samples, one taken 20 min after the other. In collaboration with J. P. Van de Geer, a multiple analysis of variance was attempted. For the present purpose it seems conceptually simpler to report mainly the results from analyses based on each sample point separately. This should be regarded as cross sections at each sample point.

The results from the correlation matrix for urine and blood samples (second blood sample) are summarized in Figure 12.1. With such a high number of possible combinations, there is a possibility of spurious correlations. The important information is the comparison across the whole experiment. It was quite clear that there were more significant correlations on the day of maximum reaction (Jump Day 1). It was also clear that only one consistent

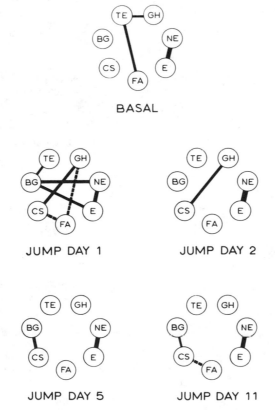

**Figure 12.1.** Correlations between plasma and urine variables for the basal day and for post-jump values of catecholamines and the variables from the second blood samples. TE, testosterone; GH, growth hormone; NE, norepinephrine; E, epinephrine; FA, free fatty acids; CS, cortisol; GB, blood glucose.

correlation pattern lasted throughout the experiment, the very strong positive correlation between epinephrine and norepinephrine.

Both sets of plasma samples, the samples obtained immediately after the jump and those obtained 20 min later, were also compared (Figure 12.2). For this comparison urine samples were excluded.

On the basal day, there were two significant correlations: Testosterone was positively correlated with growth hormone ($p < .01$) and with free fatty acids ($p < .01$). These relationships were not evident on any other day. In particular, they did not reappear when the plasma levels of hormones and free fatty acids were reduced to the basal level at the end of the training period.

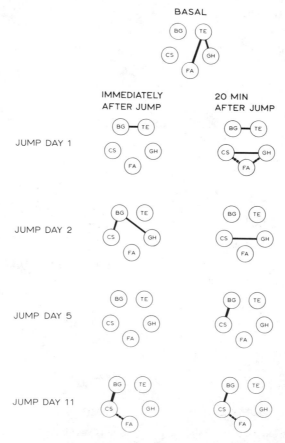

**Figure 12.2.** Comparison of correlations between variables from the first and second blood samples (immediately after and 20 min after the jump). See the legend to Figure 12.1 for a definition of the abbreviations.

On the day of maximum fear, Jump Day 1, there was a significant correlation between testosterone and the blood glucose level $(p < .01$ for the sample immediately after the jump and $p < .05$ for the sample 20 min later). This relationship did not recur throughout the training period.

A more consistent correlation was found in the 20-min sample between cortisol and growth hormone both on Jump Day 1 $(p < .01)$ and on Jump Day 2 $(p < .05)$. This relationship existed only in the blood sample obtained 20 min after the jump. The rise time for cortisol was fairly long, whereas for growth hormone it was very short. The high growth hormone levels in the second sample may be related to concern about the blood sample procedure or other events in the 20-min delay, as suggested in Chapter 10. However, the correlation with cortisol makes this less likely, at least at high activation levels. The relationship between cortisol and growth hormone disappeared when the two hormones were "at rest," when the men were coping with the jump situation. As mentioned in Chapter 10, at this time the men started talking about the blood sample procedure.

Growth hormone seems to be independent of the neural system activating the pituitary–adrenal axis (Smith & Root, 1971) and is not related systematically to arousal produced by sexual or anxiety-producing films resulting in significant increases in cortisol and free fatty acids (Brown & Heninger, 1975). In this case, a common "activation" mechanism is necessary to explain the data for the high activation levels.

On Jump Days 1 and 11 there was a puzzling negative relationship between free fatty acids and cortisol $(p < .01$ and $.05$, respectively), and on Jump Day 1 there was a negative relationship between free fatty acids and growth hormone.

The most consistent correlation found at all sample points was the highly significant relationship between epinephrine and norepinephrine $(p < .001)$. These two hormones from the urine samples correlated significantly with blood glucose on Jump Day 1 $(p < .05)$.

Finally, there was a consistent positive relationship between cortisol and blood glucose, which was observed on Jump Days 2, 5, and 11. The relationship was apparent in the first sample on Jump Days 2 and 11; on Jump Days 5 and 11 it was apparent in the second sample. This significant relationship, at least at moderate stress levels, was not surprising since cortisol is known to affect gluconeogenesis.

## Longitudinal Studies ($N = 44$): Factor Analyses

The longitudinal study may be regarded as five separate experiments, one for each sampling day. These experiments were not independent, since we measured the same hormones in the same men, although under different degrees of activation. We performed separate factor analyses for each of these five days. For the jump days, we obtained one stress sample for urine and two stress samples or post-jump samples for the blood variables. Therefore, we ran two analyses for each jump day, one with the post-jump urine samples and the first blood sample and a second analysis with the same post-jump urine sample but with the second blood sample, obtained 20 min after the jump.

The data matrices for each of these consisted of seven variables. The correlation matrices were computed in the manner described in Chapter 3. As to the number of factors used for rotation in each analysis, Kaiser's criterion (retaining the factors with eigenvalues greater than 1.0) indicated three factors in practically all of the analyses. To compare the various sample days, we selected three factors for all analyses. Percentages of variance explained by each factor are given in Table 12.1. The results from the factor analyses are evident from Figures 12.3 and 12.4. The varimax-rotated factor loadings for each factor are evident from these figures. Only one of the factor loading sets is shown in tabular form (see Table 12.2). Three principal factors were found throughout the duration of the experiment for both sets of analyses. These will be dealt with separately in the following way.

The *catecholamine factor* is Factor 1 in all five analyses, with epinephrine and norepinephrine as leading variables. This factor had a very interesting relationship to blood glucose. At high levels of activation, the catecholamine factor loaded heavily on blood glucose, for both blood samples. At more moderate stress levels this relationship was less evident, and only for the second blood sample. For low levels of activation, as on the basal day and the last jump day, there was no such relationship. This relationship between the catecholamine and blood glucose during high activation is consistent with principles originally described by Cannon (1932).

At low levels of activation there was a consistent negative loading on this factor from testosterone, evident for both blood samples for Jump Days 5 and 11. This means that activation of testosterone at low levels goes with the catecholamine factor; it must be remembered that testosterone ultimately fell as a result of activation. However, if the testosterone rise on the first blood sample indicates arousal, as suggested in Chapter 6, this type of activation is negatively related to catecholamine activation. Testosterone showed a particular relationship on the basal day, which we will return to in Chapter 14.

The second factor is the *cortisol factor,* which consists mainly of an axis between cortisol and growth hormone, with cortisol as the most consistent and leading variable. This factor is sometimes No. 3 and sometimes No. 2 on the sample points. For the second sample, it was consistently the second factor after all jumps. The most consistent other variable in this factor is

**TABLE 12.1**
**Cumulative Percentage of Variance Accounted for by Each Factor for Each Sample Day[a]**

| Factor | Jump Day 1 | | | Jump Day 2 | | Jump Day 5 | | Jump Day 11 | |
|---|---|---|---|---|---|---|---|---|---|
| | Basal day | Post-jump Sample 1 | Sample 2, blood only | Post-jump Sample 1 | Sample 2, blood only | Post-jump Sample 1 | Sample 2, blood only | Post-jump Sample 1 | Sample 2, blood only |
| 1 | 26.9 | 34.5 | 36.0 | 32.1 | 31.2 | 33.1 | 30.8 | 31.5 | 28.9 |
| 2 | 50.7 | 52.5 | 59.9 | 55.6 | 51.5 | 53.1 | 51.9 | 58.5 | 51.2 |
| 3 | 67.2 | 69.0 | 74.8 | 70.5 | 68.1 | 69.7 | 68.3 | 74.4 | 70.4 |
| 4 | 79.5 | 82.0 | 84.8 | 82.5 | 82.1 | 85.3 | 83.0 | 86. | 84.0 |
| $r_{ms}$ | .2321 | .2775 | .3152 | .2778 | .2598 | .2840 | .2597 | .2977 | .2574 |

[a] Only three factors were Varimax rotated and interpreted.

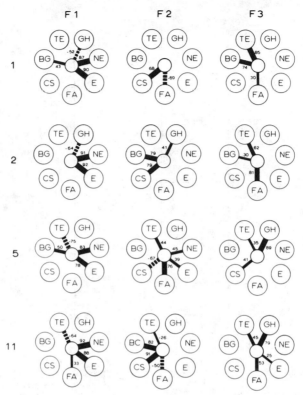

**Figure 12.3.** Factor structure for basal samples and post-jump samples; blood variables from the blood sample were taken immediately after the jump. See the legend to Figure 12.1 for a definition of the abbreviations.

growth hormone. We have already discussed the relationship between cortisol and growth hormone, which was also present during high levels of activation; the correlations were then significant (see "Longitudinal Studies: Correlation Matrices"). Even though growth hormone seemed to be independent of the neural system activating the pituitary–adrenal axis, these two hormones were activated by a particular activation mechanism, but this mechanism was in one way or another separated from or independent of the catecholamine activation system.

The cortisol factor also includes blood glucose; for the second sample, blood glucose occurred consistently at low activation levels. For the second blood sample, this was also the case except for Jump Day 5. This is almost a mirror image of the relationship between the catecholamine factor and blood glucose. At low and moderate levels of stress, the cortisol–growth hormone axis related positively to the blood glucose level, which probably

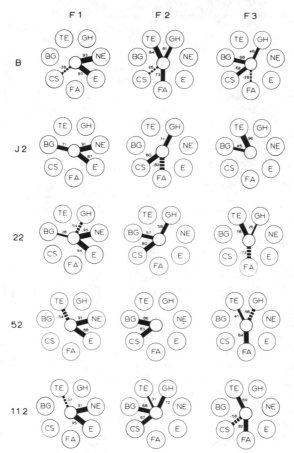

**Figure 12.4.** Factor structure for basal samples and post-jump samples, blood variables from the blood sample were taken 20 min after the jump. See the legend to Figure 12.1 for a definition of the abbreviations.

related to the gluconeogenic effect of cortisol. There was a negative relationship between this factor and free fatty acids, which was consistent at high activation levels (Jump Day 1) and occurred sporadically at other activation levels. This relationship is also evident in the next factor. The effect is probably related to the metabolic effects of cortisol.

Finally, we have a *testosterone–free fatty acid axis,* which was consistent throughout the analyses for the first sample, but less consistent for the blood sample obtained 20 min later. At high activation levels, this axis had a clear positive relationship to blood glucose and was most evident for the first sample. This seemed to be a consistent pattern and may be related to the

**TABLE 12.2**
**Varimax-Rotated Factor Loadings for Each Jump Day and the Basal Day[a]**

| | Factor | | |
|---|---|---|---|
| | 1 | 2 | 3 |
| **Basal** | | | |
| Blood glucose | — | — | .6768 |
| Cortisol | −.2823 | −.2608 | .6231 |
| Free fatty acids | — | .7285 | −.2761 |
| Epinephrine | .9293 | — | — |
| Norepinephrine | .9327 | — | — |
| Growth hormone | — | .6094 | .4814 |
| Testosterone | — | .8361 | — |
| **Day 1** | | | |
| Blood glucose | .7123 | — | .4492 |
| Cortisol | — | .7957 | — |
| Free fatty acids | — | −.8202 | — |
| Epinephrine | .8741 | — | — |
| Norepinephrine | .9058 | — | — |
| Growth hormone | — | .7124 | — |
| Testosterone | — | — | .9649 |
| **Day 2** | | | |
| Blood glucose | .2753 | .5669 | — |
| Cortisol | — | .7959 | — |
| Free fatty acids | — | — | −.7296 |
| Epinephrine | .9400 | — | — |
| Norepinephrine | .9459 | — | — |
| Growth hormone | −.5399 | .5797 | .2626 |
| Testosterone | — | — | .7752 |
| **Day 5** | | | |
| Blood glucose | — | .8585 | — |
| Cortisol | — | .8272 | — |
| Free fatty acids | — | — | .8370 |
| Epinephrine | .8840 | — | — |
| Norepinephrine | .9136 | — | — |
| Growth hormone | — | — | −.5614 |
| Testosterone | −.5365 | — | .4048 |
| **Day 11** | | | |
| Blood glucose | — | .6776 | — |
| Cortisol | — | .6658 | −.5618 |
| Free fatty acids | — | — | .8162 |
| Epinephrine | .9521 | — | — |
| Norepinephrine | .9125 | — | — |
| Growth hormone | — | .7192 | — |
| Testosterone | −.3709 | .3104 | .6867 |

[a] Second sample all variables.

116

noradrenergic innervation and activation. The reason for the apparent independence between this factor and the catecholamine values obtained from the urine analysis may simply depend on the greater sensitivity of the blood sample tests. The urine analysis was based on a 2-hr washout of the norepinephrine that escaped to the bloodstream, whereas the blood samples reflected more immediate activation, probably due to the jump itself. In particular, the free fatty acid indicator may be a more reliable indicator of fast- and short-lasting activation of the sympathetic nervous system than the urine sampling method.

The relationship to testosterone was positive, suggesting that there was a testosterone rise related to this sympathetic free fatty acid rise. This is most easy to understand if one accepts the suggestion given in Chapter 6 that there was a short-lasting testosterone increment due to activation. Even if this is not evident from the group data at the high activation levels, there may still be a delayed effect on the secondary testosterone suppression, which may explain the factor picture. If we now consider our findings both for the catecholamine factor and the testosterone–free fatty acid factor, we should conclude that the mathematical analysis is compatible with the hypothesis that there is a short-lasting testosterone activation during moderate degrees of activation that is negatively related to the activation observed in the catecholamines.

## Differences Between Accepted and Dismissed Men for "Stress" Response

At the time of the first jump, 13 men participated in addition to the 44 constituting the longitudinal study. These 13 men then withdrew or were dismissed before the mock tower training period started. The dismissed men had a higher level of epinephrine after the jump than the accepted men ($p < .01$, $t$ test) and a higher level of norepinephrine ($p < .03$). There was a tendency toward a higher level of epinephrine even before the first jump, but there was no difference in the pre-jump norepinephrine level. There was also a tendency toward a higher level of activation in other variables on Jump Day 1 in the dismissed men. The blood glucose tended to be higher in the dismissed men ($p < .06$), and there was also a nonsignificant tendency in the same direction for testosterone ($p < .09$ and .10, respectively).

When the basal level was compared among the 44 men accepted for further training and the total of 27 dismissed men, including those who resigned before Jump Day 1, very few differences appeared. Although there was again a trend in the physiological variable that indicated higher activation in the dismissed group, significant changes were only observed for two variables. The blood glucose level was significantly higher in dismissed than in accepted men ($p < .05$), and the testosterone level was lower ($p < .017$).

### Relationship to Subjective Fear Scores

The higher activation level in the dismissed men versus the accepted men during Jump Day 1 suggested that dismissed men may have had a higher degree of fear in the tower. However, even though there was a tendency toward higher mean values of subjectively reported fear in the dismissed men, at both the bottom and the top of the tower this tendency was nowhere near significance (see Chapter 4).

The fear score on Jump Day 1 was cross-tabulated against all physiology scores. An ordinary $\chi^2$ test showed no particular relationships with any other physiology variables, including the indexes, except for significant relationships between the fear level on Day 1 and the Total Fall Index for epinephrine ($p < .04$) and Fall Index 1 for testosterone ($p < .02$). This suggests that there is some relationship between the initial fear level and the starting points for the fall curve, that is, the original activation level on Jump Day 1. However, these relationships are fairly weak.

The subjectively reported fear may not represent the "real" value. It may be either that the men did not dare to report the extent of the fear they experienced or that deeper and more robust defense mechanisms were at play, to the extent that they affected the men's ability to experience the activation. We will return to this point in Chapters 13–16.

### Performance in the Mock Tower Training Apparatus

The activation in the tower and the reduction due to coping should relate to performance. However, there were very few significant correlations between evaluation of tower performance and physiological changes. Growth hormone on the last sample on the last jump day (Jump Day 11) was negatively correlated with good performance ($p < .05$). At this point in time, poor performers probably had enough feedback from peers, from themselves, and from their jump master to suspect that their performance was below the desired level. If this led to any worry or apprehension, growth hormone was the only hormone to be influenced.

In the analysis of the rise and fall indexes, only the Total Fall Index for free fatty acids showed a significant relationship with performance ($p < .05$). This, then, was the only significant correlation between the "coping effect" and tower performance. There was also a tendency for a correlation between free fatty acid rise index and performance, but this did not reach statistical significance. However, there was a significant relationship between good performers and high free fatty acid levels on Jump Day 1, first sample, with $\chi^2$ test ($p < .04$). The rise for epinephrine and norepinephrine showed a tendency in the same direction ($p < .10$). Finally, the same tendency was also observed for testosterone; Fall Index 1 was significantly related to performance ($p < .04$), and the Total Fall Index showed the same tendency ($p < .07$).

### Performance in Jumps from Airplanes

Even though we did not sample the activation level during airborne jumps, there could have been relationships between the activation profile in the tower and performance during airborne jumps. Performance both during airborne jumps and in the tower occurred under threatening circumstances, even though we might think that the threat was greater during the airborne jumps.

Blood glucose on the first sample on Jump Day 2 was significantly lower in men with good performance in jumps from the airplane. In addition, the Total Fall Index for free fatty acids showed a positive relationship with performance in jumps from the airplane ($p < .05$).

When the material was dichotomized on the medium score for good versus poor performance, no significant findings were made.

### Differences in Men Producing Urinary Specimens and Those Unable to Do So

There were only a few differences between these two groups of men. The men who did not produce urinary specimens had higher blood glucose levels on the last sample on Jump Day 11 ($p = .008$), and they also had a higher free fatty acid level on the first sample on Jump Day 2 ($p = .02$). There were marginal differences in the same direction for growth hormone, but no significant relations for cortisol. With this high number of correlations, these few differences do not warrant any general conclusions about real differences between these two groups of men, and, therefore, we have no physiological evidence that urinary specimens yield data with any systematic variation due to the sampling method. However, we shall see that there are some psychological differences between the two types of men in our material, which cautions against drawing overly general conclusions from experiments based solely on the analysis of urinary specimens.

### GENERAL DISCUSSION AND CONCLUSIONS

The group data reviewed in the previous chapters tell a very consistent story. There was a clear activation after the first jump, and all variables monitored pick up this activation. There was then a gradual coping process that reduced most of the variables. This strongly suggests the presence of one or two underlying mechanisms that influence the physiological processes monitored.

The mathematical analysis does not confirm this one- or two-process type of interpretation of the data. Activation, which is such a convenient concept both in traditional physiology and in psychophysiology, requires at least a few modifications to account for the data. Since this seems to be the case for activation, it must also hold for the reduction of activation, which we have taken as the criterion for coping.

The correlation patterns over time point to a higher degree of complexity, or less strong intercorrelations, than expected. The development over time demonstrates that there are a higher number of correlations under high levels of activation, which suggests that there may be some common activation factor after all; however, the influence of this mechanism on variance was minimal, at least for the low levels of activation. Frazier, Weil-Malherbe, and Lipscomb (1969) found a similar increased degree of correlation with increased activation of catecholamines during establishment of conditioned emotional responses in man, and Fenz and Epstein (1967) reported similar findings for autonomically innervated processes during parachute jumps.

The factor analyses also suggest common activation principles, but there seems to be more than one activation system, or at least several fairly independent activation "outlets." Three factors emerge, and at least two are very consistent—the catecholamine factor and the cortisol factor. The factor structure varies to a certain extent from low levels to high levels of "activation." Some of this variation is explicable from known physiological principles. Our general conclusion is that activation is a multidimensional and complex phenomenon for hormones also.

The importance of the lack of one "activation" superfactor should not be exaggerated. We do not suggest an individualization of hormonal responses to the same degree as that found for the autonomic nervous system (Lacey, 1950). Hormones seem to be less subject to learning factors that could selectively affect one hormone and not the others. For autonomically innervated processes, the situation is quite different, with quite obvious possibilities for feedback from response and selective control. It should be remembered that we only sampled the hormones and other physiological varibles at two points in time and that these blood variables have different rise times and half-lives. This must produce a variance that may override the influence from an activation mechanism, even if it is the activation process that regulates the whole process. The methods for studying continuous processes with multivariate techniques suggested by Cattell (1966) and Cattell and Scheier (1961) were not available to us for this reason.

The difference in the time courses may also reduce intercorrelations. In the waiting period from Blood Sample 1 to Blood Sample 2, fast indicators might pick up any possible apprehension to the blood sampling. If so, this would affect variables with a fast rise time and not those with a slow rise time. However, this would perhaps be particularly true when the tower stress was reduced, as in the later jumps. This was the first time the men had expressed any concern whatsoever about the blood samples. In these cases, we did not see any rise in growth hormone or in any other hormone.

We accept at least two consistent factors, indicating two activation types. Interestingly, the literature often treats either one or the other, probably only for technical reasons. The traditional catecholamine factor has been studied extensively, in particular in Swedish laboratories (Frankenhaeuser, 1975; Levi, 1972). The other activation factor, which we have referred to as the cortisol factor, seems to be the classical stress factor studied by Selye, Mason, and many others. The two factors may interact, which is suggested by the mathematical relationship to blood glucose and free fatty acids, and by the physiology, since both variables are influenced by cortisol, catecholamines, and growth hormone. Discrepancies or variances in the relationship between physiological activation and behavior may reflect different modes of adjusting to the environment (Block, 1957; Jones, 1950). In Chapters 13–16 we will discuss whether our data on psychology variables and performance criteria suggest that this is the case for our men.

## REFERENCES

Birk, L. Biofeedback: Behavioral medicine. New York: Grune and Stratton, 1973.

Block, J. A study of affective responsiveness in a lie-detection situation. Journal of Abnormal and Social Psychology 1957, 55, 11–15.

Brown, W. A., & Heninger, G. Cortisol, growth hormone, free fatty acids, and experimentally evoked affective arousal. American Journal of Psychiatry, 1975, 132, 1172–1176.

Cannon, J. The wisdom of the body. New York: W. W. Norton, 1932.

Cattell, R. B. (Ed.). Handbook of multivariate experimental psychology. Chicago: Rand McNally & Co., 1966.

Cattell, R. B., & Scheier, I. H. The meaning and measurement of neuroticism and anxiety. New York: Ronald Press, 1961.

Fenz, W. D., & Epstein, S. Gradients of physiological arousal in parachutists as a function of an approaching jump. Psychosomatic Medicine, 1967, 29, 33–51.

Frankenhaeuser, M. Experimental approaches to the study of catecholamines and emotion. In L. Levi (Ed.), Emotions. Their parameters and measurement. New York: Raven Press, 1975.

Frazier, T. W., Weil-Malherbe, H., & Lipscomb, H. S. Psychophysiology of conditioned emotional disturbances in humans. Psychophysiology, 1969, 5, 478–503.

Grinker, R. R. Psychosomatic research. New York: W. W. Norton, 1953.

Jones, H. E. The study of patterns of emotional expression. In M. L. Reymert (Ed.), Feelings and emotions: The moosehart symposium. New York: McGraw Hill, 1950.

Krause, M. S. The measurement of transitory anxiety. Psychological Review, 1961, 68, 178–189.

Lacey, J. I. Individual differences in somatic response patterns. Journal of Comparative and Physiological Psychology, 1950, 43, 338–350.

Lazarus, R. S., & Eriksen, C. W. Psychological stress and its personality correlates: Part I. The effects of failure stress upon skilled performance. *Journal of Experimental Psychology,* 1952, *43,* 100–107.

Levi, L. *Stress and distress in response to psychosocial stimuli.* Stockholm: Almqvist & Wiksell, 1972.

Malmo, R. B. Studies of anxiety: Some clinical origins of the activation concept. In C. D. Spielberger (Ed.), *Anxiety and Behavior.* New York: Academic Press, 1966, Pp. 157–177.

Martin, B. The assessment of anxiety to physiological behavioral measures. *Psychological Bulletin,* 1961, *58,* 234–255.

Smith, G. P., & Root, A. V. Dissociation of changes in growth hormone and adrenocortical hormone levels during brain stimulation of monkeys. *Neuroendocrinology,* 1971, *8,* 235–244.

# Part III

# PSYCHOLOGY

# 13

# Psychological Tests

EIVIND BAADE, KRISTIAN HALSE,
PER ERIK STENHAMMER, BJØRN ELLERTSEN,
TOM BACKER JOHNSEN, FRED VOLLMER,
and HOLGER URSIN

The general conclusion from the study of the physiological variables was that it was not the physical situation itself that determined the physiological response. When the men met the same situation repeatedly, there was a dramatic reduction in the physiological response. The men reported reduced or eliminated subjective fear, and their performance gradually improved according to the instructors. This indicates that the men were coping with their new situation, and we have suggested that the reduction in the internal state should be regarded as the criterion for coping having taken place.

Our conclusions so far have been based mostly on group means. However, since the physiological response depended on the subject's evaluation of the situation, there probably were important individual differences due to variations in psychological factors. This chapter deals with such individual differences and with some psychological characteristics of these men. We wanted to elucidate what type of men approached this school, why they joined the course, and what strategies they used when they developed their coping skills.

A large number of factors were relevant to the total motivational situation for the individual. This was true for each step—from application to the course, to standing at the top of the tower ready for each jump, to deciding to stay in the course despite hardships and dangers.

PSYCHOBIOLOGY OF STRESS:
A Study of Coping Men

The physiological indicators related primarily to the situation in the tower itself. On the other hand, the factors that compelled the men to stay in the course were also involved in the motivational situation when they were standing on the top of the tower. These psychological factors, therefore, will be of relevance in explaining the variance in the physiological variables and the performance.

We attempted to evaluate the resources and coping strategies of each man by using a fairly broad battery of psychological tests administered before the actual training started. We felt it necessary to design this battery so that we covered at least four areas: the interests of the subject in general, his resources, his motivations, and the defenses that could be used against threatening stimuli.

The *interests* of the subjects were elucidated by asking the men about their leisure time activities and by testing for a particular types of knowledge, for instance, technical comprehension. The *resources* of each subject were examined by tests of general intellectual abilities and particular skills. *Motivation* was tested by evaluating the preference for activities of the "Thrill and Adventure" type. The *general defense strategies* against threat were evaluated by a particular task in which the perceptual defense is thought to reveal basic defense strategies against threat. In addition to illuminating the strategies and resources used by each man to meet and master this threatening situation, the test battery should also be able to suggest predictive factors for performance.

We refrained from interviews or other direct attempts to obtain their coping strategies or what kind of defense and support they utilized. Since they lacked any special training in introspection, we thought that such procedures would make it necessary to reveal information about the project to the extent that it would interfere with the original nature of the situation. We were also afraid that this communication might have "therapeutic" effects, at least for some of the individuals, which again might affect the strategies used. We therefore avoided this approach to eliminate this possibility of self-fulfilling prophecies. Finally, individual differences in stress reactions might be attributable to any differences in the therapeutic effect of such interviewing.

However, simple questions referring to interests were used, in addition to two simple questions after the first jump: "What did you think of just before you jumped?" "What did you think of while you were gliding down the wire?" We also used our questionnaire for subjectively experienced fear (Chapter 4), which had response categories given in very general terms. This did not interfere with the defensive processes or any other aspects of coping strategies.

Most of the psychological tests are in regular use in military selection work in Norway, where norms exist for Norwegian military personnel. Some tests were also developed for our project. The tests had different formats (questionnaires, projective tests, performance tests) to counteract response biases.

In 1975 and 1976, the years after our main investigations, we investigated the same school with supplementary tests. We will present data from these investigations whenever appropriate.

## METHODS

Men were rotated in groups of about 25 between the various testers. The rotation schedule also included the medical examinations on the test days. Care was taken not to put too heavy a load on the men; there was ample time between the tests, and we attempted to keep a relaxed and noncompetitive atmosphere. As we stressed in the preceding chapters, we also tried to make it quite clear that the results from these psychological tests would not be used in the evaluation by the School Selection Board. The psychologists and most of the team members in the medical testing were civilians. In addition to the psychological tests we also asked each man to state his leisure time activities, the activities he engaged in, and what activities he would engage in if all possible resources were available. These were quite open, unstructured questions.

Brief descriptions of the tests will be given. For the tests developed for our project, and for particular tests where test descriptions are scarce or unavailable in English, a more detailed account will be offered.

### General Ability Level (GAL)

This is the general classification test used in connection with conscription in the Norwegian Armed Services. GAL is based on three subtests: one arithmetic reasoning test, one reasoning test with figures, and one vocabulary test. For every subtest the score is the number of items correctly answered, without penalty for wrong answers or for guessing. Raw scores are converted to standard scales, and the standardized scores are approximately normally distributed with $M = 50$ and $SD = 20$. These standardized scores are then added, and the sum is converted to a stanine-score ("standard-nine"), which should be approximately normal with $M = 5$ and $SD = 2$. These tests were standardized on the population of 19-year-old men meeting for conscription board examinations in 1954. We still use the norms from that time, although the distribution of stanines for the latest cohorts of conscripts is considerably skewed; the mean is now about 6. In unselected samples the corrected odd–even reliabilities of these subtests range from about .75 (reasoning test with figures) through about .80 (arithmetic reasoning test) to above .90 (vocabulary). Timing of the tests is lenient; they are not meant to be completed quickly. Correlations between subtests are about .55.

The subjects took these tests some time before they applied for the Ranger School, from .5 to 1.5 years before entry into the school. The results were known to the personnel officer at the basic training centers where the representatives from the Ranger School made their recruiting visits. There is no formal minimum score for admittance to the Ranger School, but the result undoubtedly enters into the general selection policy used by the representative. There was no score below 5 among the men we tested, except for one man who had not taken the tests before and was tested with GAL after having arrived at the Ranger School.

## Technical Comprehension (TEC)

Previously, this test was used together with the GAL in connection with conscription. The Psychological Services now uses this test only for selection of personnel for technical training. Items consist of illustrated problems in elementary mechanics, hydraulics, and electricity. The format is multiple choice, and the raw scores are the number of correct answers, with no penalty for errors or omissions. The final score is the raw score converted to stanines.

There is a strong relationship between test performance and formal educational level or occupational experience. However, a fair amount of the actual knowledge asked for in the TEC Test may be acquired through everyday observations or by reading popular material. We believe that the test score reflects technical interest as well as ability.

## Surface Development (SUD)

This is a "speeded" spatial relation test. Each SUD item consists of a "folded-out" drawing of a metal plate, together with four other drawings suggesting alternative answers to what kind of object will appear if the metal plate is folded according to the dotted lines on the drawing. This test is used together with the TEC Test in selection of personnel for training that involves technical insight. We included both in the present study because much of the communication during parachutist training is related to technical matters in a loose sense. We believe that men who obtain high scores on these tests have a certain background knowledge and attitudes that help them in structuring and accepting such "technical" environments.

## Complicated Instructions Test (CIT)

This kind of test was originally developed by British psychologists during World War II for selection of clerical workers. It was found valid for officer selection as well, and in Norway the CIT has been used for this purpose for many years. The test begins with a standard 10-min period during which the individual to be tested reads and learns a set of rules. A 10-min test period follows; the rules are applied to test problems, each item consisting of a sequence of symbols and empty spaces to be filled in with other symbols according to the set of rules. We believe that the test measures concentration and resistance to confusion. Performance is scored according to an elaborate system of points; the final sum of points is converted to the usual stanine scale. In contrast to the preceding tests, the CIT is standardized on samples of applicants for officer training; these applicants have at least a high school education ("gymnas").

## Sorting Test (SORT R−W)

This test is used in the selection of antitank missile operators in the Norwegian Army. The task is a complicated coordination task. The subject is asked to follow a relatively complicated sequence of instructions and perform actions according to these instructions. The test was developed by the Psychological Services of the Norwegian Armed Forces. The individual to be tested is asked to place cardboard pieces of four different colors in a box with nine holes (3 × 3). Each hole has been given two conflicting marks of identity (a color and the name of a different color written in letters). The pieces are to be put down according to acoustic signals and verbal orders given from a tape. Each order first gives the word for the color of the piece to be selected. A series of beats follows indicating which row the correct hole is in. Finally, the tape gives one of the two characteristics given on the correct hole. A letter indicates the color word, a whole word the color of the ring around the correct hole. The orders are given at a faster and faster speed until a speed is reached at which it is impossible to put down all pieces correctly. The instructions make it clear that, if the subject is unable to follow, he should concentrate on one order at a time and perform every second or third order or test item if necessary.

The test score is the number of pieces placed correctly (R) minus the number of erroneously placed pieces (W). The ability to cope with this "information overload" is assumed to indicate an ability to withstand or control the emotionality this type of test situation seems to involve.

### Blocks R−W

This is a paper and pencil test that depicts a stack of blocks. The task is to determine the number of blocks that are in contact with or touch one particular block. The score is the number of correct answers minus the number of wrong answers. The items of this test were given as "distraction" tasks during the test of time estimation (TEV, second test below).

### Blocks R+W

This test is not different from the Blocks R−W Test; a variable is established by scoring the test differently. Instead of giving the subject a score according to the number of correct responses, the score is the total number of problems that the subject made an attempt to solve, regardless of the right or wrong solutions. This score should therefore indicate speed of performance.

### Time Estimation Variability (TEV)

The subject is asked to give an estimate of 20 short time intervals in succession during the previous mental task. The intervals are also filled with different sounds. The mental task functions as a distraction and makes it impossible, or at least very difficult, to concentrate on the time estimation by counting.

The differences between the time estimate and the actual time are expressed as percentages of real time to make the responses comparable for different intervals. The mean and the standard deviation of these relative time estimates are computed for each subject. The score used is the coefficient of variation: $100\,SD/M$.

We assumed that the TEV Task would be vulnerable to "emotional interference" since it demands attention for two different and partly incompatible tasks. A low score on the Blocks and/or a high coefficient of variability on TEV might indicate low stress tolerance.

### Rod and Frame Test (RF)

A simple transportable Rod and Frame Test apparatus was used (Oltman, 1968). The subject looked into a $30 \times 30 \times 70$-cm box made from translucent plastic material with heavy black edges made from tape. In the background, within the black, quadratic frame formed by the bottom edges, the subject saw a solid black line ("rod"). The experimenter could tilt the rod and the frame independently. The frame was tilted approximately 28° in either direction before the subject started his observation. The rod was then rotated in small steps (3°) from a horizontal position while the subject watched. The subjects were asked to determine when the line appeared vertical. The line was always rotated toward the vertical with some adjustment back and forth, but only for the last fine adjustment; eight measurements of movement of the rod (two measurements of each of the four frame/rod combinations) were used. The score was the arithmetic mean of the eight angular deviations in degrees of arc, disregarding the direction. The score represents degrees of difficulty in judging the true vertical line independently of the external frame. This is referred to as "field dependence"; a high score indicates "field dependence," and a low score indicates "field independence."

## Internal–External Locus of Control (EXT)

A short version of the Rotter Scale for Internal–External Locus of Control using 12 items was used (Rotter, 1966; Rotter, Seeman, & Liverant, 1962). The test is meant to measure "generalized expectations of internal vs. external control of reinforcements." The short, Norwegian version has been produced by Solem and Traeldal (1970). Each item in this test consists of a pair of opposing statements, and the subject indicates which statement he endorses; for example:

(a) I often think that I do not have very much influence on what happens to me. ("External" response.)
(b) I have some difficulty in believing that chance or luck plays a significant role in my life. ("Internal" response.)

The score used is the number of items that are endorsed in the "external" direction. Persons with high external scores have been suggested to show low tolerance of external stress (Joe, 1971).

## Resultant Achievement Motivation (RAM)

This test purports to measure what has been called "resultant achievement motivation," which is defined as the strength of achievement needs minus the strength of anxiety in a test situation (Kukla, 1972). Heckhausen (1963) used the term "Net Hope" for the same variable, defined as the difference between "hope of success" and "fear of failure."

The defining characteristics of an achievement situation are as follows.

1. The individual is faced with a task/problem.
2. To solve this task or problem, the person must do something or *perform* some act (mentally, physically, or both).
3. The performance itself or some product of it may be *evaluated* (success/failure) in relation to some *standard of excellence* (individual or social norm).

In such situations, the person may react with a number of psychological processes,he may entertain a more or less strong wish to do well or to avoid failure, he may experience negative or positive emotions of varying intensity, he may have high or low expectancy, he may set himself high or low goals, he may intend to work more or less energetically, he may entertain different beliefs as to what factors will determine performance outcome (ability, effort, task difficulty, luck), and he may initiate concrete action with the goal, either to succeed or to avoid failure. It is assumed that such reactions may be grouped into two broad classes: the positive or approach reactions (hope, high expectancy, etc.) and the negative or inhibiting reactions (fear, low expectancy, etc.). The basis for such a dualistic categorization is partly the consideration that fear or avoidance reactions (fear of failure motivation or achievement-related anxiety motivation) are *inherently* different from positive or approach reactions (hope of success or achievement motivation), but also the assumption that the two kinds of reactions frequently *make* a difference, that is, have differential effects on *the quality* of actual performance.

For all individuals, both types of processes will be activated in achievement situations. Which kind of process will dominate and to what extent may vary from person to person and, to a certain extent, from situation to situation; however, a certain amount of trans-situational *consistency* in reaction pattern and strength is assumed to exist. The goal of measurement in this area is thus to construct a relatively simple test situation on the basis of which it is possible to predict psychological reactions in actual achievement situations and the quality of actual performance in such situations (it goes without saying that the quality of actual performance has many determinants, one of which is intellectual ability).

The considerations that the two kinds of motivational reactions are inherently different and that they may also affect actual behavior differentially constitute the rationale for attempting to assess the *relative strength* of the two reaction systems and to arrive at measures like *Resultant Achievement Motivation* or *Net Hope*, indicating which of the two tendencies is the dominant one and how strong the domination is. In the United States such measures are typically based on the Projective Need Achievement Score (McClelland, Atkinson, Clark, & Lowell, 1953) and scores on the Test Anx-

iety Questionnaire (Sarason, 1972). Heckhausen's Net Hope Index is calculated on the basis of two separate projective measures (Heckhausen,
1963).

The Resultant Achievement Motivation Test attempts to arrive at a measure of resultant achievement motivation by the use of a questionnaire with
an objective scoring procedure. The subject is presented with verbal descriptions of eight different achievement situations; four of them are described as
having to do with examinations, and the other four as being athletic
achievement situations. Within each of these two broad types of situations
(intellectual versus physical), the four subtasks are described as varying in
*difficulty* (high/low) and in the amount of *effort* (high/low) expended. Under
each situational description 18 different possible reactions are described.
Half of these reactions are typically fear of failure reactions; the other half
are typically hope of success reactions. The different types of described
reactions are based on various categories used in Heckhausen's (1963) system for scoring TAT responses. The subject is asked first to read through the
whole list of reactions and then to check off the six reactions that he thinks
would have the highest probability of occurring were he himself involved in
the situation described. The score for each item is simply the number of
hope of success reactions checked off. A high number thus indicates a high
frequency of hope of success reactions. A sum score across all eight items
was computed.

## Defense Mechanism Test (DMT)

This test is a method for clinical diagnosis and personnel selection and has
been used by the Swedish Institute of Military Psychology for selection of
airplane pilots. The technique consists roughly of repeated subliminal exposures (12 in all) to a TAT-like picture, exposure time being increased by steps
from 20 to 500 msec. Two such series are used. At each exposure, the
subject makes a sketchy drawing (or a marking) of what he has seen and
writes a short comment (Kragh, 1960a). For the first series, a boy with a small
toy car is placed in the center foreground, and the head and shoulders of a
threatening, ugly, middle-aged, male person is placed at the right, above the
boy. The second series has a similar picture, a young male with a stringed
instrument in the foreground and the threatening figure in the upper left
corner. The responses of the subject are classified on the basis of their
thematic content and the development of the percepts in the course of the
series of exposures. The scoring follows a procedure described in detail by
Kragh (1955, 1960b). The theoretical basis of this test is referred to as the
"Percept–Genetic Model of Perception and Personality," and the classification is performed in accordance with psychoanalytic theory of defense

mechanisms (Kragh, 1960b). A manual with operational definitions of the response types (with examples) has been produced by Kragh (1969; only available in Swedish).

Prognoses based on this test have been validated repeatedly against attrition among aviation cadets in Sweden (Kragh, 1960a) and adaptation to military aviation (Neuman, 1967). Correlations with the performance rating have been reported for frogmen also (Kragh, 1962). Kragh (1960a) explained these findings by assuming that persons in whom defense mechanisms are constantly at work also have difficulties in resisting the stress of, for example, aviation.

### Testing Procedure

The DMT can be used as a group test; we tested the men in groups of 20. An ordinary slide projector (150-W bulb) was equipped with a camera shutter allowing exposure times to vary. The pictures were presented on a translucent screen (65 × 75 cm). The projected picture on this screen was 60 × 40 cm. The room was shielded against light; it was usually used for film projection. The subjects were placed in four rows: four persons in the first row, six in the next two rows, and the remaining four in the last row. The distance from the screen thus varied from 6 to 10 m. Two control lamps were placed on the sides of Rows 2 and 3, one on each side. The lamps were directed toward the ceiling, furnishing the subjects with indirect and fairly equal amounts of weak and diffused light. There was only enough light in the room to allow subjects in the last row to give a correct description of the stimulus motif at exposures without time limits.

Each subject had a pile of papers in front of him; on one side of the paper pre-drawn squares were located. The subjects were asked to draw in these squares what they saw on the screen. On the right side of the paper they were asked to comment and interpret what they thought they saw. The subjects were asked to do this after each stimulus presentation. They were told that sometimes the pictures would change radically and that at other times there would not be much difference between one picture and the next. During the instruction a demonstration picture was shown at an exposure time of 500 msec; then the same picture was shown for a long time, and the project leader explained simple symbols, such as P for person, K for woman (*kvinne*), G for boy (*gutt*), and an arrow for threat.

The experiment then started with a presentation of a distraction picture with an exposure time of 100 msec. Picture 1 was then shown 12 times, with exposure times of 20 msec (one exposure), 40 msec (three exposures), 100 msec (two exposures), 200 msec (four exposures), and 500 msec (two exposures). The distraction picture was presented again for 100 msec, followed by 12 exposures of Picture 2 with the same exposure times as for Picture 1.

The session ended with a presentation of the distraction picture for 100 msec. The experiment took approximately 65 min per group (instruction excluded).

The protocols were all analyzed by one psychologist (K. Halse) with special training in using this test. This psychologist did not have access to any of the information about the subjects at the time of scoring; however, it was accidently revealed that one subject with a remarkably "negative" DMT protocol was exluded by the selection board from further training.

The scoring of the protocols follows a detailed manual. The operational definitions used are quite complex, and space does not allow us to give the full details. Unfortunately, the manual is at present only available in Swedish. Briefly, the variables generated by this test are defined as follows:

*Masculine/Feminine (MF).* The number of times the subject identified the central figure as a woman or a girl was scored, but only if he persisted in his conclusion, if he changed his answer from male to female, or if both persons in the picture were identified as females.

*DMT "Prognosis" (DMT PROG).* This is a "global" evaluation of the defense strategies evident throughout the entire protocol. The evaluation follows certain guidelines and has been found to predict perseverance and performance in training for execution of dangerous jobs. The evaluation is given as a rating from one (bad prognosis for perseverance and performance) to 9 (good prognosis). Even without any fixed norm or ideal with respect to the distribution of these ratings, empirically the end results seemed to follow a normal distribution.

*Defense Mechanisms (DMT DEF).* The score represents the number of repressions, reaction formations, and two variants of isolation. One of these types of isolation mechanisms is represented when the threat figure (face) is perceived as a relatively homogeneous, bright spot without any threatening properties (e.g., sun, window). The other variant of isolation is observed when the threat figure is referred to as belonging to other "worlds" or frames of reference, for instance, when the subject sees a ghost.

*Type of Mechanism (DMT MEC).* This is a nominal scale where values from 1 to 9 indicate the dominant defense mechanisms of the subject. These mechanisms are (1) Repression, (2) Isolation, (3) Denial, (4) Reaction Formation, (5) Identification with the Aggressor, (6) Turning against the Self, (7) Identification with a Female Role, (8) Polymorph Identification, (9) Projection, and (10) Regression. Only Mechanisms 1, 2, 4, 7, 8, and 9 were observed in our subjects. If the number is used as a score for a subject, it indicates the dominant defense mechanism used by that individual. It should be noted that, in the following analyses, a high score on this variable will be interpreted as "feminine identification," since we found very few scores in Categories 8 (Polymorph Identification) and 9 (Projection).

*Frequency of Defense Mechanisms (DMT FMEC).*    This is the number of times the predominant mechanism of a given individual is recorded in that individual's protocol.

## Preference for Thrill and Adventure (PTA)

Eleven activities were listed in a random order: parachute jumping, ski jumping, big game hunting, alpine skiing, hitchhiking through Europe, photo safari, diving, salmon fishing, sailing, mountain climbing, and gliding. The subject was then asked to indicate the four activities he preferred most and then rank these four activities. We then ordered the activities on the basis of the frequency with which they were selected in the total sample. Each subject was then given a score that was proportional to the correspondence between his ranking and that of the total sample. The score, therefore, reflects the "conformity" of the subject with respect to the expectancy of the group, or the group norms. We refer to this variable as a preference for activities "involving elements of speed or danger" (Zuckerman, Bone, Neary, Mangelsdorff, & Brustman, 1972). The main reason for this choice of terms is that the resultant ranking of activities quite clearly corresponded to the "Thrill and Adventure Factor" of the Sensation-Seeking Scale (SSS) of Zuckerman *et al.* (1972).

## Boredom Susceptibility (BORE)

A modified Zuckerman's Scale (SSS) was used. The BORE score was based on the response to four statements selected from a total of 11 items with a clustering program (Hierarchical Clustering Schemes, Johnson, 1967). The subject indicated whether he agreed or disagreed with the statement or whether he was in doubt. The four statements were as follows.
1. I get tired of seeing the same old faces.
2. I cannot stand being around boring people.
3. Even if it's necessary, I dislike routine jobs.
4. I get restless being home for a long time.

A high score on the BORE Scale therefore indicates that the individual gets bored easily.

We also tested for questions that gave a cluster corresponding very closely to the "swinging" factor or subscale of the SSS. However, since this cluster had less inner coherence it was not included as a variable in the main analysis. We felt that only clusters with small mean interpoint distances between items should be included since we found it to be more likely that such clusters would contribute to the interpretation of eventual correlations with other variables.

## Performance Criteria

### Tower Performance (K1)

The performance in the tower was recorded and evaluated following the procedures described in Chapter 4. For the present analysis, the percentage of accepted jumps was the score (K1) for the performance of each man in the sample of 44.

### Air Performance (K2)

Jumps from the airplanes or helicopters were also scored (K2), based on the recordings of the instructor's evaluations of the jumps. Each jump in the series was rated as acceptable or not acceptable. Among the unacceptable jumps, some were also classified as dangerous. If the trainee performed two or more dangerous jumps he had to leave the course. There were fairly clear rules for classifying the jumps as "dangerous": body spin, inverted body position, or releasing the parachute too late (>2 sec). The number of jumps evaluated varied a little from individual to individual, but consisted of about 20 jumps, beginning with the automatic (line) opening of the parachute and proceeding with increasing periods of free fall and increasing demands for maneuvers during the free fall.

We condensed the series of jump ratings into a 6-point scale, where Score 1 implied two or three dangerous jumps resulting in dismissal, Score 2 implied one dangerous jump and many unaccepted jumps, and so on. Score 6 was given for a series of accepted jumps only. The frequency distribution of these scores was approximately rectangular.

## RESULTS

Summarizing the information in these test results for the subjects may be approached in several ways, where the principal objectives are (a) to characterize the men who applied for this type of training and (b) to explore any differences between the two subgroups in the sample (the accepted and the dismissed men). In this chapter these objectives are mainly limited to the "psychological" variables, that is, performance in the test sessions.

The results oriented toward these objectives are based on several different types of analyses. First, the total material is characterized with respect to *univariate distributions* on these variables. In the same vein, the *second* set of results is based on a factor analysis of the same variables using the complete set of subjects. The interest is centered on the structure of relations between the different tests. Obviously, these two types of analyses are oriented toward the first objective. To cope with the second objective, the differences between the two subgroups, three different types of analyses were employed. The *third* set of results is based on tests for any differences between the two groups on each single variable. The *fourth* and *fifth* sets of results are comparable to the second analysis, where the same factor analysis is performed (this time on each of the two sets of subjects separately) and the results are compared. Finally, the *sixth* set of results is, in principle, an extension of the third set, this time with the total set of test results as dependent variables in a discriminant analysis.

## General Characteristics of the Complete Sample

The men who apply for this type of training do not differ in any dramatic way from the ordinary Norwegian soldier. As mentioned in the introduction, several of the tests we used are in general use in the Norwegian Army, and the mean scores of the group may be compared with the standard scores of the average Norwegian young male. The General Ability Level of the 72 men we tested was about .5 SD above the mean for the general population; the Technical Comprehension Test showed a level of performance about .75 SD above the mean for the general population of conscripts. The general educational level was not recorded systematically. An earlier sample of applicants to the Ranger School was tested with the Minnesota Multiphasic Personality Inventory and showed no evidence of pathology. The average profile was very flat, with small standard deviations.

These men do have special interests, evident from the fact that they did apply for this type of training. We asked the men to list their leisure time activity and told them that they could list as many activities as they wanted. We also asked the men to list all of the leisure time activities they would engage in if they had the necessary resources. The same questions were given to the recruits in an infantry company (about 100 men) at the same time in a nearby infantry training center. The results are given in Tables 13.1 and 13.2.

The types of activities mentioned were about the same in the two groups, but there were a few clear differences. The parachute training applicants had a high preference for skiing, even in August; this was not mentioned by the infantry trainees at all. In this latter group, music as an active or passive

**TABLE 13.1**
**Ranking of Real Leisure Time Activity Based on Number of Times Mentioned**

| Parachutist trainees | | | Infantry training center recruits | | |
|---|---|---|---|---|---|
| Rank | Type | Frequency | Rank | Type | Frequency |
| 1 | Soccer | 21 | 1 | Soccer | 25 |
| 2 | Alpine skiing | 15 | 2 | Music, active and passive | 17 |
| 3 | Cross-country skiing | 12 | 3 | Sports fishing | 13 |
| 4 | Unspecified skiing and ski jumping | 12 | 4 | Hunting and fishing | 12 |
| 5 | Outdoor sports | 12 | 5 | Outdoor sports | 9 |
| 6 | Hunting and fishing | 11 | 6 | Handball | 8 |
| 7 | Swimming | 10 | 7 | Reading | 7 |
| 8 | Sports fishing | 9 | 8 | Party-going | 7 |
| 9 | Diving | 8 | 9 | Athletics | 5 |
| 10 | Reading | 8 | 10 | Unspecified athletics | 5 |

interest was very frequent; this was not mentioned by the parachute trainees. There was a clear preference for dramatic activities in the parachute trainees. Both groups gave travel the highest preference as a group. The preference for dramatic and tough leisure time activities was further analyzed in our Preference for Thrill and Adventure Scale, and we will return to this in the discussion.

**TABLE 13.2**
**Rank of Preferences in Leisure Time Activity**

| Parachutist trainees (N = 72) | | | Infantry training center recruits | | |
|---|---|---|---|---|---|
| Rank | Type | Frequency | Rank | Type | Frequency |
| 1 | Travel | 19 | 1 | Travel | 16 |
| 2 | Diving | 11 | 2 | Hunting and fishing | 7 |
| 3 | Parachute jumping | 8 | 3 | Fishing | 6 |
| 4 | Alpine skiing | 8 | 4 | Music | 6 |
| 5 | Airplane pilot | 7 | 5 | Parachutist jumping | 5 |
| 6 | Around the world, boat | 6 | 6 | Outdoor sports | 4 |
| 7 | Mountain climbing | 5 | 7 | Car racing | 4 |
| 8 | Sailing | 4 | 8 | Around the world | 3 |
| 9 | Car racing | 4 | 9 | Airplane pilot | 3 |
| 10 | Hunting and fishing | 4 | 10 | Vacation | 3 |
| 10 | Unspecified athletics | | 10 | Unspecified athletics | 3 |
| | | | 10 | "Playboy activity" | 3 |

**TABLE 13.3**
**Reasons Given for Applying to the Ranger School (1975 Applicants)[a]**

| Reasons given for applying | All (N = 81) | Quit (N = 30) | Remain (N = 51) |
|---|---|---|---|
| Better use of military service | 44 | 18 | 26 |
| Test oneself, a challenge | 35 | 11 | 24 |
| Interested in jumping | 24 | 6 | 18 |
| Get in better physical shape | 23 | 7 | 16 |
| Adventure, excitement | 20 | 10 | 10 |
| Other answers | 12 | 3 | 9 |
| Sum, number of answers | 158 | 55 | 103 |

[a] Number of answers exceeds total number of subjects since more than one reason was permitted.

**TABLE 13.4**
**Means and Standard Deviations for the Variables in the Full Sample**

| Variable | M | SD |
|---|---|---|
| GAL | 6.96 | 1.27 |
| TEC | 72.89 | 14.62 |
| SUD | 71.04 | 14.28 |
| CIT | 41.97 | 18.29 |
| SORT R−W | 19.04 | 8.77 |
| Blocks R−W | 10.10 | 8.61 |
| Blocks R+W | 26.15 | 4.04 |
| TEV | 15.16 | 7.59 |
| RF | 2.41 | 1.96 |
| EXT | 3.90 | 2.07 |
| RAM | 29.65 | 4.86 |
| DMT MF | 4.4 | 5.12 |
| DMT PROG | 5.98 | 1.83 |
| DMT DEF | 2.79 | 3.38 |
| PTA | 55.29 | 16.50 |
| BORE | 4.74 | 2.06 |

In our supplementary investigations in 1975, we also asked the applicants to the Ranger School why they applied for this training. Eighty-one men were asked to state their reasons. The results are given in Table 13.3. It is evident that the reasons varied, the most common reason being to test oneself and to meet a challenge. To get in better physical shape was also an important reason. However, the most prevalent answer was to make better use of the military service.

In summary, the means and standard deviations for each of the variables described in the methods section are shown in Table 13.4.

### Factor Analysis of the Complete Sample

As a further step in the characterization of the test battery and the total set of subjects, a factor analysis was performed on the complete set of subjects, that is, on all of the accepted and dismissed men. This analysis followed the general rules outlined in Chapter 3.

The analysis included a total of 15 variables, where five factors were indicated using Kaiser's criterion (eigenvalues greater than 1.0). These five factors accounted for 60.9% of the variance. However, to simplify comparison with the other analyses in this chapter, six factors are used and discussed. These six factors account for 72.6% of the total variance.

The factor matrix was then rotated in the usual manner (by varimax) and the resultant values are given in Table 13.5. To simplify inspection of the matrix, loadings with an absolute value of less than .25 were omitted. This factor analysis gives information about the psychological characteristics of the applicants to the Rangers School, as well as a summary of the test battery as a whole. None of the six accepted factors is test specific in the sense that it loads on variables derived from one test; all of the factors contain fairly large loadings on two or more different tests.

The first factor was a general intellective factor commonly found in this type of test battery, whereas the other factors indicated combinations of tests that suggest descriptive labels. If we call the first factor a "General Intellective Factor," the second factor could be called "Defense" because of the combination of DMT PROG and DMT DEF. This factor also contained a weak loading on the test Blocks R−W in the opposite direction. The third factor may be called "Activity Need," based on the prevalence of "success reactions" on the RAM inventory and a low tolerance for monotonous activities (BORE). The fourth factor may be called "Control" due to the control or stability of time estimation (TEV) and the loading (in the same direction) on the EXT variable (Internal−External Locus of Control).

The fifth factor was related to the first, with an emphasis on CIT (Complicated Instructions Test) and SORT R−W. Subjects often reported tenseness

**TABLE 13.5**
**Varimax-Rotated Factor Loadings from Full Sample**

|            | 1       | 2       | 3       | 4       | 5      | 6      |
|------------|---------|---------|---------|---------|--------|--------|
| GAL        | .5964   | —       | —       | —       | .4891  | —      |
| TEC        | .7849   | —       | —       | —       | —      | —      |
| SUD        | .7283   | —       | —       | —       | —      | —      |
| CIT        | .4150   | —       | —       | —       | .7096  | —      |
| SORT R−W   | —       | —       | —       | —       | .8305  | —      |
| Blocks R−W | .5866   | −.4072  | —       | −.2690  | —      | —      |
| Blocks R+W | .6657   | .3634   | —       | .2503   | —      | —      |
| TEV        | —       | —       | —       | .7444   | —      | —      |
| RF         | −.6134  | −.2523  | —       | —       | —      | —      |
| EXT        | —       | —       | −.2862  | .6834   | —      | —      |
| RAM        | —       | —       | .8533   | —       | —      | —      |
| DMT MF     | —       | —       | —       | —       | —      | −.7422 |
| DMT PROG   | —       | .7528   | —       | —       | —      | .3010  |
| DMT DEF    | —       | −.6530  | —       | .3000   | —      | —      |
| PTA        | —       | —       | —       | —       | —      | .8433  |
| BORE       | —       | −.3804  | .6624   | —       | —      | —      |

during the SORT Test, and we refer to this factor as "Low Test Anxiety." The final factor ("Masculine Role Taking") was clearly related to a low number of feminine identifications on the DMT, as well as to a high score on the Preference for Thrill and Adventure Test (PTA).

## Differences between the Accepted and Dismissed/Quit Men

To compare the two subgroups of subjects, that is, the accepted men ($N = 44$) and the dismissed/quit men ($N=28$), the differences in means were tested with a simple *t* test on each of the 15 variables included in the factor analysis of the total material. These results are shown in Table 13.6. There were only two significant differences between the two groups: TEC (Technical Comprehension) and EXT (External Locus of Control). The difference between the two groups for GAL (General Ability Level) was fairly close to the significance limit ($t = 1.89$). The accepted men tended to score higher on Technical Comprehension and low on External Locus of Control.

### Factor Analysis of the Accepted Men

The same set of variables was analyzed for the 44 men who completed both the mock tower period and the parachute jumps. In this case, Kaiser's criterion indicated the use of six factors, which accounted for 68.6% of the

**TABLE 13.6**
**Comparison of Test Results for Accepted and Dismissed/Quit Men**

|            | Accepted (N = 44) | | Dismissed/quit (N = 28) | | |
|------------|------|------|------|------|--------|
|            | M    | SD   | M    | SD   | t      |
| GAL        | 7.2  | 1.01 | 6.6  | 1.6  | 1.885  |
| TEC        | 77.1 | 13.7 | 66.3 | 14.0 | 3.232**|
| SUD        | 72.9 | 13.7 | 68.0 | 15.1 | 1.407  |
| CIT        | 42.5 | 16.7 | 41.2 | 20.8 | 0.289  |
| SORT R−W   | 20.2 | 7.8  | 17.2 | 10.2 | 1.410  |
| Blocks R−W | 9.9  | 7.8  | 10.5 | 10.0 | 0.285  |
| Blocks R+W | 26.7 | 3.2  | 25.2 | 5.0  | 1.516  |
| TEV        | 13.9 | 6.3  | 17.1 | 9.2  | 1.312  |
| RF         | 2.2  | 1.5  | 2.7  | 2.6  | 1.156  |
| EXT        | 3.5  | 1.9  | 4.5  | 2.2  | 2.098* |
| RAM        | 29.6 | 4.2  | 29.8 | 5.9  | 0.134  |
| DMT MF     | 4.16 | 5.2  | 4.78 | 5.2  | 0.5    |
| DMT PROG   | 6.2  | 1.9  | 5.6  | 1.7  | 1.212  |
| DMT DEF    | 2.6  | 3.4  | 3.1  | 3.4  | .625   |
| PTA        | 57.5 | 17.6 | 51.8 | 14.5 | 1.424  |
| BORE       | 4.4  | 1.9  | 5.2  | 2.2  | 1.575  |

*$p < .05$ (two tailed).
**$p < .01$ (two tailed).

total variance. The first six factors were then rotated by a simple varimax procedure, and the rotated factor loadings are shown in Table 13.7. To simplify the inspection of the matrix, loadings with an absolute value of less than .25 have been omitted.

The first factor corresponded to the "General Intellective Factor" in the total material, except for the loss of RF. The second factor corresponded to Factor 2 in the total material ("Defense"), but there were important differences. In the accepted men, this factor had a heavy contribution from BORE and an influence from EXT (External Locus of Control). The contribution from Blocks R−W was lost. The third factor had the variable RAM in common with the third factor in the total material, but there were no other common loadings. The factor had contributions from the SORT Test and Defensive Mechanisms (DMT DEF). The fourth factor was quite similar to the "Masculine Role Taking" in the total material (Factor 6), except for a more pronounced loading on DMT PROG, the variable that has been used as a predictor for continuing this type of training. The fifth factor contained loadings on both TEV and Blocks R−W with a negligible contribution from EXT.

**TABLE 13.7**
**Varimax-Rotated Factor Loadings from the Accepted Men**

|            | 1      | 2      | 3      | 4      | 5      | 6      |
|------------|--------|--------|--------|--------|--------|--------|
| GAL        | .8152  | —      | —      | —      | —      | —      |
| TEC        | .7983  | —      | —      | —      | —      | —      |
| SUD        | .5996  | —      | —      | —      | —      | −.5362 |
| CIT        | .6735  | —      | .3977  | —      | —      | —      |
| SORT R−W   | .3493  | —      | .6633  | —      | —      | —      |
| Blocks R−W | .4633  | —      | —      | —      | −.5754 | —      |
| Blocks R+W | .5927  | —      | —      | —      | .4432  | −.4070 |
| TEV        | —      | —      | —      | —      | .8376  | —      |
| RF         | —      | —      | —      | —      | —      | .8598  |
| EXT        | −.3006 | .4709  | —      | .3379  | .2728  | —      |
| RAM        | —      | —      | −.6778 | —      | —      | —      |
| DMT MF     | —      | —      | —      | .8459  | —      | —      |
| DMT PROG   | —      | −.4057 | —      | −.5193 | —      | −.3124 |
| DMT DEF    | —      | .4819  | −.4053 | —      | —      | .4565  |
| PTA        | −.2871 | —      | .3498  | −.7330 | —      | —      |
| BORE       | —      | .8318  | —      | —      | —      | —      |

Tentatively, this factor may be labeled "Control," as in the total sample. The "controlled" direction of this factor (low TEV) was positively related to the "controlled" test behavior reflected in the R−W score on Blocks, whereas it was negatively related to the speed of performance (R+W). "Controlled" subjects perform correctly under time pressure. We do not have any suggestions for a label for Factor 6. It showed a connection between field dependence, defense, and low performance under time pressure.

In principle, therefore, we found the same general results in this subsample as in the total material. There was a "General Intellective Factor," which is to be expected, and we also found the "Masculine Role Taking Factor" and the "Defense Factors," as in the total material. The factors "Low Test Anxiety" and "Activity Need" found in the total material were less clear in the corresponding analysis for the accepted men. The "Low Test Anxiety Factor" from the total material was changed. These last two factors were not interpreted in this analysis.

### Factor Analysis of the Dismissed/Quit Men

To complete the picture, a factor analysis was also performed on the other subgroup within the total sample, that is, the 28 men who did not complete the mock tower training. Most of these subjects did not even start this training period.

**TABLE 13.8**
**Varimax-Rotated Factor Loadings from the Dismissed/Quit Men**

|            | 1      | 2      | 3      | 4      | 5      | 6      |
|------------|--------|--------|--------|--------|--------|--------|
| GAL        | .3841  | —      | —      | .5948  | —      | −.3255 |
| TEC        | .8295  | —      | —      | —      | —      | —      |
| SUD        | .5237  | —      | —      | .5673  | .3155  | —      |
| CIT        | .5154  | —      | —      | .6473  | −.2607 | —      |
| SORT R−W   | —      | —      | —      | .8491  | —      | —      |
| Blocks R−W | .7762  | —      | —      | —      | —      | —      |
| Blocks R+W | .4526  | .4778  | −.3131 | —      | —      | —      |
| TEV        | —      | —      | —      | .2511  | .6599  | —      |
| RF         | −.5296 | −.6438 | —      | —      | —      | —      |
| EXT        | —      | —      | −.7148 | —      | —      | —      |
| RAM        | —      | —      | .6238  | .4882  | —      | .2607  |
| DMT MF     | —      | −.7282 | —      | —      | —      | —      |
| DMT PROG   | —      | .8492  | —      | —      | —      | —      |
| DMT DEF    | .2756  | —      | —      | —      | .7813  | —      |
| PTA        | —      | —      | —      | —      | —      | .9083  |
| BORE       | —      | —      | .8596  | —      | —      | —      |

The analysis was performed in the same manner as reported for the two previous analyses, using six factors; this was also indicated by Kaiser's criterion. In this case, the six factors accounted for 74.1% of the total variance. This pattern matrix was rotated by a varimax procedure, and the results from this rotation are shown in Table 13.8. As in the preceding reports on factor loadings, absolute values of less than .25 were omitted to improve the "readability" of the matrix.

The first two factors in this material were similar to factors found in the two other analyses, that is, the "General Intellective Factor" and the "Masculine Role Taking Factor." Two other factors were somewhat different in this analysis: Factor 3 combined "Activity Need" with "Internal Locus of Control," whereas the other aspect of "Control" related to DEF in Factor 5.

### Comparison of the Dismissed/Quit and Accepted Men

The total sample size is too small to permit any detailed analysis of the three sets of factor patterns. However, even so, there are quite interesting points arising from a comparison of the three analyses.

Factor 1, *"General Intellective Factor,"* was common to all three analyses. Within this factor, some differences occurred between the two groups. The only variable that discriminated between the two groups in a univariate test loaded on this factor, where the accepted men had a significantly higher score on TEC (Technical Comprehension, $t$ (70) = 3.232, $p$ < .01). The same group of men also tended to have higher scores on GAL (General Ability Level, $t$ (70) = 1.885, $p$ < .10). In the dismissed/quit men, GAL did not contribute to this factor at all. Nonsignificant tendencies in the same direction were present in some of the other tests in this factor (SUD, Blocks R+W). Biersner and Rynan (1974) found that divers admitted to psychiatric service had less technical insight and less general skills than their controls. A combination of general ability tests and a test similar to TEC would reduce attrition rate significantly. Basowitz, Persky, Korchin, and Grinker (1955) found similar evidence in parachutist trainees; there were poorer performances on tests like digit memory and serial subtractions in their dismissed/quit group.

The Rod and Frame Test (RF) loaded on Factor I both in the total material and in the dismissed/quit group but not in the remaining men.

The *"Defense Factor"* was present in both groups, as in the total material. There are considerable differences in the factor structure around the defense mechanism. In both groups, Defense must be assumed to be an important variable, but the correlations between Defense and the rest of the psychological variables are different, suggesting that different strategies may be involved in the two groups.

*"Masculine Role Taking"* was also a consistent factor across groups. In the dismissed/quit men, this factor loaded not only on MF, but also on PROG, RF, and one of the performance tests that is assumed to measure activity in a demanding, time-pressed task (Blocks R+W). We do not find the Preference for Thrill and Adventure in this group; in the accepted men this is a leading variable on this factor. On the other hand, in the accepted men, we do not find the RF or the Blocks R+W.

Masculine role taking is of obvious importance for total adaptation to the course. Even though there was no significant difference between the dismissed/quit group and the remaining men with regard to feminine identifications, the factor patterns suggested that the two groups differed in their relationship to this important role variable. This factor probably also interacted with the decision to stay or quit the course. It is of particular importance for this question that, in the men from the dismissed/quit group that did go through the first jump and therefore obtained one Fear score, the mean score was not significantly higher than for the accepted men.

*"Low Test Anxiety,"* which is our label for Factor 5 in the total sample and for Factor 4 in the dismissed/quit men, was absent in the accepted group. Our interpretation is that test anxiety and emotionality may have entered the performance of the dismissed/quit men to a larger extent than for the ac-

cepted men. This is further illustrated by the correlation matrices, which showed higher average correlations between personality tests and intellective tests in the dismissed/quit group.

## Discriminant Analysis

Yet another approach to exploring the differences between the two groups of subjects is to extend the "univariate" analysis of variance to a discriminant analysis. Again, the same set of variables is used as in the previous analyses, and the problem is to find an optimal linear combination of these variables that discriminates between the two groups.

Table 13.9 shows the discriminant weights (standardized) for defining the linear combination that discriminates between the two groups in an optimal manner and the correlations between the variables employed in the computations and the discriminant score, that is, the value computed by the linear combination. These results confirmed that the variables TEC and EXT show the highest correlations with the discriminant scores; these variables are the same as those discriminated in the univariate case. Other sizable correlations were found with respect to GAL (General Ability Level), Blocks R+W, TEV, and BORE.

**TABLE 13.9**
**Discriminant Weights and Correlations**

|  | w | r |
|---|---|---|
| GAL | .8504 | .3756 |
| TEC | .1181 | .6157 |
| SUD | −.0169 | .2834 |
| CIT | −.0826 | .0591 |
| SORT R−W | .0367 | .2840 |
| Blocks R−W | −.0889 | −.0581 |
| Blocks R+W | .0524 | .3048 |
| TEV | −.1127 | −.3443 |
| RF | −.1179 | −.2338 |
| EXT | −.1129 | −.4155 |
| RAM | .1244 | −.0273 |
| DMT MF | .0302 | −.1019 |
| DMT PROG | −.0206 | .2448 |
| DMT DEF | −.0811 | −.1272 |
| PTA | .0455 | .2866 |
| BORE | −.4230 | −.3161 |

### Factor Analysis of the Accepted Men Including Jump Performance

Using the results from the 44 accepted men, another factor analysis was performed including the variables Fear, K1, and K2. Table 13.10 shows the rotated factor pattern from this analysis, and it is clear that Factor 1 was the same "General Intellective Factor" found in all of the previous analyses. As Factor 2, we found "Masculine Role Taking," which was also close to the corresponding factors in the preceding analyses, but with the addition of Fear.

In the remaining men there was a very strong relationship between DMT MF and Fear ($r = .51, p < .01$). There was also a significant negative correlation between DMT MF and the Preference for Thrill and Adventure (PTA, $r = -.46, p < .01$), but no significant correlation between Fear and PTA.

As Factor 3 we found "Defense." This factor loaded on defense and RAM and negatively on Fear. Under "Subjective Fear Ratings" (see "Discussion"), we discuss that fear reported in the situation may be of two types: fear of dying or of physical damage and fear of failure. However, there is no reason

**TABLE 13.10**
**Varimax-Rotated Factor Loadings for the Accepted Men, Including K1, K2, and Fear**

|            | 1       | 2       | 3       | 4       | 5       | 6       |
|------------|---------|---------|---------|---------|---------|---------|
| GAL        | .7189   | —       | —       | —       | .2586   | —       |
| TEC        | .7413   | —       | —       | —       | .2524   | —       |
| SUD        | .4454   | —       | —       | .4428   | .5583   | —       |
| CIT        | .7763   | —       | —       | —       | —       | —       |
| SORT R−W   | .5861   | —       | —       | —       | —       | —       |
| Blocks R−W | .4088   | —       | —       | —       | .7085   | —       |
| Blocks R+W | .3876   | —       | —       | .7655   | —       | —       |
| TEV        | −.3720  | —       | —       | .5344   | −.3555  | —       |
| RF         | —       | .2734   | —       | −.4502  | −.2563  | —       |
| EXT        | −.2653  | .3805   | —       | —       | —       | —       |
| RAM        | —       | —       | .7026   | —       | —       | —       |
| DMT MF     | —       | .8418   | —       | —       | —       | —       |
| DMT PROG   | —       | −.5370  | —       | .2930   | —       | .5508   |
| DMT DEF    | —       | .2537   | .7294   | −.2967  | —       | —       |
| PTA        | —       | −.6610  | −.2617  | −.3703  | —       | —       |
| BORE       | —       | —       | .3088   | —       | .3063   | −.6401  |
| K1 (tower) | —       | —       | —       | —       | .2669   | .6993   |
| K2 (jump)  | —       | —       | —       | —       | .7913   | —       |
| Fear       | —       | .5328   | −.5303  | —       | —       | −.3417  |

to believe that these should end up in separate factors after this pattern. However, the loading on Fear in the Masculine Role Taking Factor may be related to the "unmanliness" of reporting fear.

Factor 4 had no clear relationship to any of the previous analyses, and the loadings gave us no cue to a label for it.

Factor 5 was related to quality of performance in jumps from the airplane and to performance on the Blocks R−W; we termed this the *Air Jump Factor*. The last factor, Factor 6, was related to the performance in the tower. It is of interest that these two performance criteria loaded on separate factors.

## DISCUSSION

In the rest of this chapter we will discuss the results obtained in the analyses. First, we will discuss the psychological variables that are important for the various performance criteria. We will then discuss particular psychological variables that we believe to be of particular importance for coping with parachute training.

### Mock Tower Performance

In the last factor analysis, only one factor (Factor 6) included K1, but there were no significant correlations between this variable and any of the other variables. The correlations within the factor were negligible, and there were no other significant correlations with any other variable in the total correlation matrix. However, when the material was broken down into good performers versus poor performers (good performers were those for whom 30% of their jumps were rated acceptable) there was one significant finding: The good performers had significantly less variance in their time estimate (TEV, $p < .05$). During tower training, the timing is important; the men were counting during the sliding down the wire and marking when they were supposed to open the chute.

The evaluation of the performance in the tower is the feedback to the men about their skills, and it should be an important factor for the development of coping. The relationship between this variable and their Resultant Achievement Motivation (RAM) is discussed in Chapter 15.

The lack of a significant correlation between the performance in the mock tower and the performance in the jumps from the airplane is remarkable ($r = .18$). The defense mechanisms did not seem to have any decisive importance for performance during mock tower training, but these variables were important for jumps from the airplane.

## Performance in Parachute Jumps (K2)

In the factor analysis in which K2 was included, it loaded on one of the factors (Factor 5, "Air Jump Factor").

In the correlation matrix, K2 correlated significantly with two variables, Blocks R−W ($r = .42, p < .01$) and SUD ($r = .30, p < .05$). There were no other significant correlations with K2.

Low Performance Scores 1 and 2 on K2 were significantly related to the defense mechanisms Repression and Isolation ($p < .005$, Fisher's exact test). The finding of a relationship between particular types of defense mechanisms and performance in the air jump is a point of major interest.

Factor 4 in the total material ("Control Factor") showed a significant relationship with K2, but only for the group of men that were poor in the tower training ($N = 20, p < .025$). In other words, the men with a below average performance in the tower might obtain a very good performance in the real jump if they had high scores on the "Control Factor" (Internal Locus of Control and Stable Time Estimation).

High scores on the Preference for Thrill and Adventure (PTA) are predictive of poor performance on airborne jumps. When extremely poor performance (K2, Classes 1 and 2) was compared with higher performance (K2, Classes 3–6), there was a significantly higher frequency of poor performance among the men who had the high PTA (greater than 70) ($p < .005$). A possible interpretation is that the men with the high PTA "overidentified" with the ranger role or image. It is possible that this overidentification rendered them more insensitive to cues of poor performance at an earlier stage

TABLE 13.11
Relations between Levels of Fear and Levels of Performance
in Parachute Jumps[a]

|  |  | K2 | | | |
| --- | --- | --- | --- | --- | --- |
|  |  | 1,2 | 3,4 | 5,6 | Σ |
| Fear | 1,2–1,9 | 1 | 9 | 6 | 16 |
| Fear | 2,0–2,9 | 12 | 1 | 3 | 16 |
| Fear | 3,0–3,9 | 0 | 1 | 5 | 6 |
| Fear | ≧4,0 | 0 | 1 | 3 | 4 |
| Σ |  | 13 | 12 | 17 | 42[b] |

[a] $\chi^2 = 29, —p < .005$.
[b] Two subjects without a Fear rating were omitted here.

**TABLE 13.12**
**Relations between Types of Dominant Defense Mechanisms (DMT MEC) and Levels of Subjective Fear**

| DMT MEC | Mechanism number | Fear | | | | | $\Sigma$ |
|---|---|---|---|---|---|---|---|
| | | 1,0–1,9 | 2,0–2,9 | 3,0–3,9 | 4,0–4,9 | $\geqq$5,0 | |
| Repression | 1 | 5 | 4 | 1 | 0 | 0 | 10 |
| Isolation | 2 | 4 | 7 | 1 | 0 | 0 | 12 |
| Reaction Formation | 4 | 1 | 1 | 0 | 0 | 0 | 2 |
| Identification with a Female Role | 7 | 4 | 9 | 4 | 5 | 2 | 24 |
| Polymorph Identification | 8 | 3 | 2 | 0 | 0 | 0 | 5 |
| Projection | 9 | 1 | 0 | 1 | 0 | 0 | 2 |
| $\Sigma$ | | 18 | 23 | 7 | 5 | 2 | 55 |

of the training. They also used isolation or repression as their defense against threats, more often than men with low PTA ($p < .05$).

There was also an interesting relationship between subjectively reported fear before the first jump in the mock tower training apparatus and the performance in jumps from the airplane ($p < .005$, see Table 13.11).

The product–moment correlation between these two variables was quite low ($-.19$), but it is clear from Table 13.11 that the relationship between the two variables was U shaped. Moderate levels of fear in the tower before the first training jump were related to poor performance in the jump from airplanes. The middle level of fear was also characterized by repression or isolation as the dominant defense mechanism (see Table 13.12). Low and moderate levels of fear were associated with the defense mechanisms Repression and Isolation ($p < .01$).

Our men did not reach a level of excellence and coping as quickly during the airborne jumps as was the case in the mock tower; fear was very quickly reduced in the mock tower training period. When they jumped from the plane the situation was more life-threatening, and coping developed more slowly. We have seen from the heart data (Chapter 9) that the initial arousal did not vary much between the two situations. Even so, defense mechanisms affected jumps from the airplane more than jumps from the tower. The threatening aspects may be more important for performance in jumps from the airplane. This activation of their defense mechanisms interfered with the perception of the situation and therefore also with their performance in this task. This may be particularly true for the men who experienced relatively little fear and had high repression and isolation. Of the 8 men who had a moderate Fear score and Repression or Isolation, 7 were poor in airborne jumps, whereas, of the 34 other men who jumped from the aircraft, only 6 had poor performances in the air ($p < .001$).

The task also demanded spatial organization and time estimation and this may explain some of the correlations with psychology variables.

## Preference for Thrill and Adventure (PTA)

A high PTA score indicated that the subject identified with the group norms, or those he expected the group to have. Few subjects with very high scores left the course.

The preference was as follows: parachuting, diving, alpine skiing, and gliding. The ranked activity preferences seem to be a very stable characteristic of applicants to parachutist training. The rankings were nearly the same among the applicants the following years (1975 and 1976); the only exception among the four top rankings was that instead of gliding they ranked mountain climbing as No. 4 in 1975.

Preference for Thrill and Adventure correlated significantly with GAL ($r = -.30, p < .05$), Blocks R+W ($r = -.35, p < .05$), and DMT MF ($r = -.46, p < .01$). The interaction with Defense Mechanisms is discussed under "Defense Mechanisms."

## Subjective Fear Ratings (Fear)

The Fear Scale showed several interesting relationships with other variables. We have already commented upon the relationship between middle Fear level and poor performance in jumps from the airplane. This moderate use of the Fear Scale was associated with Repression and Isolation.

It is also evident from Table 13.12 that usage of the relatively *high* scores on the Fear Scale was associated with feminine identifications on the Defense Mechanism Test. This may be due to an absence of Repression and Isolation as leading defense mechanisms, but there was a significant positive correlation ($r = .51, p < .01$) between DMT MF and Fear. The percentage of men with DMT MF scores above median rose in an almost linear manner from 27 to 100 with Fear (Figure 13.1).

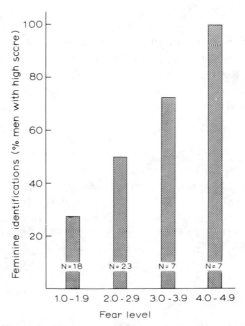

**Figure 13.1.** The relationship between feminine identification scores and fear level. The fear level is derived from the scores on the Fear Scale.

The results may indicate that the tower training situation was perceived as a test of "masculinity" by most of the subjects. High feminine identification is indicative of uncertainty about the sex role identity (Kragh, 1960a). When such subjects apply for paratroop training it could imply a kind of counter-phobic behavior, possibly as a result of cultural and social pressures.

It seems to be a truism that in our male youth culture it is still "unmanly" to show fear. If this were true, we should expect men with high femininity identification to suppress or deny their fear. Our data do not seem to support this, quite to the contrary. On the other hand, we should keep in mind that our Fear Scale contained 10 steps, and only the lower half of it was used. The lowest 3 or 4 intervals had verbal characterizations indicating quite modest amounts of fear (see Table 3.1 in Chapter 3). This is quite compatible with the maintenance of a satisfying self-image.

Our findings demonstrate that subjective fear ratings depend on the defense of the individual and that the type of defense mechanism is crucial. We find that defense mechanisms that may be effective at low levels of threat, as in the tower, lose this effectiveness at higher levels of threat, as in the airborne jump. This may be because these defense mechanisms act on perceptual factors, which leads to defective "reality testing" and interference with an adequate perception of the task requirements.

Basowitz et al. (1955) found that men reported a relatively low level of fear in the same training situation as we have used. They discussed the possibility that, in the failing men in particular, such low reports of fear might have been due to higher defense or denial, which no longer worked at the actual jumps. If that were true, their fear would then become overwhelming and interfere with their jumps. The relationship between subjectively reported fear and other important variables, like performance, is curvilinear. This seems to be a function of the defense mechanisms, and it must be taken into consideration when such scales are employed.

Basowitz et al. (1955) found that, for their parachutist trainees, the main concern was not fear of injury, but fear of failure. Basowitz et al., therefore, defined two sets of Fear scores: fear of death and injury and fear of failure. These two were not correlated. Fear of failure was most pronounced at the beginning of the training, whereas fear of injury occurred mainly later in the training. However, the type of training also differed during their test period, with more life-threatening situations in the later phases, particularly in jumping from the aircraft. We will return to the fear of failure concept in Chapter 15.

## Defense Mechanisms

As pointed out in the preceding section, the defense strategy of the individual is important both for his subjective fear and for his final performance in jumps from the airplane.

Perception and reproduction of geometrical forms have been found to be related to cortical maturation, integration, and anxiety (Bender, 1938; Pascal & Suttell, 1951) or simply to the ability to perceive and respond to reality (Basowitz et al., 1955). Tachistoscopic presentations of pictures have also been used with even better results, including Bender pictures (Bender, 1938; Basowitz et al., 1955) and Rorschach presentations (Stein, 1949). Projective tests by themselves have failed to predict flying performance (Holtzman & Sells, 1954). Basowitz et al. (1955) showed that the quality of perception of the Bender figures was reduced in parachutist trainees with high anxiety. The perception and interpretation of pictures with contents from parachutist jumping were influenced both by situational and by personality factors and therefore probably also by the defense mechanisms of the individual. Tachistoscopic presentation of stimuli has been developed further by Kragh in his "percept–genetic" method (Kragh, 1955, 1960a,b). Essential to his method is that the picture is presented repeatedly. There is, therefore, a gradual buildup of the percept. The method permits not only a diagnosis of the defense mechanism used, but a quantification of the mechanisms. It has previously been used for prediction of performance in Swedish air pilots (Kragh, 1960b) and in Danish attack divers (Kragh, 1962). We found the results from the test to be clearly related to the performance in the jumps from the airplane, but not for the performance in the mock tower. We believe the latter finding to be due to the fast development of coping and the corresponding reduction in the threat. In Chapter 14, we shall see that these mechanisms are also important to the internal state.

Repression and isolation mechanisms were also used by some of the men who performed well in the airborne jumps. This type of defense may be effective, therefore, when the stress is moderate or coping develops quickly. This was probably the case in the mock tower training period: The threat was reduced very quickly, and there was no handicap to have Repression and Isolation as leading defense mechanisms. In the jumps from the airplane, these mechanisms may have been a serious handicap for performance, depending on the fear level or the intensity of the threat. In the least fearful individuals, Repression and Isolation may have been leading mechanisms, but in these cases the mechanisms are effective enough. These men therefore remained unaffected, and their performance was good. However, in the men who perceived the threat, there was a resulting moderate activation: Something got "through." The inadequacy of these defenses would then become evident.

Fenz and Epstein (1967) evaluated the defense strategies used by sky divers by testing their subjects with a Thematic Apperception Test (TAT) just before entering the aircraft. They compared these data with tests from a day remote from the jump day and found interesting differences. On the jump day, there was a very clear denial of fear and "displacement" of fear to previously neutral objects. This denial of fear seemed to be a very effective strategy, since the 8 men (of 16 tested) who showed the most denial each had a significantly lower Galvanic Skin Response (GSR) (Fenz, 1973). There were also possible effects of training; with increasing experience there was a shift from high relevant to low relevant cues. Fenz has pointed out that the differences they previously ascribed to experience may be the variables that select those that go on with the voluntary training and become experienced (see Chapter 1 for a discussion).


## GENERAL DISCUSSION

Our main hypothesis is that when a man is in a threatening situation it is not the objective situation or his performance that determines the internal state. No matter how the man solves his problem, it is his own evaluation of his situation that is the important factor for determining whether or not coping will occur. We know that our parachutist trainees coped with their situation; they showed a clear reduction in all indicators of their internal state.

In this chapter we have tried to elucidate the various psychological factors that are involved in the development of the coping behavior. Even if some of the results seemed highly successful in predicting at least the airborne jumps, and whether the men continued their training or not, prediction as such was not the main purpose of this investigation. Coping with the *task* was not the primary focus of our interest; we wanted to study the effect of coping for the internal physiological state.

In summing up the results in this chapter, we will have this perspective in mind. Our main hypothesis is that coping is a function of what the subject learns about his status in the stressful situation. The key input variable here is the task itself. As to the basis of our findings, we have reason to believe that other concepts of the situation may play a part, for example, the multitude of social signals from peers and instructors. Furthermore, the subjects select among these inputs according to their personality. Coping, therefore, is a function not only of task performance, but also of a series of intervening variables.

Important elements in this connection were classified into three main areas. We tried to evaluate the *resources* of each man, his interests and *identification* with this role and motivation, and, finally, his *strategies*, that is, emotional management and control of the situation. For each of these three areas, we used a number of tests; however, some of these covered more than one of these areas. Finally, we described several interactions and relationships between our variables, which illustrate these three original fields of interest.

*Resources.*   To evaluate the resources of each man, we used several intellective tests. The scores on these tests were higher among the accepted men than among the dismissed/quit men. We found that particular tests within this cluster also related positively with performance in the jumps from the airplane.

*Interests, identification, and role motivation.*   The particular skills and interests evaluated in this area were technical comprehension, the reasons for applying for this training, preference for thrill and adventure, masculine/feminine identification, and leisure time activities and tolerance of boredom. Several of the sets of results clustered together in our second factor, Masculine Role Taking. Several of the variables were related to the accepted/dismissed criterion; accepted men had a stronger identification with the masculine role and a higher preference for thrill and adventure. The most striking difference was their much higher score for technical abilities. We also found that an especially high preference for thrill and adventure was negatively related to performance in airplane jumps. There was also a relationship between preference for thrill and adventure and defense mechanisms in that the subjects with especially high scores on the Preference for Thrill and Adventure Test more often indicated repression or isolation. This may perhaps explain the negative relation between preference for thrill and adventure and the airborne jump performance. There were also clear relationships between feminine identifications and preference for thrill and adventure and between feminine identifications and the subjectively reported fear level. We also found a positive relation between feminine identification and the airborne jump criterion, possibly because these subjects had less repression and isolation.

*Strategy, emotional management, and control.*   The Defense score and the type of mechanism from the DMT contributed to this area; we also found that the Time Estimate Variability and the Internal–External Locus of Control were important variables. We found that there was a relationship between the subjectively reported Fear level and the type of defense mechanism and between the type of defense mechanism and performance in the jumps from airplanes. This is one of our most important findings. Defense mechanisms affect perception, and may interfere negatively with adequate perception of danger. They also affect the total evaluation of the situation and can be seen as a moderator variable in the relationship between danger, adequate behavior, and the experience of fear. We also found that there was no relationship between these types of defense mechanisms and performance in the tower. This may be due to a lower level of threat in this situation, at least in the later stages of training. There were also several other variables that related curvilinearly with fear. In particular, the relationship between performance in the airborne jumps and fear was curvilinear, which is probably explained by the defense mechanisms. Men with high levels of repression and isolation used only the lower level of the Fear score axis, and men with feminine identifications and low Repression and Isolation used the higher parts of the Fear curve also. Therefore, the subjectively reported fear is very dependent on the defense mechanisms of that individual. This also makes the relationship between a score like subjectively reported fear and performance in the jumps from the airplane a very complicated phenomenon. Along the same lines, the number of feminine identifications showed a very clear and linear relationship with fear; in this case, we believe that there is no interaction with the defense mechanisms Repression and Isolation. The end result of this is that there is perhaps an initial surprising relationship between good performance in airplane jumps and high levels of subjective fear. It should be noted that our Fear Scale was used very moderately by our whole group. It was possible to score up to 10 points, but we never obtained scores higher than about 5.

## CONCLUSION

The men who approach this type of training enter this environment with certain expectations. For example, it is reasonable to assume that they expect this particular environment to reward personality characteristics that we have referred to as Masculine Role Taking. This will apply to all men, even to those who have some difficulties with this role. The difficulties resulting from this inadequate masculine identification manifest themselves in their Fear scores. On a deeper level, subjects with a sufficient masculine role identification experience little fear, but it may be that they pay for this by having defense styles like Repression and Isolation. These defense mechanisms interfere with task performance. In contrast, subjects with feminine identifications and less masculine interest experience more fear, but have less of the defense mechanisms Repression and Isolation, which interfere with performance. Therefore, these men perform better.

The consequences for studies of activation are that one must take these complex interactions into account. Performance, subjective experience of task difficulties, subjective evaluation of performance, subjectively experienced fear, and the defense mechanisms of each person all interact and determine the final internal state evident in a psychophysiological study of activation. In our opinion, this necessitates multidimensional analyses, and we have attempted to do this by descriptive factor analyses as our first approach.

We will follow this strategy for the final relationship between the psychology variables and the physiological variables in the next chapter. The factor analyses will be used at the first approximation, and we will also follow up particular factors and variables we found of interest in this chapter.

## REFERENCES

Basowitz, H., Persky, H., Korchin, S. J., & Grinker, R. R. *Anxiety and stress. An interdisciplinary study of a life situation.* New York: McGraw–Hill (Blakiston Division), 1955.

Bender, L. A visual-motor gestalt test and its clinical use. *American Ortopsychiatric Association Research Monograph.* 1938, No. 3.

Biersner, R. J., & Rynan, D. H. Psychiatric incidence among military divers. *Military Medicine,* 1974, *139,* 633–635.

Fenz, W. D. Stress and its mastery: Predicting from laboratory to real life. *Canadian Journal of Behavioural Sciences,* 1973, *5,* 332–346.

Fenz, W. D., & Epstein, S. Gradients of physiological arousal in parachutists as a function of an approaching jump. *Psychosomatic Medicine,* 1967, *29,* 33–51.

Heckhausen, H. *Hoffnung und Furcht in der Leistungsmotivation.* Meisenheim/Glan: Hain, 1963.

Holtzman, W. H., & Sells, S. B. Prediction of flying success by clinical analysis of test protocols. *Journal of Abnormal and Social Psychology,* 1954, *49,* 485–490.

Joe, U. C. Review of the internal–external control construct as a personality variable. *Psychological Reports,* 1971, *28,* 619–640.

Johnson, S. C. Hierarchical clustering schemes. *Psychometrica,* 1967, *32,* 241–254.

Kragh, U. *The actual-genetic model of perception-personality.* Lund: Gleerup, and Copenhagen: Munksgaard, 1955.

Kragh, U. Pre-cognitive defensive organization: review, discussion and preliminary operational definitions. *Acta Psychiatrica et Neurologica Scandinavica,* 1960, *35,* 190–206. (a)

Kragh, U. The Defense Mechanism Test: A new method for diagnosis and personnel selection. *Journal of Applied Psychology,* 1960, *44,* 303–309. (b)

Kragh, U. Predictions of success of Danish attack divers by the Defense Mechanism Test (DMT). *Psychological Research Bulletin,* Lund University, Sweden, 1962.

Kragh, U. *Defense Mechanism Test.* Test Manual. Skandinaviska Testförlaget AB, Stockholm, 1969.

Kukla, A. Foundations of an attributional theory of performance. *Psychological Review,* 1972, *79,* 454–470.

McClelland, D. C., Atkinson, J. W., Clark, R. A. & Lowell, E. L. *The achievement motive.* New York, Appleton-Century-Crofts, 1953.

Neuman, T. Personality and adjustment to military aviation. A study of correlations between variables from the DM-test and criterion variables. Follow-up, validation and decision— theoretical evaluation. Report No. 59 from the Swedish Institute of Military Psychology, Stockholm, 1967 (mimeographed in Sweden).

Oltman, P. K. A portable rod-and-frame apparatus. *Perceptual and Motor Skills,* 1968, *26,* 503–506.

Pascal, G., & Suttell, B. J. *The Bender-Gestalt Test.* New York: Grune & Stratton, Inc., 1951.

Rotter, J. B. Generalized expectancies for internal control of reinforcement. *Psychological Monograph,* 1966, *80,* Whole No. 609.

Rotter, J. B., Seeman, M., & Liverant, S. Internal versus external control of reinforcements: A major variable in behavior theory. In N. F. Washburne, (Ed.), *Decisions, values and groups.* Oxford: Pergamon Press, 1962. Pp. 473–516.

Sarason, I. G. Experimental approaches to test anxiety: Attention and the uses of information. In C. D. Spielberger (Ed.), *Anxiety. Current trends in theory and research.* New York: Academic Press, 1972. Pp. 381–403.

Solem, P. E., & Traeldal, A. Internalitet/externalitet, 1970. Available only in Norwegian, from Forsvarets Psykologitjeneste, Akershus Festning, Oslo 1.

Stein, M. I. Personality factors involved in the temporal development of Rorschach responses. *Rorschach Research Exchange and Journal of Projective Techniques,* 1949, *13,* 355–360.

Zuckerman, M., Bone, R. N., Neary, R., Mangelsdorff, D., & Brustman, B. Personality trait and experience correlates of the sensation-seeking scales. *Journal of Consulting and Clinical Psychology,* 1972, *39* (2) 308–321.

## Part IV

# PSYCHOBIOLOGICAL IMPLICATIONS

# 14

# Physiology, Psychology, and Performance

EIVIND BAADE, BJØRN ELLERTSEN,
TOM BACKER JOHNSEN, and HOLGER URSIN

In this chapter we will discuss the interaction between the physiological and psychological variables. At least some of the variance in the physiological responses must depend on psychological factors such as general abilities, defensive strategies, and the motivation for completing the training. The physiological changes taking place in the individual were presumably dependent on the psychological state. However, there was also a feedback principle working; the physiological changes in themselves may have contributed to the experience of the situation for each man. The perception of these bodily changes was probably affected, for instance by defense mechanisms, and these mechanisms probably did not only influence the perception of the external world. The performance and, in particular, the subjective evaluation and expectations of performance were of major importance for the subjective experience of the situation. Therefore, performance was also reciprocally influenced by psychological and physiological factors.

The interaction between physiology and psychology variables may be regarded as a complex feedback system between the brain and the rest of the body. For this reason it will be difficult to approach this material by simple methods of data analysis. We decided to attack the problem in several stages, starting with a more descriptive use of factor analyses and then

163

PSYCHOBIOLOGY OF STRESS:
A Study of Coping Men

proceeding to ordinary significance testing of correlations between variables from the two sets of data.

We will first discuss the variance in the basal values. The basal or reference value obtained was not the absolute resting value and probably showed a variance that was influenced by psychological variables. First we will describe particular findings for the dismissed/quit men. We will then analyze the accepted men in more detail. It should be remembered from Chapters 5–12 that the physiological variables followed a very consistent picture. Three distinct phases were identified, and these will be discussed separately: the basal state, the activation level, and the "coping slope."

## RESULTS FROM THE FACTOR ANALYSES

The results from the factor analyses consist of three sets of data, depending on the subset of the cases to be used. First, the results from the total material will be presented, using the hormone basal values and the psychological variables that were sampled for all men. Next, a similar analysis is presented for the dismissed/quit men ($N=28$), using the same set of variables as in the first analysis to compare the results from the two analyses.

We then proceed to the longitudinal analyses of the accepted men, and in these analyses we include all of the variables from the tower training and the performance in the jumps from the airplane. As to the decision of number of factors, we refer the reader to Chapter 3. For the comparisons between the total material and the dismissed/quit men, we chose the four-factor solution, which accounted for 54.8% of the variance for the total material and 52.4% of the variance for the dismissed/quit group.

### Basal Values

#### Factor Analysis of the Total Material (N=72)

In this analysis, we included all psychology variables except those to which only accepted men contributed, that is, the variables from the mock tower training and the performance in airplane jumps. From the physiology data we used the basal values, which were obtained from the 72 men. As mentioned in the introduction, the basal values did not represent the lowest possible value obtainable from awake men ("resting level"). It is questionable whether such values may be obtained at all in humans, except perhaps with implanted catheters and extremely well-trained men. Even though we made a considerable effort to obtain a relaxed and nonstressed atmosphere, the men were not only awake, but also apprehensive about their new environment and the risk of not being able to master it. There was probably also some concern about the blood sampling itself, even though we felt that this was kept to a minimum during the waiting period. Therefore, we expect that some of the individual variance may be due to psychological factors, and we expect at least some of the psychology variables to explain some of this variance.

When the whole matrix (consisting of these two different sets of variables) was analyzed by factors, we predicted some pure psychology and some pure physiology factors. However, the interesting factors were the joint factors (see Table 14.2). Only loadings with absolute values larger than .40 were included in order to clarify the general picture. The abbreviations used are given in Table 14.1.

**TABLE 14.1**
**Abbreviation Code**

| | |
|---|---|
| Blocks R−W | Block Task, right minus wrong answers; given as "distraction" tasks during TEV |
| Blocks R+W | Block Task, total number of answers given |
| BORE | Boredom Susceptibility |
| CIT | Complicated Instructions Test |
| DMT DEF | Defense Mechanism Test, Defense Mechanisms, the number of Isolation, Repression, and Reaction Formation types of responses |
| DMT MF | Defense Mechanism Test, Masculine/Feminine, number of feminine identifications |
| DMT PROG | Defense Mechanism Test "Prognosis," evaluation of prognosis for continued training in and execution of dangerous occupation; high score indicates good prognosis |
| EXT | Internal–External Locus of Control; high scores indicate external control |
| Fear | Subjective Fear score (see Chapter 4) |
| GAL | General Ability Level |
| K1 | Performance in tower |
| K2 | Performance in airplane jumps |
| PTA | Preference for Thrill and Adventure, agreement with preference of the group |
| RAM | Resultant Achievement Motivation; high scores indicate hope of success |
| RF | Rod and Frame Test; high scores indicate field dependence |
| SORT R−W | Sorting Test, difference between the number of right and wrong responses |
| SUD | Surface Development |
| TEC | Technical Comprehension |
| TEV | Time Estimation Variability |

**TABLE 14.2**
**Varimax-Rotated Factor Pattern from Total Sample, Basal Values, and Psychological Tests**

|                | 1       | 2       | 3       | 4      |
|----------------|---------|---------|---------|--------|
| Blood glucose  | —       | —       | .3088   | —      |
| Cortisol       | —       | —       | —       | .3033  |
| Free fatty acid| —       | .3169   | —       | —      |
| Epinephrine    | —       | .7437   | —       | —      |
| Norepinephrine | —       | .7848   | —       | —      |
| Growth hormone | —       | —       | −.3250  | —      |
| Testosterone   | —       | −.3412  | −.4828  | —      |
| GAL            | .7623   | —       | —       | —      |
| TEC            | .7786   | —       | —       | —      |
| SUD            | .7337   | —       | —       | —      |
| CIT            | .6915   | —       | —       | —      |
| SORT R−W       | .4477   | —       | —       | —      |
| Blocks R−W     | .5247   | −.2547  | —       | —      |
| Blocks R+W     | .6229   | .2562   | —       | —      |
| TEV            | —       | .2871   | —       | .3367  |
| RF             | −.5259  | −.2458  | .3097   | —      |
| EXT            | —       | .3842   | .3266   | —      |
| RAM            | —       | —       | −.3338  | .6198  |
| DMT MF         | —       | —       | .6796   | —      |
| DMT PROG       | —       | .2501   | −.6484  | —      |
| DMT DEF        | —       | −.3676  | .2751   | .6162  |
| PTA            | —       | —       | −.5897  | —      |
| BORE           | —       | —       | —       | .6775  |

*Factor 1* corresponds to Factor 1 in the Psychology Only analysis ("General Intellective Factor," see Chapter 13) and remained purely a psychological factor in this analysis.

*Factor 2* is a pure physiology factor, the catecholamine factor. The loading for Externality approached our limit for significance, but no correlations were significant.

*Factor 3* is the only joint factor. The psychology variables are for the most part identical to the "Masculine Role Taking Factor" in the Psychology Only matrix. It is very interesting that the hormone that loads on this is the basal value of testosterone. Men with low identification with the masculine role showed a low testosterone value. One of the correlations within this factor was significant (testosterone versus PTA = .24, $p < .05$), and another was close to that significance level (testosterone versus DMTMF = −.23, $p \sim .05$). It seems unreasonable to assume that Masculine Role Taking depended on testosterone. The low testosterone value was probably due to a stress factor; these men may have had difficulties with identification and adaptation to this highly "masculine" environment.

*Factor 4* is, again, a pure psychology factor. It contains elements from "Defense" (Factor 2) and "Activity Need" (Factor 3) in the total Psychology Only material.

## Factor Analysis of the "Dismissed/Quit Men" (N=28)

It is reasonable to assume that this factor structure is considerably less reliable than the first analysis because of the large number of variables in relation to the number of subjects (23 variables versus 28 subjects). Even worse, the number of valid pairs used as the basis for some of the correlations is considerably lower in this group (i.e., all correlations with epinephrine and norepinephrine, where $N = 7$). Since these specific variables load high on more than one factor and the basis for the correlations may be weak, the results could be considerably changed with a higher $N$.

**TABLE 14.3**
**Varimax-Rotated Factor Pattern from Dismissed Men ($N = 28$), Basal Values, and Psychological Tests**

|                | 1      | 2       | 3       | 4       |
|----------------|--------|---------|---------|---------|
| Blood glucose  | —      | −.9372  | —       | —       |
| Cortisol       | —      | —       | .5070   | −.3297  |
| Free fatty acid| —      | —       | —       | −.6842  |
| Epinephrine    | .2989  | .6625   | —       | −.4073  |
| Norepinephrine | −.3210 | .7591   | −.5161  | −.5223  |
| Growth hormone | −.2771 | —       | .5760   | —       |
| Testosterone   | —      | .6268   | —       | .4154   |
| GAL            | .7458  | —       | —       | —       |
| TEC            | .8055  | —       | —       | —       |
| SUD            | .7779  | —       | —       | —       |
| CIT            | .6899  | —       | —       | —       |
| SORT R−W       | .4266  | —       | —       | −.4218  |
| Blocks R−W     | .4758  | —       | —       | —       |
| Blocks R+W     | .5550  | —       | —       | —       |
| TEV            | .3298  | —       | —       | —       |
| RF             | −.6250 | —       | —       | .4718   |
| EXT            | —      | .3040   | −.5509  | —       |
| RAM            | —      | .3901   | .5442   | —       |
| DMT MF         | —      | —       | −.4385  | —       |
| DMT PROG       | —      | —       | .3009   | −.7522  |
| DMT DEF        | .3919  | —       | —       | .6344   |
| PTA            | —      | .1734   | .4276   | —       |
| BORE           | —      | —       | .6883   | —       |

*Factor 1* is again the "General Intellective Factor" and very close to Factor 1 in the analysis of the dismissed men in the Psychology Only analysis.

*Factor 2* is a pure physiology factor, but RAM was very close to our limit (.39) and showed a significant correlation with testosterone ($r = .38$, $p < .05$). The correlation with epinephrine was high (.46), but did not reach significance due to the low number of observations. RAM was also found in the next factor.

*Factor 3* points to the relationships between psychology variables from "Masculine Role Taking" and cortisol, norepinephrine, and growth hormone. Cortisol and growth hormone had signs opposite to those of norepinephrine. The only significant relationship was between cortisol and Resultant Achievement Motivation (RAM, .39, $p < .05$). There were also high correlations within the factor between norepinephrine and External Locus of Control (EXT, .45) and Boredom (BORE, −.46), but none of these reached statistical significance.

*Factor 4* is, again, a joint factor. It contains elements from the Defense Factor in the Psychology Matrix combined with the results from the Rod and Frame Test (RF, shows field dependency) and poor performance in the SORT Test (SORT R−W). From the physiology matrix, free fatty acids, epinephrine, norepinephrine, and testosterone all showed loadings in the direction of low activation values. Since the tendency of the difference was in the opposite direction, this pole of the factor may be the most interesting. A high activation level on all hormones except growth hormone may be most pronounced in men with low defense and, paradoxically, a good prognosis. This may be related to their quitting the course. The other men (the other pole of the factor), with high defense and low activation, were able to ignore or defend themselves against the apprehensive or environmental factors that were operating on the first days. They ignored these cues in the same way they ignored the threatening aspects in the DMT. However, in more provocative test situations, like SORT R−W, the defense was not effective and performance was impaired.

*Conclusion—dismissed/quit men.* In the dismissed/quit men, there were very few significant correlations. The only correlations found were between Resultant Achievement Motivation (RAM) and cortisol and testosterone. These two significant correlations were found in two separate factors, corresponding to the conclusions from the Physiology analysis; basal values of cortisol and testosterone were not correlated and did not load on the same factors. The interpretation is complicated by the finding that the men who quit had greater extreme RAM scores, both higher and lower, than the accepted men. The factor analysis suggests relationships between basal day activation and "Masculine Role Taking" in this group also.

In the dismissed men, we found a higher level of at least some of the indicators, in particular the catecholamines, testosterone, blood glucose, and free fatty acids, but not the cortisol–Defense Factor. The dismissed/quit men tended to have low defense and high fear levels, which tended to give a higher arousal level on the basal values. In Chapter 13, we concluded that test anxiety and emotionality may have entered the performance of the dismissed/quit men to a larger extent than for the accepted men.

### Factor Analysis of the Basal Values of the Accepted Men Including Variables from the Tower Training

In the analysis of the total material, only the variables on which all men were tested could be included. We also ran a four-factor solution for the accepted men to investigate possible differences in the factor structure between the two groups. This analysis did not yield any new information.

To obtain a better picture of the important variables for the accepted men, all of the variables from tower training and airplane jumps were included. We tried several analyses with four, five, and six factors and found that the six-factor solution is conceptually the best one, since the two performance criteria, which we know to be almost uncorrelated, separated into two different factors. This solution explains 54.6% of the variance.

*Factor 1* is again a General Intellective Factor (see Table 14.4).

*Factor 2* is a joint factor. It contains the testosterone–free fatty acids and growth hormone factor from the Physiology basal data analysis. The psychology variables added to this factor were leading variables from the Masculine Role Factor (DMT MF) and DMT PROG plus performance in the tower (K1) and the subjective fear level reported on Jump Day 1.

The only significant correlation between variables from the two matrices within this factor was between free fatty acids and performance in the tower (.30, $p$ <0.05). Free fatty acids also correlated significantly with External Locus of Control (EXT, $-.33, p < .05$), which was very close to inclusion in this factor (.36).

Free fatty acids showed a remarkable relationship to performance in the tower, and we will return to this relationship in the discussion. This factor also suggests that Internal Locus of Control was related to high levels of free fatty acids. Free fatty acid activation seemed related to low fear, good performance in the tower, and a low number of feminine identifications. This factor suggested that high identification with the "masculine role" was related to good tower performance, low fear, and high growth hormone and free fatty acid activation. The testosterone activation, however, was low.

Men with a high number of feminine identifications, the other aspect of the factor, tended to perform poorly in the tower, and their prognosis for further training was poor. In these men, the free fatty acid and growth

**TABLE 14.4**
**Varimax-Rotated Six-Factor Solution on Basal Values, Psychology Variables, and Performance[a]**

| | Factor | | | | | |
|---|---|---|---|---|---|---|
| | 1 | 2 | 3 | 4 | 5 | 6 |
| Blood glucose | — | — | — | — | — | .5711 |
| Cortisol | — | — | — | .4508 | −.5286 | — |
| Free fatty acid | — | .5323 | — | — | — | — |
| Epinephrine | — | — | .8813 | — | — | — |
| Norepinephrine | — | — | .8885 | — | — | — |
| Growth hormone | — | .4438 | — | — | — | — |
| Testosterone | — | .5016 | — | — | .3148 | −.3300 |
| GAL | .5326 | — | .3532 | — | .3965 | — |
| TEC | .5583 | — | .4038 | — | .3234 | — |
| SUD | — | .3249 | — | — | .6785 | — |
| CIT | .7169 | — | — | — | — | — |
| SORT R−W | .6796 | — | — | — | — | — |
| Blocks R−W | — | — | — | — | .7740 | — |
| Blocks R+W | — | — | .4185 | — | — | .4547 |
| TEV | −.5121 | — | — | — | — | .3379 |
| RF | — | .3929 | — | — | — | — |
| EXT | — | .3620 | — | — | — | — |
| RAM | — | .3427 | — | .6499 | — | — |
| DMT MF | .3183 | −.5081 | — | — | — | .5007 |
| DMT PROG | — | .7179 | — | — | — | — |
| DMT DEF | — | — | — | .7775 | — | — |
| PTA | — | — | — | — | — | −.7170 |
| BORE | — | — | — | .4654 | .3101 | — |
| K1 | — | .4309 | — | — | — | — |
| K2 | — | — | — | — | .5704 | — |
| Fear | — | −.4275 | .3389 | — | — | .3009 |

[a] Accepted men, $N = 44$.

hormone activation was low, whereas the testosterone activation was high. Their fear score was high, and it may be that the lack of identification with the masculine role permitted a more liberal use of the Fear Scale. This could explain their relatively low activation on free fatty acid and growth hormone activation. The particular relationship between testosterone and the "feminine" scores remains puzzling.

*Factor 3* is also a joint factor, but there were no significant correlations between the two sets of variables. This factor suggested that a high basal level of catecholamines was associated with good performance on TEC and with a high number of responses (right or wrong) on the Blocks Test; these men worked fast, but their responses were not necessarily correct.

*Factor 4* suggests a very interesting relationship between cortisol and the Defense Factor. The correlation between DMT DEF and the cortisol basal value was significant (.37, *p* < .05). There was also a contribution from Resultant Achievement Motivation (RAM).

*Factor 5* is again a joint factor, and the basal value of cortisol also loads on this factor. Low basal values of cortisol were found in men who performed well in the airplane jumps. There was also a negative relationship between cortisol and performance on the two tests Blocks R−W and SUD, which were significantly correlated with performance on jumps from the airplane (Chapter 13). The correlations between the cortisol basal value and the performance criterion (K2) and SUD were not significant. However, the cortisol basal value was negatively correlated with Blocks R−W (−.33, *p* < .05).

Cortisol activation as expressed by increased basal levels related negatively to performance in the air jumps. The free fatty acid factor, however, was positively related to performance in the tower. This confirms our suggestion that these two types of activation may be independent or perhaps negatively interrelated.

*Factor 6* is also a joint factor, the leading components from the "Masculine Role Factor" from the Psychology analyses related to blood glucose basal level, although none of the single correlations between blood glucose and other components reached significance.

*Conclusion—basal values.* From the Physiology analyses, three factors emerged. All three factors are clearly present in the combined material.

The catecholamine factor showed a significant relationship with performance on one of the psychology tasks (Blocks R+W). Pre-jump levels of epinephrine fell below basal level when coping had been established. This suggested a particular sensitivity for epinephrine for whatever psychological factors might have been working on the first days of the course. However, there are no simple explanations evident from the correlation matrix or from the factor analyses. High basal values of epinephrine may be related to test performance, or at least to the activity level in the Blocks Test.

The second factor, *cortisol–growth hormone,* showed clearly different relationships, at least for cortisol. Growth hormone was more related to the testosterone–free fatty acid axis. There was a positive relationship between cortisol basal values and Defense. There was also a clear relationship between cortisol and low performance in jumps from the airplane. Cortisol also related to those tasks in the psychology battery that were predictive of poor performance in jumps from airplanes.

The third factor, the *testosterone–free fatty acid* axis, also showed particular relationships to performance different from those of the other two factors.

It related to performance, but was related in particular to Masculine Role Taking. Free fatty acids had a clear relationship to tower performance, fear, feminine identification, and prognosis for going through this type of training. Testosterone also showed a particular relationship to feminine identifications. It seemed to be a relationship between low identification with the masculine role and low testosterone level mainly on the first days, when the difficulties in adapting to this "masculine" environment were supposedly at their worst.

## Activation Levels

All analyses that follow are from the 44 accepted men. We performed several factor analyses with various indexes of "Rise" and compared these with the Psychology matrix. These analyses yielded a fairly consistent picture of the relationships between physiology and psychology variables. Two of these analyses are reported.

### Absolute Rise Levels

For these comparisons, we decided to use the second blood sample, from Jump Day 1, and the post-jump ("stress") urine samples. The six-factor solution explained 57.3% of the variance. *Factor 1* (see Table 14.5) is again the General Intellective Factor. The catecholamine factor was close to inclusion in this factor, but appeared strongly in Factor 3.

*Factor 2* is a joint factor with loadings on tower performance and jumps from the airplane and cortisol, free fatty acids, and growth hormone. Cortisol and, in this case, growth hormone were related to poor performance, whereas free fatty acids related to good performance. High levels of cortisol rise related negatively to performance in jumps from the airplane ($\chi^2$ test, $p < .01$). There was again a significant correlation between free fatty acids and performance in the tower ($.37, p < .05$), as was also the case for basal values of free fatty acids.

*Factor 3* is a joint factor; the catecholamine factor and blood glucose appeared together with low tolerance of boredom, and a few of the psychology performance tests were close to inclusion. However, BORE did not correlate significantly with any of the physiology variables except growth hormone rise ($-.32, p < .05$), which did not load on this factor. TEC was close to inclusion on this factor and correlated significantly with epinephrine rise ($.45, p < .05$) and with glucose ($.38, p < .05$); both physiology indicators were found most strongly in this factor.

*Factor 4* suggests a relationship between testosterone activation (fall) and jumps from the airplane, low tolerance of boredom, and achievement

**TABLE 14.5**
**Absolute Rise Levels plus Psychology and Performance Variables, Six-Factor Rotated Solution**

| | Factor | | | | | |
|---|---|---|---|---|---|---|
| | 1 | 2 | 3 | 4 | 5 | 6 |
| Blood glucose | — | — | −.7795 | — | — | — |
| Cortisol | — | .8218 | — | — | — | — |
| Free fatty acid | — | −.7320 | — | — | — | — |
| Epinephrine | −.3872 | — | −.7121 | — | — | — |
| Norepinephrine | −.3071 | — | −.7938 | — | — | — |
| Growth hormone | — | .6086 | — | — | — | — |
| Testosterone | — | — | −.3366 | −.4942 | — | — |
| GAL | −.6632 | — | — | — | — | −.3358 |
| TEC | −.5379 | — | −.3967 | — | — | −.4412 |
| SUD | −.5872 | — | — | — | — | −.4199 |
| CIT | −.6252 | — | — | — | — | — |
| SORT R−W | — | — | .3384 | −.3659 | — | −.3689 |
| Blocks R−W | — | — | — | — | — | −.7274 |
| Blocks R+W | −.8141 | — | — | — | — | — |
| TEV | — | — | — | — | — | .7111 |
| RF | — | — | — | — | −.4097 | — |
| EXT | — | — | — | — | −.3636 | .3127 |
| RAM | — | — | — | .6049 | .3356 | — |
| DMT MF | — | — | — | — | −.7646 | — |
| DMT PROG | — | −.3303 | .3223 | — | .6602 | — |
| DMT DEF | — | — | — | .5413 | — | — |
| PTA | .5303 | — | — | −.4779 | — | — |
| BORE | — | — | −.5270 | .4318 | — | — |
| K1 | — | −.3936 | — | — | — | — |
| K2 | — | −.4057 | — | .5085 | — | — |
| Fear | — | — | — | — | −.6499 | — |

motivation. These men were characterized by defense mechanisms and did not have a particularly high preference for thrill and adventure.

*Factor 5* is from the Psychology Only matrix, as is *Factor 6*.

### Activation Index

This index expresses the rise from the basal value. For the catecholamines, the second sample was the only stress sample, and the index was obtained by subtracting the basal sample value from the post-jump value. For the blood variables, both samples were stress samples. We computed the average of the two post-jump samples obtained and subtracted the basal value. The six-factor solution explained 56.7% of the variance.

*Factor 1* is again the General Intellective Factor (Table 14.6); this time, the norepinephrine rise reached the level of acceptance.

*Factor 2* again points to an interesting relationship between "Activity Need," a low tolerance of boredom, and the catecholamine factor. There was a significant correlation between BORE and norepinephrine (.50, *p* < .05). RAM was close to acceptance for this factor and correlated significantly with epinephrine (.43, *p* < .05). TEC did not reach the acceptance criterion, but there was a significant correlation between TEC and the epinephrine Activation index (.42, *p* < .05).

*Factor 3* is a pure psychology factor with variables from the "Masculine Role Taking Factor." Blood glucose was close to the acceptance level.

**TABLE 14.6**
**Activation Index**

| | Factor | | | | | |
|---|---|---|---|---|---|---|
| | 1 | 2 | 3 | 4 | 5 | 6 |
| Blood glucose | — | −.4806 | .3600 | −.3789 | — | — |
| Cortisol | — | — | — | — | .8198 | — |
| Free fatty acid | — | — | — | — | −.7452 | — |
| Growth hormone | — | .3157 | — | — | .5557 | — |
| Testosterone | — | — | — | −.6913 | — | — |
| Epinephrine | .3790 | −.4791 | — | .4783 | −.3861 | — |
| Norepinephrine | .4284 | −.4921 | — | — | — | — |
| GAL | .7398 | — | — | — | — | — |
| TEC | .7274 | — | — | — | — | −.3207 |
| SUD | .6845 | — | — | .3921 | — | — |
| CIT | .6681 | — | — | — | — | — |
| SORT R−W | .3084 | .3198 | — | — | — | −.3812 |
| Blocks R−W | .3527 | — | — | .5114 | — | −.4917 |
| Blocks R+W | .7635 | — | — | — | — | .3832 |
| TEV | — | — | — | — | — | .6966 |
| RF | −.3495 | — | — | — | — | — |
| EXT | — | — | −.4054 | — | — | — |
| RAM | — | −.3443 | — | .4034 | — | .3673 |
| DMT MF | — | — | −.8280 | — | — | — |
| DMT PROG | — | .4481 | .5272 | .3086 | — | — |
| DMT DEF | — | −.4276 | — | — | — | — |
| PTA | −.3211 | — | .5573 | — | — | −.3194 |
| BORE | — | −.7543 | — | — | — | — |
| K1 | — | — | — | .4668 | −.3384 | — |
| K2 | — | — | — | .6292 | — | — |
| Fear | — | — | −.6035 | — | — | — |

*Factor 4* is characterized by a combination of both of the performance criteria (tower jumps and airborne jumps) and the testosterone, blood glucose (negative), and epinephrine increases. The testosterone–free fatty acid factor is split; free fatty acids appear in the next factor. None of the correlations within this factor reached significance.

In *Factor 5* we find the cortisol–growth hormone factor and a negative loading on free fatty acids. The free fatty acids was negatively correlated with cortisol ($-.42, p < .01$). A negative loading on epinephrine was close to the acceptance level. A significant positive relationship was again seen between free fatty acids and performance in the tower ($.35, p < .05$).

Cortisol was negatively related to perfromance and to free fatty acids, but the negative correlations between cortisol and the performance criteria were not significant. Cortisol was also negatively correlated with SORT R−W ($-.31, p < .05$), but this task was not included in this factor. Free fatty acids also correlated significantly with DMT PROG ($.33, p < .05$), but this task was also not included in the factor.

*Factor 6* is a pure psychology factor.

## Conclusion—Activation Analyses

In the analyses of the physiology activation we found three consistent factors, and these factors seem to be meaningfully related both to psychology tests and to performance.

*Cortisol–growth hormone factor.* Cortisol and growth hormone were consistently found as one factor for basal values and for high activation levels. These two variables were negatively related to free fatty acids. This relationship disappeared at later jumps.

Free fatty acids showed consistently positive correlations with performance in the tower and with the prognosis as evaluated by the DMT. Cortisol showed the opposite relationship: High levels of cortisol were associated with poor performance both in jumps from the tower and in jumps from the airplane. The same relationship was found for growth hormone.

*Catecholamines.* Again, there was a clear relationship between the catecholamines and activity, or "Activity Need." There was also a consistent relationship between catecholamines and the important performance tests, in particular, the Technical Comprehension Test (TEC). There were also consistent correlations between epinephrine and RAM and between blood glucose and TEC. Norepinephrine was also significantly correlated to BORE. All correlations were positive, and the catecholamine factor was clearly related to performance. In Chapter 7 we pointed to the possibilities that epinephrine was related to the coping act itself, whereas norepinephrine was characterized more by passive coping and apprehension. So far, the factor analysis has not supported any differentiation between the two hormones. However, we have previously mentioned that the strong correlation between epinephrine and norepinephrine may, at least in part, be due to an artifact, because these hormones follow each other throughout the chemical analyses. The relationship between activity, performance, and catecholamines has been described by Frankenhaeuser (1975).

In general, our results are compatible with the data of Roessler (1973), who demonstrated that in coping individuals there is more of a psychophysiological reactivity in autonomic processes influenced by the sympathetic nervous system; when coping is established, this activation is reduced.

*Norepinephrine and fear.*    There was no direct significant relationship between norepinephrine and fear. However, in the seven men who quit after the first jump and who were able to produce urinary specimens, there was a striking relationship between the norepinephrine value and the level of fear reported in the tower. There was a significant correlation between the norepinephrine value obtained on the day of basal sampling and the fear reported in the tower ($r = .93, N = 7, p < .01$). Even with this small value for $N$, the relationship is so striking that it demands particular attention. The same relationship was evident on the day of the first jump the fear level reported on that day correlated strongly with both the norepinephrine levels reported before the jump ($.7, p < .05$) and the value obtained at 1000 hr, the time at which approximately half of these men had jumped ($r = .62, p < .05$).

We have suggested that norepinephrine related to passive or cognitive tasks, and no support was found for any differentiation of the catecholamine hormones along the fear–aggression axis. The fear rating may not express a clear fear of death or fear of destruction, but may also involve a "fear of failure," at least in the group of men who left the course after the first jump. We have also pointed out that the dismissed men, with relatively low defense and high femininity scores, tended to use the fear score more liberally than the accepted men. The lack of a similar relation in the accepted men may therefore be due to their defense mechanisms and their reluctance to use the high scores on the Fear Scale.

*Impatience and activation.*    A final significant relationship is the positive correlation between intolerance of routine and boredom (BORE) and growth hormone and norepinephrine. This correlation suggests high reactivity in individuals who are easily bored. It is as if they become activated easily and strongly, at least on growth hormone and norepinephenne, but decrease quickly in arousal and engagement. The epinephrine arousal, on the other hand, was related to performance or achievement motivation. The growth hormone basal value correlated significantly with Resultant Achievement Motivation. Preference for Thrill and Adventure (PTA) did not show any significant relationship to this score.

## Fall Index

The central thesis in this book is that adequate coping behavior is characterized by a significant reduction in internal physiological activation. We expect psychological variables to be of importance for this fall, which depends not only on performance and feedback from the environment, but also on each man's experience and appraisal of the situation. To investigate the possible relationships, we constructed a "Fall Index" by using the difference between the top activation (the second sample on Jump Day 1) and the average activation level reached on the last two jumps (second sample on Jump Days 5 and 11). This index was used in a factor analysis (see Table 14.7). Explained variance was 57.0%.

*Factor 1* is the usual General Intellective factor.

*Factor 2* is a joint factor, with contributions from the catecholamine and cortisol factors. As expected, cortisol had a negative loading.

As surmised from our previous findings, good performance in jumps from the airplane and a low tolerance of boredom (BORE) were associated with high levels of catecholamines and blood glucose; also as expected, cortisol was negatively related to these psychological variables. This factor suggests a particularly pronounced fall in catecholamine in the men who were good performers in the tower and in the psychological tests. Since both of the performance criteria were related to the catecholamine factor, it did not surprise us that the performance variable that loaded on this factor was air performance rather than tower performance.

*Factor 3* is the relevant performance, K1, which is performance in the tower. Again, we found a relationship between K1 and free fatty acids ($.34, p < .05$). In this case, the free fatty acids fell very rapidly in men with good performance in the tower. It should be noted that free fatty acids showed a very fast decrement for the group as a whole. This physiological variable seems very sensitive not only to performance, but also to feedback from this performance.

The decrease in free fatty acids also related significantly to the prognosis for continuing this type of training (DMT PROG, $.41, p < .01$). The other

**TABLE 14.7**
**Fall Index**

| | Factor | | | | | |
|---|---|---|---|---|---|---|
| | 1 | 2 | 3 | 4 | 5 | 6 |
| Blood glucose | — | .5464 | — | — | −.3163 | .3587 |
| Cortisol | — | −.6439 | — | — | — | .4040 |
| Free fatty acid | — | — | .6015 | — | — | — |
| Epinephrine | — | −.3365 | — | — | — | .3711 |
| Norepinephrine | .3211 | — | — | −.6514 | — | — |
| Growth hormone | — | .8179 | — | — | — | — |
| Testosterone | — | .8576 | — | — | — | — |
| GAL | .7013 | — | — | — | — | — |
| TEC | .7084 | .3632 | — | — | — | — |
| SUD | — | — | — | .3606 | — | .6899 |
| CIT | .7801 | — | — | — | — | — |
| SORT R−W | .5778 | — | — | — | — | — |
| Blocks R−W | — | — | — | .5848 | — | — |
| Blocks R+W | .4137 | — | — | — | — | .5562 |
| TEV | — | — | — | −.5158 | — | — |
| RF | — | — | — | — | — | −.6531 |
| EXT | — | — | — | — | — | — |
| RAM | — | — | — | — | .6979 | — |
| DMT MF | — | — | −.6768 | .3970 | — | — |
| DMT PROG | — | — | .7650 | — | — | — |
| DMT DEF | — | — | — | — | .7651 | −.3320 |
| PTA | — | — | .3327 | −.2299 | −.4329 | — |
| BORE | — | .5348 | — | — | .3702 | — |
| K1 | — | — | .4307 | .4826 | — | — |
| K2 | — | .4076 | — | .5357 | — | — |
| Fear | — | — | −.6315 | — | — | — |

psychology variables in the factor, together with DMT PROG, derive from the Masculine Role Taking Factor.

In *Factor 4* there is again a suggestion of a relationship between norepinephrine activation and performance criteria, but none of the correlations reached statistical significance.

*Factor 5* is a pure psychology factor; *Factor 6* is a joint factor, but the correlations between the variables from the two sets did not reach significance. The direction of the relationship between cortisol fall and performance was opposite to the direction we found in activation.

## DISCUSSION

### Catecholamines and "Apprehension"

The pre-jump values for epinephrine fell below the basal values in the later part of the training phase. This suggested a specific type of apprehension affecting epinephrine on the day of basal sampling and that this apprehension must be sensitive to the coping effect. It disappeared after repeated sampling and repeated exposures to the situation.

The difference between the basal level and the pre-jump values for the last two jumps was computed as an index. The correlation matrix showed that there was only one significant correlation: RAM correlated negatively with the Fall Index for epinephrine ($-.52$, $p < .05$). This means that a pronounced decrease was seen in the men with the least achievement motivation. In Chapter 15 we will return to the importance of RAM for the activation pattern obtained on these later stages of training.

Norepinephrine also showed an "apprehension" effect, but on a different day. This type of apprehension was only evident before the first jump. In Chapter 7 it was suggested that norepinephrine was related to more cognitive tasks and cognitive preparations, in line with previous suggestions made by Frankenhaeuser (1975) and by Obrist (1976).

The values of norepinephrine obtained before the first jump showed only one significant correlation: Norepinephrine correlated positively with TEC ($.42$, $p < .05$). This correlation was found in the "General Ability Level Factor" (GAL), in a factor analysis comprising only this hormone value and all psychology variables. The hormone did not load on any other factor. This finding supports our interpretation and suggests that this pre-jump value was related to the resources and strategies used in the more cognitive-oriented performance of the individual. The relationship between fear and norepinephrine was found only in the dismissed men. There are also other phenomena for which we tend to use the term apprehension. In particular, we have already discussed the "apprehension" present in the men who experienced difficulties (or at least different identifications) with this type of "masculine" role, evident in the testosterone activation. This hormone may also have picked up a fourth type of apprehension, fear of failure, which is tapped by the negative "pole" of the RAM Test. There was a tendency for fear of failure to be associated with low testosterone values. The epinephrine decrease related to RAM, but this was, of course, dependent on the level on the basal day, even though it did not turn up in the analysis directly.

Epinephrine increased after every jump, throughout the whole experiment, and we have referred to this as "phasic" activation (Chapter 7). The same short-lasting activation was also found in the heart rate (Chapter 9). An analysis of the relationship between the increase in epinephrine from pre-jump to post-jump values each day and the psychology variables did not reveal a consistent picture.

## Cortisol–Growth Hormone Factor

This hormone axis was particularly characterized by cortisol, with less consistent findings for growth hormone. The striking finding is that, at least in the 44 accepted men, this type of activation was related to high defense and low performance. There is a possibility of 63 correlations for the performance tests; cortisol showed 52 negative correlations. The largest negative correlations were found for the timed tests. The increase in cortisol was also associated with field dependency.

The relationships for the dismissed men are less clear; cortisol basal values and psychology variables correlated significantly only with Resultant Achievement Motivation. With high achievement motivation, there was also a high cortisol activation. These men were able to quit, and it could perhaps be said that, in this connection, cortisol activation was "good." We have no concrete information on the degree of defense in the cortisol-activated dismissed men.

## Testosterone–Free Fatty Acid Factor

This axis also showed distinct relationships to the psychology variables.

*Testosterone* was particularly associated with feminine identifications and the Masculine Role Taking factor, at least for the basal values. The low testosterone values were negatively related to Preference for Thrill and Adventure. It may be that testosterone picked up particular types of threats to the individual, mainly when this was related to the "masculine" role.

*Free fatty acids* were very clearly related to good performance for basal values, rise factors, and the coping effect. This held for performance in the tower and for several of the performance tests. It also held to a certain extent for jumps from the airplane. Free fatty acids were also related to Internal Locus of Control. The free fatty acid activation, therefore, was characterized by a strong rise and a fast fall in the men who were effectively coping.

*Blood glucose* showed a mixed relationship with performance and defense. This was most likely due to the fact that it related partially to the catecholamine factor and partially to the cortisol factor; this seemed to depend on the degree of activation. At low levels of activation, blood glucose correlated with cortisol. At high levels of activation, blood glucose correlated with the catecholamines, as predicted from the traditional physiological view concerning activation (Cannon, 1932).

## REFERENCES

Cannon, J. *The wisdom of the body*. New York: Norton, 1932.
Frankenhaeuser, M. Experimental approaches to the study of catecholamines and emotion. In L. Levi (Ed.), *Emotions. Their parameters and measurement*. New York: Raven Press, 1975.
Obrist, P. A. The cardiovascular-behavioral interaction—as it appears today. (Presidential address, 1975). *Psychophysiology*, 1976, *13*, 95–107.
Roessler, R. Personality, psychophysiology, and performance (Presidential address, 1972). *Psychophysiology*, 1973, *10*, 315–327.

# 15

# Motivational and Physiological Arousal

FRED VOLLMER

## PHYSIOLOGICAL AROUSAL AS RELATED TO ACHIEVEMENT MOTIVATION

The subjects in the present study were faced with the task of learning basic parachutist jumping techniques. To this end they were subjected to several weeks of training involving jumping from a tower. Performance gradually improved during the training phase. The reason for selecting this task for study was that it was judged to be a highly threatening and fear-provoking situation. As such, it was considered an ideal situation in which to test a number of hypotheses regarding relationships between degree of threat experienced in a situation, on the one hand, and physiological arousal/subjective fear on the other. For instance, will improvement in performance/skill lead to a change in experience of the situation's degree of threat and thereby to a change in subsequent physiological arousal/subjective fear? Will defense mechanisms to some degree determine how threatening the situation is perceived to be and therefore also be related to physiological activation?

In characterizing the task situation as threatening and fear provoking, however, the question arises: What kind of threat was experienced by the

PSYCHOBIOLOGY OF STRESS:
A Study of Coping Men

subject, that is, what was the object of his fear? One obvious answer is that the situation (jumping from a tower) was experienced as physically threatening by the subject and that he was afraid of bodily injury. Besides being physically dangerous, the task situation had a number of other characteristics that also involved threat. The subject was faced with the task of learning a *skill,* he had to *perform,* and his performance was *evaluated* by an expert. Moreover, the subject performed together with others. His level of skill was seen by his peers in addition to an expert and himself. Furthermore, his acceptance for airborne jump training was contingent on good performance in the tower training. It is highly probable, then, that the subject experienced a threat in the possibility that his performance would not reach a high standard of excellence, that his level of skill would be judged as low by expert, peers, and himself, that he would fail in the competition with his peers, and that he would not be accepted for further training. Fear and motivation related to such threats are termed *fear of failure.*

The task characteristics described in the preceding paragraph make the training session a typical achievement situation. In such situations, not only are fear and failure avoidance motivation aroused, but more positive psychological states such as hoping and wishing to do well, expecting future success, intending to work hard, and expending high levels of actual effort to reach success are also brought into play.

To sum up, it is reasonable to assume that the parachutist trainees perceived that they were in an achievement situation, that the situation experienced as such was likely to arouse *motivation,* and that such motivation may be related to physiological arousal. The question we now turn to is: What factors may be thought of as decisive for degree of motivational arousal in an achievement situation and therefore also possibly related to physiological activation in that same type of situation?

## ATKINSON'S THEORY OF ACHIEVEMENT MOTIVATION

According to Atkinson (1957) and Atkinson and Feather (1966), motivational arousal in an achievement situation is determined by two sets of factors: task characteristics and individual characteristics. Starting with the latter, individual characteristics are conceived of as relatively stable motives or dispositions. There are two types of such dispositions relevant to achievement situations: the motive to succeed ($M_s$), and the motive to avoid failure ($M_{af}$). $M_s$, when aroused, leads to *motivation* to perform, that is, an impulse/tendency/force to take action. $M_{af}$, when aroused, leads to motivation *not* to perform, that is, an impulse/tendency/force resisting or inhibiting action. The two tendencies add up to a resultant tendency/impulse/force that determines the intensity of achievement-oriented activity. When $M_s > M_{af}$, the resultant force will be positive. When $M_{af} > M_s$, the resultant force will be negative. The stronger $M_s$ is relative to $M_{af}$, the stronger will be the resultant force facilitating action and the more intense the resulting behavior. The stronger $M_{af}$ is relative to $M_s$, the stronger will be the resultant force inhibiting action. In all cases where $M_s$ is not stronger than $M_{af}$, there should be no behavior, unless some other extrinsic tendency overcomes the resistance of the negative resultant achievement-oriented tendency. As to the *quality* of performance, this is normally assumed to be positively related to the strength of the resultant (achievement-oriented) force and to the *intensity* of the behavior. In some cases, however, it is thought that a very high behavioral intensity may lead to a decrement in the quality of performance, in line with the Yerkes–Dodson Law (1908). In such cases, a relatively strong inhibiting force, in producing a decrement in positive resultant force and behavioral intensity, may be related to better performance than a relatively weak inhibiting tendency.

In interpreting the behavior-determining resultant force, then, *motivational arousal* should be strong when one of the motives is clearly stronger than the other. When the two motives are about equally strong, motivational arousal should be weak. If motivational arousal, in turn, is assumed to have somatic concomitants, it follows that physiological arousal in an achievement situation may be expected to be relatively high when $M_s > M_{af}$ or when $M_{af} > M_s$ and relatively low when $M_s = M_{af}$.

As an alternative line of reasoning, however, it is possible to take the predicted intensity of actual *behavior* in an achievement situation as the starting point for making assumptions about relationships between personal dispositions and physiological arousal. Regarding this issue, the Atkinson theory clearly assumes that behavior intensity/effort expenditure on an achievement-related task will be higher the stronger (more positive) the resultant force is. When the resultant force approaches zero and becomes negative, effort expenditure is believed to diminish and disappear (the person is no longer *trying* at all). Thus, the assumption may be made that, in achievement situations, effort expenditure and physiological arousal will be relatively high for individuals in whom $M_s > M_{af}$ (positive resultant force) and relatively low for individuals in whom $M_{af} \geqslant M_s$ (zero and negative resultant forces).

Turning now to situational determinants of motivation, the Atkinson theory assumes that for all individuals such arousal will be highest when the achievement-related task is of intermediate difficulty and the subjective probability of success ($P_s$) is about .50. Thus, for individuals in whom $M_s >$

$M_{af}$, the positive resultant force will be strongest when $P_s = .50$, and for individuals in whom $M_{af} > M_s$, the negative resultant force will likewise be maximal when $P_s = .50$.

The implication for physiological arousal, then, could be that the difference between individuals with $M_s = M_{af}$, on the one hand, and those with $M_s > M_{af}$ or $M_{af} > M_s$, on the other, with regard to such arousal, will be largest when $P_s = .50$ and become smaller as the probability approaches either unity or zero. The alternative prediction is that the difference in behavior intensity/effort expenditure and concomitant phyiological arousal between individuals with $M_s > M_{af}$ and those with $M_{af} \geqslant M_s$ will be largest when $P_s = .50$ and become smaller as the probability approaches unity or zero.

## KUKLA'S THEORY OF ACHIEVEMENT MOTIVATION

The most notable novel feature of work on achievement motivation in the 1970s was the increasing utilization of concepts stemming from Heider's (1958) analysis of causal attribution. Attributional theories of achievement-related behavior thus typically assume that performance will be related to beliefs on behalf of the actor as to how outcomes (success/failure) are caused by degree of *ability*, amount of *effort* expended, *difficulty* of the task, and *chance* factors.

Kukla (1972) presented such a theory where the *intensity* of task performance is the main focus of interest. As the energetic aspect of behavior may be thought of as related to physiological arousal, it is of interest to note how variations in behavioral intensity are explained by Kukla. In theorizing, Kukla introduces a number of simplifying assumptions. First, the task is of a type that has two possible outcomes: success (s) or failure (f) (this is also assumed in Atkinson's theory). Second, the utility (value) of success is assumed to be greater than the utility of failure. Third, in performing a task, there are a finite number (0–1) of possible levels of effort exertion. And fourth, each such possible effort level will on a given task be expected to lead to success or failure with subjective certainty ($P_s = 1/0$).

Since the utility of success is greater than the utility of failure, it is assumed that, when faced with a task, the subject will choose/intend to exert the least level of effort that for him is associated with $P_s = 1$. This intended level of effort is, in turn, thought of as positively related to the actual level of effort expenditure.

Some tasks will be perceived by the subject as requiring little effort to ensure success. Such tasks will be judged as easy by the subject, and his intended and actual effort expenditure will be low. Other tasks will be perceived by the subject as requiring much effort to ensure success. Such tasks will be judged as difficult, and intended and actual effort level will be high. Still other tasks will be perceived to have failure as the certain outcome even when maximal effort level is exerted. On such tasks intended and actual level of effort expenditure will be zero. Unfortunately, Kukla does not specify what independent *task characteristics* are decisive for a given subject in forming beliefs as to the amount of effort required to ensure success on different tasks. Kukla's reasoning on this point seems to be somewhat circular in that perceived difficulty is assumed to determine the level of effort believed to be required to ensure success, which in turn determines perceived difficulty.

Whatever the decisive task characteristics may be, however, it is assumed that for a given task the subject's *perceived ability* will be related to the level of effort the subject thinks is required to ensure success. On some types of tasks subjects with low perceived ability are expected to manifest higher levels of intended and actual effort than subjects with high perceived ability. These tasks, which Kukla calls *easy,* are such that both the subject with high perceived ability and the subject with low perceived ability believe that success can be reached by exerting effort. The subject with low perceived ability, however, believes that more effort is required than does the subject with high perceived ability. The former's intended and actual effort is consequently higher than the latter's. On other tasks subjects with high perceived ability are expected to show higher levels of intended and actual effort than subjects with low perceived ability. These tasks, of *intermediate* difficulty, are such that, while the subject with high perceived ability believes success can be ensured by exerting a high level of effort, the subject with low perceived ability believes that failure will be the outcome even when maximal effort is expended. Finally, there are some types of tasks, called *difficult,* of such a nature that both the subject with high perceived ability and the subject with low perceived ability believe that success cannot be reached even by exerting maximal effort. In this case, the subject with high perceived ability and the subject with low perceived ability are not expected to differ as to expended effort.

If behavioral intensity and motivation, in the sense of how hard a person *intends* and does *try* to perform a task, are thought of as related to physiological arousal, then such arousal should be higher for subjects with high perceived ability than for those with low perceived ability on tasks of intermediate difficulty. On easy tasks, motivational and physiological arousal can be expected to be higher for subjects with low perceived ability than for subjects with high perceived ability.

## MEYER'S THEORY OF ACHIEVEMENT MOTIVATION

Another such attributional theory, making predictions about intensity of task performance and therefore relevant in the present context, has been presented by Meyer (1973, in preparation). Meyer assumes that the main goal or incentive for a person in an achievement situation is to gain new information on personal ability. The theory also presupposes tasks with two possible outcomes: success and failure. $P_s$ on a task, however, can take on any value between zero and unity.

$P_s$ for an actor is determined by three factors: (a) the perceived difficulty of the task, which in turn is defined as the actor's belief as to how many individuals, in the group of which he is a member, can solve the task (perceived percentage of successful persons); (b) the actor's own perceived ability; and (c) the level of effort he intends to exert on the task. If, for different subjects, intended effort level and perceived task difficulty are the same, subjects with high perceived ability will have higher $P_s$ than subjects with low perceived ability. If, for different subjects, perceived task difficulty and perceived ability are the same, $P_s$ will be higher for those subjects who have decided to exert a high level of effort than for those whose intended effort level is low. If, for different subjects, perceived ability and intended effort are the same, $P_s$ will be higher for those subjects who are confronted with easy tasks than for those who are confronted with difficult tasks.

Individuals with high perceived ability, presented with an easy task, believe that a high level of effort expenditure will make success almost certain, that is, result in a high $P_s$. On such tasks where there is certainty of success, which are not, therefore, expected to yield any new information on personal ability, motivational arousal (intended and actual level of effort expenditure) will be low. Individuals with high perceived ability, presented with a difficult task, believe that a high level of effort expenditure will make performance outcome highly *uncertain*, $P_s = .50$. On such tasks where new information on personal ability is expected to ensue, motivational arousal will be high.

Individuals with low perceived ability, presented with a difficult task, believe that a high level of effort exertion is not capable of changing the certainty of failure. On such tasks no new information is expected and motivational arousal will be low. Individuals with low perceived ability, presented with an easy task, will be highly uncertain of the outcome if a high level of effort is exerted. New information on personal ability is perceived to be obtainable, and motivational arousal will be high.

It follows that if motivational arousal, in the sense of intended and actual effort expenditure, is thought of as having somatic concomitants, individuals with high perceived ability may be expected to be more physiologically aroused on difficult tasks, and less aroused on easy tasks, than individuals with low perceived ability.

## A GENERAL HYPOTHESIS

All three theories reviewed agree, in general, that differences in motivational arousal may be expected between individuals, but that such differences will depend on perceived task characteristics (difficulty or probability of success).

The relevant individual dimension, according to Atkinson, is the relative strength of a motive to succeed and a motive to avoid failure. In the following, this relative strength between motives will be called *resultant achievement motivation*, in accord with Kukla (1972) and Weiner (1972). This use of terminology, it should be noted, is not in accord with Atkinson, who uses the term *"motivation"* to refer to an arousal dimension and *"motive"* in speaking of stable dispositions. The relevant individual dimension, according to Kukla and Meyer, is perceived ability. Both Kukla and Meyer, however, assume that the main difference between individuals with varying resultant achievement motivation is a difference in perceived ability. Kukla argues for this conclusion by citing empirical studies showing that subjects high in resultant achievement motivation report higher estimates of their own ability, and expectancy on novel tasks, than do subjects with low perceived ability. Meyer points to the fact that subjects with high resultant achievement motivation have been found to attribute success more to their own high ability and failure less to a lack of ability than subjects with low resultant achievement motivation and concludes that subjects with high resultant achievement motivation probably have higher perceived ability than those with low motivation. There is also some evidence (though it is scanty, cf. Weiner, 1972) that high resultant achievement motivation is related to internal locus of control on Rotter's Internal–External Locus of Control Scale (Rotter, 1966), again pointing to the conclusion that resultant achievement motivation and perceived ability may be related dimensions.

The conclusion that seems to follow is that if the parachutist training session is considered an achievement situation, motivational arousal and concomitant physiological arousal in the situation may be related to the resultant achievement motivation of the men. That is, resultant achievement motivation should be a relevant dimension to measure in the present context, and possible empirical relationships between this dimension and other variables may be interpreted in terms of perceived ability.

In *what way* RAM (the measure of resultant achievement motivation) may be expected to relate to motivational arousal and somatic concomitants in the present situation is, however, a more difficult question. According to Atkinson, a strong relationship between RAM and motivational arousal may be expected on tasks of intermediate difficulty ($P_s = .50$). One interpretation of Atkinson is that, when $P_s = .50$, a curvilinear relationship may be expected, that is, subjects with high (positive) or low (negative) resultant achievement motivation will be more motivationally and somatically aroused than subjects with intermediate (zero) resultant achievement motivation. The alternative interpretation is that, when $P_s = .50$, a positive linear relationship may be expected, that is, subjects with high resultant achievement motivation will be more aroused motivationally and somatically than subjects with low resultant achievement motivation. Following Kukla and Meyer, subjects with low RAM (low perceived ability) may be expected to be more motivationally and physiologically aroused on easy tasks, and less aroused on difficult or intermediately difficult tasks, than subjects with high RAM (high perceived ability). To make predictions about relationships between RAM and arousal in the present task situation, it would thus seem desirable to know something about perceived difficulty and/or probability of success on this task.

A possible indicator of task difficulty in the present situation is the expert's evaluation of the jumps. Starting with Jump Day 2, namely, every time a jump was made by a soldier, he was given a detailed critique of the jump and a summary evaluation in terms of accepted/not accepted.

Over a given period of days, then, it is possible to estimate the proportion of accepted jumps for a man and consider this proportion as a measure of the perceived difficulty of the *subsequent* task. Following the theories described above, it now becomes possible to formulate the general hypothesis that physiological arousal (as concomitant with motivational arousal) in the present achievement situation will be related both to RAM and to previous performance level.


## METHOD


### Motivation

The various subscores on RAM (cf. Chapter 13) were not found to be highly interrelated, indicating the feasibility of examining relationships to physiological measures for motivational subscores separately. To gain some information on validity, however, and a preliminary notion as to which subscores might be expected to relate to physiological arousal, relationships between the various RAM subscores and other psychological variables were investigated. One subscore in particular (termed "$RAM_1$") was related in a meaningful way to other psychological variables. $RAM_1$ was the score obtained on the test item describing an intellectual achievement situation as highly difficult and for which a low level of effort had been expended in preparation. This subscore was found to be positively related to general ability level ($r = .35, p < .05$, two tailed) and negatively related ($r = -.40, p < .01$, two tailed) to vulnerability to emotional interference in an achievement situation as indicated by time estimation variability (cf. Chapter 13).

## Previous Performance Level

To test the motivation theories previously reviewed, a situation is required where performance level (or probability of success) varies from low to high. Previous to Jump Day 5 (first day of blood and urine sampling preceded by evaluated jumping), mean performance level and variability were low. For instance, the mean proportion of accepted jumps across Days 2, 3, and 4 was .11 ($s = .17$).

A more appropriate situation is found prior to Jump Day 11. The mean proportion of accepted jumps across Days 8, 9, and 10 was .54 ($s = .25$). Previous to Day 11, in other words, a fair number of subjects had reached a performance level of about .50; some were at a higher level (easy task) and some were at a lower level (difficult task). On day 11, then, it is possible to relate physiological arousal to $P_s$ values pointed to as critical for motivational arousal by Atkinson, Kukla, and Meyer.

Three different measures of performance level prior to Day 11 were computed: (a) proportion of accepted jumps on Day 10; (b) proportion of accepted jumps across Days 9 and 10; and (c) proportion of accepted jumps across Days 8, 9, and 10. These three measures were highly interrelated (a and b, .82; a and c, .78; b and c, .91).

## Physiological Arousal

In relation to the motivational line of reasoning adopted, the meaningful dimension to study as the dependent variable is physiological arousal *during* or immediately *preceding* performance (i.e., jumping). Values from the *first* blood and urine samples on Day 11 were consequently used as the bases for constructing indexes of physiological arousal.

For each hormone, absolute as well as relative arousal values for Day 11 were used. The rationale for using relative values was that individuals may vary as to what constitutes normal and high arousal values. What is a normal or low level for one person may be a high level for another. Consequently, each person's level of arousal on Day 11 was compared with his degree of arousal on Day 5. A high score thus indicated that the subject showed an increase (or little decrease) in arousal from Day 5 to Day 11, whereas a low score indicated a drop (or little increase). Day 11 values were also compared to basal and Day 1 values.

## Data Treatment

One way of testing the hypothesis that physiological arousal will be determined by task difficulty and motivation, and that the relationship between arousal and motivation will depend on the level of task difficulty, would be by traditional analysis of variance. The task difficulty variable could be split in three (low, intermediate, high) and the motivation variable at the median (high/low), yielding a 3 × 2 design with $F$ values for two main effects and interaction. However, such a practice of transforming originally continuous variables to dichotomies or trichotomies to make them fit the traditional analysis of variance design has been criticized for leading to a loss of information and statistical power (Cohen, 1968; Cohen & Cohen, 1975). Instead, it is suggested that a multiple regression analysis approach be adopted using continuous variables and their products as predictors. With two continuous variables $A$ and $B$, an estimate of the interaction effect $A \times B$ is achieved when $A$ and $B$ are partialled from $A \times B$, that is, $R^2(A \times B) = R^2(A,B, A \times B) - R^2(A,B)$ (Cohen & Cohen, 1975; Overall & Spiegel, 1969). The partialled $R^2(A \times B)$ is, according to Cohen and Cohen (1975), independent of the absolute scale values of $A$ and $B$ and may be interpreted in the same way as the traditional analysis of variance interaction effect, namely, as indicating whether the relationship between $Y$ and $B$ depends on the level of $A$.

In the present study, then, with physiological arousal as the dependent variable $(Y)$ and previous performance $(A)$ and motivation $(B)$ as continuous independent variables, the multiple regression analysis approach was adopted. The specific meanings of significant $A \times B$ interaction effects were interpreted by investigating the slopes of the regression lines for $Y$ (arousal) on $B$ (motivation) for three different levels of $A$ (previous performance: high, intermediate, low) (Cohen & Cohen, 1975).

## RESULTS

Physiological arousal measures $(Y)$ were examined for linear as well as curvilinear relationships to previous performance indexes $(A)$. While no significant linear correlations were found between $Y$ and $A$, the addition of $A^2$ in the regression equation in several instances led to significant increases in explained $Y$ variance, indicating curvilinear relationships between physiological indicators and previous performance measures. $R$ $(A, A^2)$ for the proportion of accepted jumps across Days 9 and 10 and the various arousal measures is presented in the third column of Table 15.1.

No curvilinear relationships were found between any $Y$ measures and RAM subscores. The subscore showing the most consistent and meaningful relationships to physiological arousal measures was $RAM_1$ (cf. Method section). As this subscore was also found to possess some degree of validity as a measure of resultant achievement motivation compared to other psychological variables (cf. Method), $RAM_1$ alone was used as the motivation measure. Linear relationships between $RAM_1$ ($B$) and $Y$ measures are presented in the fourth column of Table 15.1.

Multiple correlations ($R$) between $Y$ measures and $A$, $A^2$, and $B$ and between $Y$ measures and *partialled* interactions (cf. Method section) are shown in Columns 5 and 6, respectively, of Table 15.1. (Free fatty acid was not found to be related to previous performance or to $RAM_1$.)

Blood glucose, epinephrine, and norepinephrine were related in a U-shaped fashion to previous performance. An inverted U-shaped relationship was found between testosterone and previous performance. These relationships were particularly strong for relative arousal values $11-5$.

Growth homone $11-$basal and cortisol $11-1$ showed inverted U-shaped relationships with previous performance. $RAM_1$ was also related in a consistent way to blood glucose, epinephrine, and norepinephrine (all positive relationships) and to testosterone (negative relationship). $RAM_1$ was negatively related to growth hormone $11-$basal and unrelated to cortisol.

Relationships between motivation and epinephrine/norepinephine (11, 11–basal, and 11–5) varied over different levels of previous performance (interaction effect). For all of these interactions, the slope of the regression line for $Y$ (arousal) on $B$ (motivation) was found to be steeper at high and low levels of $A$ (previous performance) than at the intermediate level. For low levels of previous performance negative slopes were found, and for high levels positive slopes occurred. In other words, motivation was negatively related to physiological arousal for subjects whose previous performance level was low and positively related for subjects whose performance level was high. Motivation was least related to arousal for subjects whose performance level was intermediate.

## DISCUSSION

The dominant U-shaped relationship found between physiological arousal (blood glucose, epinephrine, norepinephrine, and testosterone) and previous performance level was unexpected, and it is unexplainable in relation to both the Atkinson and the Kukla–Meyer theories. The Atkinson

**TABLE 15.1**
**Relationships between Hormone Values and Previous Performance and Motivation**

| Physiological arousal measures (Y) | $R (A, A^2)$, performance | $r (B)$, motivation | $R (A, \ddot{A}, B)$ | $R (A \times B)$ |
|---|---|---|---|---|
| 11[a] | | | | |
| BG | .38** | .19 | .40 | .17 |
| E | .35 | .59*** | .61** | .59*** |
| NE | .30 | .43** | .46 | .59*** |
| TE | .22 | −.21 | .28 | .10 |
| CS | .21 | −.02 | .22 | .05 |
| GH | .13 | −.03 | .13 | .11 |
| 11−basal | | | | |
| BG | .40** | .17 | .42** | .11 |
| E | .35 | .51** | .55* | .63*** |
| NE | .52** | .52** | .62** | .41*** |
| TE | .35* | −.19 | .36 | .18 |
| CS | .10 | .11 | .18 | .03 |
| GH | .42** | −.32** | .45** | .20 |

| | | | | |
|---|---|---|---|---|
| 11–1 | BG | .32* | .22 | .34 | .19 |
| | E | .33 | .01 | .37 | .00 |
| | NE | .28 | .00 | .32 | .00 |
| | TE | .25 | −.07 | .26 | .17 |
| | CS | .35* | .05 | .40* | .13 |
| | GH | .13 | .20 | .27 | .20 |
| 11–5 | BG | .40** | .34** | .44* | .08 |
| | E | .61*** | .45*** | .65*** | .70*** |
| | NE | .63*** | .38* | .64*** | .41*** |
| | TE | .32* | −.45*** | .48** | .10 |
| | CS | .25 | −.14 | .18 | .11 |
| | GH | .29 | −.19 | .30 | .11 |

[a] 11, arousal values on Day 11; 11−basal, difference in arousal between Basal and Day 11 values; 11−1, difference in arousal between Day 1 and Day 11 values; 11−5, difference in arousal between Day 5 and Day 11 values.

[b] BG, blood glucose; E, epinephrine; NE, norepinephrine; TE, testosterone: CS, cortisol; GH, growth hormone.

*p < .10.
**p < .05.
***p < .01.

theory predicts an inverted U-shaped relationship (between $P_s$ and *motivational* arousal), and the Kukla–Meyer theories predict no simple relationship at all, that is, different relationships (between task difficulty and *effort* level) for different levels of perceived ability (or resultant achievement motivation).

The dominant positive linear relationship found between physiological arousal (blood glucose, epinephrine, norepinephrine, and testosterone) and RAM is not in accord with the Kukla–Meyer theories, which predict different relationships between perceived ability and expended/intended effort for tasks of varying difficulty. To some extent, the present findings are in accord with Atkinson's theory, which does predict a general positive relationship between motivational arousal and RAM, though this relationship is only expected to be marked on tasks of intermediate difficulty.

The interaction effects found for epinephrine and norepinephrine, however, are not explainable in terms of the Atkinson theory or the Kukla–Meyer theories. As already mentioned, Atkinson assumes that RAM will be more strongly (positively) related to motivational arousal for tasks of intermediate difficulty than for easy or difficult ones. Kukla and Meyer assume that RAM will be positively related to actual/intended effort on difficult or intermediately difficult tasks and negatively related for easy tasks. In the present situation, RAM was positively related to physiological arousal for subjects whose performance level was high and negatively related for subjects whose performance level was low.

Taken as a whole, then, the relationships found in the present study between blood glucose, epinephrine, norepinephrine, and testosterone, on the one hand, and previous performance level and RAM, on the other, do *not* fit well with the assumptions about motivational arousal found in the reviewed theories of achievement motivation.

One way of coming to terms with this discrepancy would be to point out that the Atkinson and Kukla–Meyer theories make assumptions about *motivational*, not *physiological,* arousal. The psychological factors that determine motivational arousal need not affect physiological arousal in the same way. A high level of motivational arousal need not be accompanied by a high level of physiological arousal, and, conversely, a high level of physiological arousal need not be associated with a concomitant high level of motivational arousal. It may be inappropriate, in other words, to interpret physiological arousal in an achievement situation like the present one in motivational terms.

This line of reasoning would be strongly supported if it were possible to demonstrate that physiological arousal in the present situation, besides being hard to interpret in relation to the Atkinson and Kukla–Meyer theories, does not make sense at all in motivational terms.

This, however, is not the case. For, in the kind of achievement situation under study in the present context—a competetive situation where it is highly probable that the subject will be evaluating who may be likely to win and who to lose, what his own position is relative to the positions of others, and how he is evaluated by the others—it intuitively makes sense that the individuals at the top will be trying very hard to stay at the top and perhaps be best, instead of second or third. This makes sense when viewed in relation to athletic contests, where effort expenditure and concentration may be seen to be very high among the few men competing for the top positions. The present achievement situation does bear resemblance to an athletic contest. That effort expenditure among good performers should be especially high for those with high resultant achievement motivation also seems to be psychologically meaningful.

In the present situation, where the subjects themselves chose to go through a great deal of trouble to be accepted, and were probably highly motivated to do well in advance, it also seems psychologically meaningful that the really bad performers should experience being in an embarrassing and threatening situation (the situation of the loser). That this threat (and embarrassment/anxiety) should be experienced as especially acute by the subjects with low resultant achievement motivation (high fear of failure, low perceived ability) also seems to make good psychological sense.

To sum up, then, though the present data (where physiological arousal is understood as being concomitant with motivational arousal) do not fit in very well with the Atkinson and Kukla–Meyer theories, a meaningful motivational interpretation may still be given.

This "meaningful interpretation," however, runs into some problems since it applies only to the *dominant* relationships found between physiological arousal and previous performance/motivation. An inverted U-shaped relationship was found between growth hormone (and to some extent cortisol) and previous performance, and $RAM_1$ was shown to be negatively related to growth hormone. This pattern of relationships found between growth hormone–cortisol and motivational variables, while generally being weaker (only growth hormone $11 - basal$ related significantly to motivational variables, and cortisol $11 - 1$ related only at the .10 level) than the pattern found for blood glucose, epinephrine, norepinephrine, and testosterone is the exact converse of the latter. Physiological arousal as indicated by growth hormone and cortisol was highest for the subjects with an intermediate performance level (in accord with the Atkinson theory) and high (as far as growth hormone is concerned) for subjects with low resultant achievement motivation (high fear of failure, low perceived ability) (in accord with neither the Atkinson nor the Kukla–Meyer theories). In other words, the motivational variables related to physiological arousal differently for the different hormone groups. If previous performance and resultant achievement motivation determine motivational arousal (in whatever way) and *thereby* physiological arousal, why should a given level of motivational arousal be related to one level of physiological arousal for blood glucose, epinephrine, norepinephrine, and testosterone and a different level for cortisol and growth hormone? This is hard to explain.

One way out is to trust the *dominant* pattern. The U-shaped relationship found between physiological arousal and previous performance is more dominant than the inverted U, both with respect to the number of hormones showing the respective patterns and with respect to the strength of the relationships and how reliably they show up over different indexes (11, 11−basal, 11−1, 11−5).

Another solution may be that the two hormone groups indicate arousal at different points in time. Epinephrine and norepinephrine as the only hormones sampled *before* jumping are clearly pre-performance measures of arousal, and as such the hormones that most unambiguously give information on relationships between motivational variables and physiological arousal immediately prior to performance. Since blood glucose and testosterone show the same relationships to motivational variables as epinephrine and norepinephrine perhaps the former may also be interpreted as indicating arousal immediately preceding or during *performance*. Cortisol and growth hormone, on the other hand, instead of indicating arousal in connection with performance itself, may be indicative of arousal *after* the jump, related to the subject's uncertainty as to how well he has performed and what the jump leader's evaluation will be. That subjects with low resultant achievement motivation (high fear of failure, low perceived ability) should be most anxious and concerned (aroused) about this future evaluation is psychologically meaningful. In addition, the finding that subjects with intermediate previous performance level show the highest physiological arousal level *after* performance also makes sense if $P_s = .50$ is interpreted as the performance level entailing the highest subjective uncertainty.

## REFERENCES

Atkinson, J. W. Motivational determinants of risk-taking behavior. *Psychological Review*, 1957, 64, 359–372.

Atkinson, J. W., & Feather, N. T. *A theory of achievement motivation.* New York: Wiley, 1966.

Cohen, J. Multiple regression as a general data-analytic system. *Psychological Bulletin*, 1968, 70, 426–443.

Cohen, J., & Cohen, P. *Applied multiple regression/correlation analysis for the behavioral sciences.* New Jersey: Lawrence Erlbaum, 1975.

Heider, F. *The psychology of interpersonal relations.* New York: Wiley, 1958.

Kukla, A. Foundations of an attributional theory of performance. *Psychological Review,* 1972, *79,* 454–470.

Meyer, W. U. *Leistungsmotivation und Ursachenerklärung von Erfolg und Misserfolg.* Stuttgart: Klett, 1973.

Meyer, W. U. Leistungsoritentiertes Verhalten als Funktion von wahr-genommener eigener Begabung und wahrgenommener Aufgabenschwierigkeit. In H. D. Scmalt & W. U. Meyer (Eds.), *Leistungsmotivation und Verhalten.* Stuttgart: Klett. In preparation.

Overall, J. E., & Spiegel, D. K. Concerning least squares analysis of experimental data. *Psychological Bulletin,* 1969, *72,* 311–322.

Rotter, J. B. Generalized expectancies for internal versus external control of reinforcement. *Psychological Monographs,* 1966, *80,* 1–28.

Wiener, B. *Theories of motivation.* Chicago: Markham, 1972.

Yerkes, R. M., & Dodson, J. D. The relation of strength of stimulus to rapidity of habit-formation. *Journal of Comparative and Neurological Psychology,* 1908, *18,* 459–482.

# 16

# Activation, Coping, and Psychosomatics

## HOLGER URSIN

The findings reported in this book are very consistent, at least with regard to the group data. We found a relative basal or reference value in our "basal" sample, a very clear and significant change from this basal value on the first jump, and a general return to basal levels when the jumps were repeated. We regard this change as crucial evidence for coping having taken place. Our main hypothesis was confirmed for all of the physiological variables except heart rate.

In Chapters 14 and 15 we discussed which psychological variables influence bodily processes. This final chapter will discuss the psychophysiological and psychosomatic implications of our findings. At first, activation theory will be discussed, and then the implications for this theory from our findings. The gate or filtering functions that were evident from our study of the coping effect will also be treated. Finally, the implication of this type of research for psychosomatic theory will be dealt with specifically.

The appraisal of the "stressor" (Lazarus & Averall, 1972), or the subjective, psychological factors, is often ignored in medical literature on the possible relationships between environment and disease. In particular, coping mechanisms and the development of coping to environmental factors have been largely ignored in psychosomatics. Furthermore, the physiology

201

of activation is also too often taken lightly. When activation is referred to as "stress," the lay reader, as well as large parts of the medical profession, is led to expect pathological consequences. When activation is referred to as activation only, we tend to think in positive terms of health and "adaptive" processes. In this interface between medicine and psychobiology, there should be room for at least one more attempt to review the pertinent literature.

We have tried to elucidate the psychological mechanisms that are involved both in the activation and in the return to the reference values in our own data. Both for physiological and psychological variables there is a considerable variance in spite of the very clear group data. We have used much of this variance for our analyses. The complex picture emerging from our analyses is, of course, completely dependent on our selection of tests. Our conclusions are clearly limited to the variables we have studied. The true picture may be simpler or, probably, more complex.

The multivariate techniques used suggest that the important variables from our heterogeneous and complex test battery cluster in a fairly limited and consistent pattern. The general ability level, the defense mechanisms, and various motivational and role identification factors explain considerable portions of the variance. This is particularly true for the first stages of our experimental period. In the later stage of training, when the subjects coped with the situation, the variance became increasingly dependent on the relationship between resultant achievement motivation and the actual performance of that individual (Chapter 15).

## ACTIVATION

Even though the psychological situation was quite complex during the first jump from the tower, it seems clear that fear was the dominant variable. It has long been known that fear is accompanied by profound changes in physiological processes. Cannon (1932) emphasized the "energy mobilizing" aspects of these changes and saw such changes as evidence of the "wisdom of the body." The early theories of emotions were centered on what was most essential or primary for the emotional experience, the bodily changes (James–Lange theory), or the central nervous system processes (Cannon–Bard theory, see Cannon, 1932). Within activation theory (see Lindsley, 1951), this controversy may be reduced to a debate of which is most important of two parts of a positive feedback loop.

Cannon emphasized adrenergic activation and the sympathetic nervous system, but also the interaction with the parasympathetic nervous system, which is engaged in the bodily responses during emotional states. There was evidence that the parasympathetic system was more concerned with "normal" functions, or building functions, but it was evident during emotional states (Gellhorn & Loofbourrow, 1962). The interaction is obviously quite complex (Lindsley, 1951), and this may be one reason why the various indicators used do not always agree. Even so, autonomically innervated processes were studied intensely and were the basis for the early development of psychophysiological studies (see Woodworth & Schlosberg, 1954, for an early review). *Activation theory* (Lindsley, 1951) was not formulated until Moruzzi and Magoun (1949) described the brain stem activation "system." The concept of a general level of "activation" has many roots, therefore, but was not formulated until the possible nervous substrate had been suggested. It was not until this time that the importance of the electroencephalogram (EEG) as a research tool for experimental psychologists was realized (see, for instance, the very brief mention of this method in Woodworth & Schlosberg, [1954]). In his original description of the electroencephalogram, Berger (1930) defined both the alpha rhythm, which is seen during relaxation, and the "blockage" of this rhythm, the faster and "desynchronized" rhythm seen during states we refer to as activation.

## Definition of Activation

Activation is most simply defined as any increment in activity; however, it remains to define activity. In the literature on the brain stem reticular formation, activation simply refers to EEG desynchronization and the accompanying behavioral signs of increased wakefulness, arousal, or even "awareness." There is very little reason to question that the individual or the brain as a whole is more "active" when the EEG is desynchronized. For clarification of the activation concept it should be stressed that it remains an empirical observation that when an individual reports or demonstrates clear overt behavioral signs of activation his cortex shows the desynchronized EEG pattern.

There is no simple relationship between activity on the neuronal level and behavioral "activation." Recordings of unit activity during various states of activity reveal a very complex interaction between facilitation and inhibition of neurons, where the pattern of firing seems to be more important than the number of "facilitated" versus the number of "inhibited" units. On the neuronal level, activation should be regarded as a highly integrated process setting the neural system for coordinated function (Jasper, 1963). The desynchronized EEG pattern that is used as an indicator for arousal may be the result of a breakdown or inhibition of the feedback system producing the alpha oscillation in thalamic neurons (Andersen & Andersson, 1968).

Most authors have treated activation and arousal as synonymous concepts. Feldman and Waller (1962) found a dissociation between EEG activation and behavioral arousal in subjects given atropine or small, surgically induced lesions in the brain stem. However, in all practical situations, no such differentiation is apparent, at least in intact brains. When scoring systems are used to evaluate behavioral activation, at least in the cat, there is an acceptable degree of agreement with the EEG activation, measured as the length of desynchronization to the activating stimulus (Ursin, Wester, & Ursin, 1967).

In this chapter, the term "activation" will be used, except in quotations from other authors who show a preference for the term "arousal." The same strategy was followed by Malmo (1966).

## The Neural Substrate for Activation

During stimulation of brain stem reticular formation in a conventional neurophysiological experiment in anesthetized cats, Moruzzi and Magoun (1949) found a consistent "activation" in the electroencephalogram. This activation was independent of classical sensory pathways, but acted through a "diffuse projection system" via the thalamus (Lindsley, Bowden, & Magoun, 1949). Electrical stimulation of the same structures through implanted electrodes in freely moving animals produced behavioral "arousal," which coincided with EEG arousal (Segundo, Arana-Iniquez, & French, 1955). The behavioral response these authors observed was probably the Pavlovian orienting response (see Ursin, Wester, & Ursin, 1967). Finally, lesions in the same structures were claimed to produce coma (Lindsley, 1951; French & Magoun, 1952), but later research has made it necessary to modify this conclusion. At least in the cat, wakefulness is not necessarily impaired even after large reticular formation lesions (Sprague, Chambers, & Stellar, 1961).

The reticular formation receives afferent inputs from all sensory sources, directly or indirectly, and from diencephalic and telencephalic structures. The physiological and the anatomical findings constitute the basis for the well-known model of activation, which is often referred to as the Moruzzi–Magoun model.

This model states that when there is information transmitted through the classical sensory pathways, there are also impulses sent directly to the reticular formation of the brain stem, either through collaterals from the sensory pathways or via direct fibers running in parallel with these pathways. The brain stem reticular formation, or specific parts of it, "activates" the diencephalic and telencephalic structures. When sensory information reaches the cortex for analysis, the arousing or activating system is already at work (Lindsley, 1951; Magoun, 1958). The activation of the hypothalamus acts on the endocrine system, and there is also a flow "downstream" through the spinal cord, acting on the autonomic nervous system and the muscle tension (Granit & Kaada, 1952; Sprague, Schreiner, Lindsley, & Magoun, 1948).

Moruzzi and Magoun (1949) and Lindsley (1951) pointed to the importance of this system for the waking effect of external stimulation, but also suggested that the system played an essential role in the regulation of wakefulness as a continuum from sleep to wakefulness. Later work suggested that sleep may be qualitatively different from wakefulness rather than a part of a sleep/wakefulness continuum (Jouvet, 1972; Sterman & Clemente, 1974). Activation theory is still, however, a powerful model for the explanation of physiological and psychological mechanisms in wakefulness, emotional states, and sleep.

The essence of the activation model is that the sensory events do not only have a signal effect, but also an activation effect. The signal or cue effect is supposed to be dependent on the activation effect. In this sense, there is an obvious relationship to the drive concept; Hebb (1955) held that activation (arousal) in this sense was synonymous with a general drive state.

The close anatomical and physiological relationship between the hypothalamus and reticular formation makes activation theory essential for physiologically acceptable formulations of drive registration and drive reduction mechanisms (Lindsley, 1951). Malmo (1966) treated the relationship between physiological drives and activation and demonstrated that the physiological indicators of activation change as a monotonic function of the deprivation level when measured in situations with relevant stimuli.

Finally, the cortical and telencephalic inputs to the reticular formation (see Ursin, Wester, & Ursin, 1967, for references) make it possible to account for centrally induced variations in activation level. Hebb (1955), in particular, hypothesized that this cortical feedback to the activation system had relevance for drive effects and cognitive processes.

The input to the reticular formation from cortex must be assumed to be capable of eliciting, maintaining, and increasing activation (Hebb, 1955). The brain is a network with its own activity persisting for as long as it is alive. It will generate behavior even in the absence of external stimuli. Even though it is well established that the functioning is abnormal when there is no or low input to the brain, there is still activity going on.

Activation, therefore, may be initiated, maintained, decreased, or increased by loops that may be strictly intracerebral. The loops may also involve peripheral bodily processes (the Cannon–Bard/James–Lange loop), and, finally, such loops may involve interaction with the environment.

The existence of intracerebral, neural loops is the morphological basis for the contemporary view of the brain as a "conceptual nervous system" (Hebb 1955). The cognitive aspects of the intracerebral events may be treated in terms of information theory (see Hamilton, 1975). There are also cognitive factors involved in the experience and interpretation ("attribution") of the bodily changes during activation (the James–Lange effect). If the individual expects the somatic changes to be due to anger, this is what he experiences. If, on the other hand, the individual expects the changes to be due to an injection or to environmental factors, there is much less of an "emotional" effect (Rule & Nesdale, 1976; Schachter & Singer, 1962).

In the early formulations of activation theory (Lindsley, 1951) it was made explicit that the physiological phenomena observed under fear and aggressive states were easily accounted for by activation mechanisms. In summary, activation may be looked upon as a "final common path" for all phenomena that lead to higher activity in the CNS. Activation, therefore, is the phenomenon we have studied.

### Endocrinological "Activation"

The original formulation of activation theory (Lindsley, 1951) was not restricted to cortical activation, but also comprised activity in the autonomic nervous system and the somatomotor system as well as endocrine responses. With improved methods for determining plasma levels of hormones, it has become increasingly clear that the whole (or at least very large parts) of the endocrine system is subject to influence from psychological factors. These phenomena are easily treated within activation theory, but, unfortunately, some confusion arises from particular developments and traditions tied to specific hormone systems. In particular, the tradition surrounding the adreno-corticotropic hormone–suprarenal axis is sometimes quite remote from the available data from psychophysiological research using other indicators of activation.

A large body of literature has been published about this axis, and Mason (1971) has demonstrated that the main source of variation for this hormonal system is psychological. In this field, however, activation is most often referred to as *stress,* following the work by Selye (see 1974). Unfortunately, this nomenclature sometimes leads to quite unsubstantiated implications about relationships between activation and disease, even if Selye's own formulations seem quite clear. This topic will be dealt with under "Psychosomatics."

Some of the literature on epinephrine and norepinephrine has been formulated within this latter "stress" tradition, recognizing the relationship between catecholamines and cortisol responses during activation (Levi, 1972). For the other hormones, the bulk of the data was recorded after the development of adequate methods. The specific literature for the hormones we have analyzed is dealt with in the respective chapters.

## Activation and Performance

Several authors have described and discussed the curvilinear relationship between activation and at least certain types of performance (Malmo, 1966; Duffy, 1972). According to Malmo (1966), there is an optimal point of activation for performance. On either side of this point, performance is impaired, increasing with the distance from the optimal point. This is an essential part of the activation theory of Malmo; it has been used to explain many psychopharmacological effects and appears to be essential for models of schizophrenia (Mirsky, 1969). The theory is also essential in attempting to explain negative effects of anxiety on performance. Anxiety as a medical complaint has been suggested to be due to defective autonomic system control (Malmo, 1966). Activation has been suggested to be homeostatically controlled, and, for instance, hyperkinesy in children has been regarded as a compensatory mechanism for hypoarousal. This might explain the beneficial effect of stimulating drugs in well-defined groups of hyperkinetic children (Satterfield, Cantwell, & Satterfield, 1974).

The curvilinear relationships in some learning tasks may be seen in relation to the drive theory of Spence and Spence (1966), even though they emphasize that their "drive" concept was a mathematical concept without any direct relevance to physiological activation. Drive theory proceeds from the basic assumption of Hull that the excitatory potential determining the strength of a given response is a multiplicative function of the total effective drive state and the habit strength. High drive levels, by the definition of Spence and Spence, should not always lead to superior performance. In situations where a number of competing response tendencies are evoked, of which only one is correct, the performance will depend on the number and comparative strength of the various response tendencies. A high drive level interacts multiplicatively with the habit strength of irrelevant responses, and the high drive level subject could therefore perform poorly.

Other formulations within information theory are based on Broadbent's (1971) limited channel-capacity theory of central nervous functions. Hamilton (1975) explains the decrement in performance in anxious subjects as an information overload. Anxiety, in this context, is treated as information ("I am anxious"). The registration of being anxious is a load on the cerebral information processing; the load is related to the degree of anxiety and is reduced when anxiety is reduced (Hamilton, 1975). Attempts to improve performance by biofeedback training aimed at reducing physiological indicators of activation have very little if any effect on performance (Lawrence, 1976). The training seemed simply to represent more load on the system, more things to be done, which had no beneficial effect on performance. However, the subjects themselves felt much better.

In our situation, there was no tendency toward any curvilinear relation to performance. There were few if any competing response tendencies and very little demand on the information processing system of the men for the performance in the tower.

Only in situations in which a number of competing response tendencies are evoked may irrelevant responses interfere with the development of the correct response. In simple situations (for instance, classical conditioning), subjects with a high drive level give more conditioned responses than do low drive subjects. However, in complex learning, high drive subjects will make more errors on complex tasks and therefore require more trials to reach a learning criterion (Spence & Spence, 1966; Spielberger, 1966).

### Activation, Expectancy, and Control Theory: A General Formulation

The activation model suggested by Moruzzi and Magoun (1949) could not function very well without one important modification. The brain must be able *not* to respond to a stimulus. If all incoming stimuli should have free access to the general activating mechanisms, life would be one long and fairly continuous series of orienting responses. However, EEG desynchronization and autonomic responses are only elicited at the first presentations of a stimulus. Lindsley (1951) stated that an interesting aspect of sensory stimulation was that the effect on the alpha rhythm seemed to depend "more upon attention or conditions of anticipation, or upon suddenness and unexpectedness . . . than upon sensory stimulation per se [p. 496]."

This gradual decrement in orienting responses is *habituation*. Habituation is now a well-described phenomenon, on the synaptic level (Kandel, 1970) and on the behavioral level (Thompson & Spencer, 1966). On the "software" or cognitive level, Sokolov (1963) has offered the best-known model, which at least is useful for the extinction of the orienting reflex. Repeated presentations of a stimulus lead to a gradual buildup of a "template" for that particular stimulus or pattern of stimulation. The organism responds with an orienting response if, and only if, there is no such "template." This means that the orienting response type of activation occurs as a response to the unexpected, just as Lindsley (1951) stated in his original formulation.

The "template" or expectancy about the environment may be referred to as a *set value* and is compared constantly with the *actual value* of the sensory input. Within control theory terms, therefore, the orienting response type of activation (Activation$_{OR}$) occurs whenever there is a discrepancy between the set value for sensory input (set value$_{SI}$) and the actual value for sensory input (actual value$_{SI}$). Formally, this may be stated as

$$\text{Activation}_{OR} = f \text{ (set value}_{SI} - \text{actual value}_{SI}).$$

For exploratory behavior, the unexpected and unknown are, of course, the essence of the relevant stimulus situation (Berlyne, 1960). For the exploration type of activation, therefore, the same function is valid. The generality of the formulation helps to explain why activation is a relevant and useful concept in wide areas of psychology, for instance, studies on attitude changes in social psychology (Nuttin, 1975).

The same formulation may be used for other types of activation as well. Activation evoked by drive stimuli or physiological regulation mechanisms also occurs whenever there is a difference between the set value of a given variable and the actual value of that variable. This is easily seen for homeostatically controlled variables, for instance, osmotic pressure (OP):

$$\text{Activation}_{OP} = f \text{ (set value}_{OP} - \text{actual value}_{OP}).$$

When the set value for osmotic pressure differs from the actual value, activation occurs and persists until there is no such difference, or normal brain function is impaired by the imbalance in osmotic pressure. This principle may be generalized to all variables registered and controlled by the central nervous system. There are only two conditions: that the nervous system is able to register the variable and that there is a set value for that variable. It should be noted that there are two types of such set values. One type is the genetically predetermined and fixed set values, as for the homeostatically controlled physiological systems, referred to as *primary drive systems* in classical psychological literature. The other type is the set values that are under constant change, for instance, the templates for sensory input.

In this context, problem solving is to eliminate such differences. Activation will persist until the problem is solved. This is done either by changing the actual value of the problematic variable or by changing the set value for variables when this is an option.

The present unifactorial formulation cannot account for the activation level in one given moment, since the brain has more than one set point. It is beyond the scope of this presentation to develop a total mathematical model that takes this complexity into consideration. The problem is related to the interaction between anxiety, activation, and performance, which was treated under "Activation and Performance." It seems evident that there must be mechanisms that shift from one set point system to another, and the required gating or priority function is not well understood. The stimulus situation is of importance; Malmo (1966) found his relationship between deprivation and activation only in situations where relevant stimuli were present. Learning and expectancy are also involved. Cofer and Appley

(1968) suggested that anticipation was important for activation induced by, for instance, water deprivation. Levine, Goldman, and Coover (1972) have demonstrated that this is the case; expectancy and the predictability of reward determine the activation measured by the corticosterone level in the rat.

To the extent that this may be referred to as "theory," it does not differ essentially from drive reduction theory, except that it comprises orienting behavior and exploration and avoids too complicated distinctions between primary and secondary drives. These formulations are not original; for instance, Hunt (1963) held that "arousal" was a function of congruity and incongruity.

Similar formulations are found to an increasing degree in contemporary physiological psychology. This is due to a slowly growing influence from control theory. The essential formulation for self-controlling systems is that it is the error that is running the process or, again, the difference between the actual value and the set value. In the original formulations of the application of control theory for physiological problems, Wiener (1948) used muscle movements as an example: "Now, suppose that I pick up a lead pencil. To do this I have to move certain muscles. However, for all of us but a few expert anatomists, we do not know what these muscles are; . . . What we will is to pick the pencil up. Once we have determined on this, our motion proceeds in such a way that we may say roughly that the amount by which the pencil is not yet picked up is decreased at each stage [p. 14]."

### Anxiety and Fear, a Function of Uncertainty

The activation due to anxiety and fear may also be treated with this general activation formula. Extreme degrees of discrepancies between set values and actual values should lead to extreme degrees of activation, and such degrees of activation are generally only observed during strong emotions.

The set values that the Sokolov model and other cognitive models assume for sensory input are set values or expectancies for the relationships between the individual and the external world. If this expectancy is not met at all there is, by definition, a high degree of uncertainty. Uncertainty does not only elicit exploration, it is also the key stimulus to fear and anxiety (Cattell, 1966). Therefore, in men as well as in rats, uncertainty elicits activation as well as "fear" and exploration (Russel, 1973). Exploration will eliminate the fear through acquisition of information and thereby reduction of the discrepancy registered by the brain. There is, therefore, no paradox in the fact that novelty elicits both fear (anxiety) and exploration (Halliday, 1968). There seems to be an obvious relationship between these fundamental processes and the fact that at least some men approach a fear provoking situation like parachutist training (Berlyne, 1960).

The concept of uncertainty as the stimulus to anxiety is not new. Kierkegaard (1844) stated that anxiety was a consequence of freedom; when men were confronted with choices, anxiety was elicited. Anxiety, therefore, was the price for freedom and creativity. The more possibilities one had, the more anxiety. Within information theory, formulated 100 years later, this means that anxiety is a function of uncertainty. Uncertainty is defined by the number and probability of possible outcomes. Information is quantified by how much uncertainty is reduced or, in these terms, by how much anxiety is reduced.

According to Freud, fear is characterized by the presence of an object, or, in experimental nomenclature, fear is characterized by a clear and well-defined threat stimulus. Anxiety is characterized by the absence of any such clear stimulus. Therefore, there may be less uncertainty in a fear situation, and the distinction between fear and anxiety could be a question of intensity and possibilities to cope. Since there is a clear stimulus, it should at least sometimes be easier to cope with fear situations.

Fear, or "objective anxiety," does not involve uncertainty, at least when the stimulus situation has been well established. In experimental situations, there is usually an initial classical conditioning phase where the signal value of the stimuli is established. We have referred to this stage as "Factor 1" (Coover, Ursin, & Levine, 1973). Bolles (1972) referred to this phase as the establishment of "stimulus expectancy." This expectancy produces activation. This activation will only be reduced once there is reason to expect that the problem is solved. Coover et al. (1973) showed that, in rats, this occurred after prolonged training in active avoidance. The rats then showed a clear reduction in their corticosterone. We stressed the importance of the "expectancy to cope" concept. Bolles (1972) referred to the same stage as the development of "response expectancy." This expectancy reduces activation.

## Specific Arousal Systems

In early work, psychophysiologists postulated specific activation patterns for specific emotions, in particular, fear and anger (Ax, 1953; Schachter, 1957). This was never established. Activation is a necessary, but not sufficient, condition for a specific type of emotional experience (Lykken, 1968). Autonomic blockade interferes with avoidance learning and emotional experience, but it does not block or eliminate the emotional experience (see Lord, King, & Pfeister 1976). Cognitive aspects determine the interpretation of the experience of peripheral physiological changes ("attribution" of arousal; Rule & Nesdale, 1976; Schachter & Singer, 1962). There has been some concern to theorists about how we can experience emotions as qualitatively different if there is no specificity peripherally, and attribution determines the input interpretation anyway. The specificity of intracerebral emotional mechanisms remains a reasonable and sufficient explanation for the specificity, as in the Cannon–Bard formulations. The James–Lange principle is involved in the positive feedback loops of activation, and the continued experience of specificity may involve "attribution" mechanisms.

In psychophysiology, the remarkable lack of correlations between the various indexes of activation has been a matter of concern for a long time (Lacey, 1950). Initially, neuroanatomists may have been the first to point out the unreasonable assumption that the reticular formation of the brain stem could be so simple and homogenous as postulated in the early activation theory. Brodal (1957) has repeatedly pointed to the enormous complexity of the reticular formation and found it untenable from an anatomical point of view to accept the reticular formation as one "system." Hebb (1955) suggested that the activation system might consist of a number of subsystems with distinctive functions.

Our data point to several different types of activation mechanisms. The cortisol axis was related to defense mechanisms, the free fatty acids were related to performance, and testosterone was related to role identification. The catecholamines, in particular epinephrine, were also related to performance, and it may be that free fatty acid measurement simply is a better way of estimating adrenergic activity.

The degree of specificity is surprising and must be investigated further. It agrees with previous data, but these are scarce, and old data based on indirect estimates of endocrine activity are unreliable. Ideally, the data should be measured with multidimensional scaling and a more continuous monitoring of the hormones than we were able to perform. If there is such a specificity, it is more reasonable to expect to find this for hormone data than for the autonomic processes monitored classically, since these latter processes are under classical and instrumental control.

Some of the specificity we found may be due to differences in the time course in rise and fall of the plasma level of the hormones. It is, for instance, possible that the relationship between cortisol and defense, on the one hand, and good performance and free fatty acids–catecholamines, on the other, may simply be due to good performers not having any activation before the jump, and high defense individuals starting their worrying process long before the crucial act. The differences in time course depending on performance, and perhaps on experience, have been described by Fenz (1975). This may explain some, but not all, of the specificity we have seen. Again, this can only be solved by a more continuous monitoring of the hormone levels. This is the main difficulty with using hormones as indicators, and traditional psychophysiological measurements are superior in the ease with which they may be monitored continuously. However, they may also be monitored by the subject and, therefore, these functions are subject to individualization through conditioning processes. This is probably not the case with hormones like cortisol and testosterone.

## Phasic and Tonic Activation

Our data also demonstrated another and perhaps more important differentiation of the activation process. There were obviously two different mechanisms, one that was subject to the coping effect and one that was not.

Most of the physiological parameters we followed showed a very marked fall when training progressed. We attribute this fall to the effect of coping, in fact, it was our criterion for coping having taken place. This was seen for cortisol, testosterone, catecholamines, growth hormone, free fatty acids, and blood glucose. However, this was not the case for additional heart rate. At every jump, there was a very pronounced increment in heart rate. There was also an increase in the epinephrine level, compared with pre-jump levels, even though the level reached showed the general effect of coping.

We suggested that these two activation mechanisms should be referred to as "phasic" and "tonic" activation. Phasic activation is the short-lasting, fast-acting activation observed in heart rate. Tonic activation is the long-lasting and slow activation characteristic of cortisol. We have included all of the other plasma variables in this long-lasting slow group of variables. The terms have been used repeatedly in both neurophysiology and neuropsychology, but they have also provoked controversy. Herrick (1927), for instance, defined the direct transient effect on the spinal reflex arcs by the cerebral cortex through the pyramidal tract as "phasic" activity, in contrast to the continually acting plastic tonus from the extrapyramidal system.

In our material, "phasic" activation was not altered by the limited repeated experience. We cannot exclude, of course, that longer exposures and training effects would be without effect, but the system was at least more resistant to what we refer to as the "coping effect." The other physiological indicator involved in slower-rising, but longer-lasting, activation mechanisms was very sensitive to the effect of coping.

The existence of two types of activation with regard to the effects of experience and coping processes is essential for the understanding of the relationship between activation, health, and health risks. This is the topic of the last segment of this chapter.

**TABLE 16.1**
**Activation**

|              | Phasic             | Tonic                                      |
|--------------|--------------------|--------------------------------------------|
| Onset        | Rapid (seconds)    | Slow (1–15 min)                            |
| Duration     | Short              | Long                                       |
| Circulation  | Heart rate         | Blood pressure                             |
| Catecholamines | Epinephrine      | Norepinephrine                             |
| Other hormones | Testosterone rise? | Cortisol, testosterone fall, growth hormone |
| Blood changes |                   | Blood glucose, free fatty acids            |
| Effect of coping | Moderate, or none | Pronounced                              |

## COPING

Coping, by our definition, occurred when there was a response decrement in the physiological activation processes accompanying the response to threat. In the previous chapter, the conclusions were that activation could be explained within a rather general control theory formulation and that activation disappeared when set values and actual values coincided. Coping, then, must be related to the elimination of this difference. However, even though this formulation was very wide and could even be used for anxiety, problems remained, at least if we accept fear as being distinct from anxiety. Before this is clarified, it is necessary to specify the type of response decrement studied.

### Response Decrements, Classification, and Definitions

Several previous authors have described response decrements that we would interpret as coping, but a variety of terms have been used. Several terms used have acquired specific and conventional meanings in contemporary physiology and physiological psychology, and consistent use of this terminology should help in clarifying the issues. In the following, definitions will be given for response decrement phenomena, which hopefully are within general and accepted use.

*Adaptation.* This is perhaps the most complex term and is used to define many different responses. The term most often implies a Darwinian or teleological function: Responses are "adaptive," and we adapt to the environment. Since the present problem is to elucidate the processes that are involved in the interaction between individuals and environment, this use will be avoided since it represents only a pseudo-explanation. Adaptation in this text will not be used for any other phenomena than those strictly concerned with sensory organs. This is in accordance with common use in neurophysiology. The response decrement we observed was probably completely unrelated to sensory adaptation, and we will not use this term. Adaptation has been used in the literature relevant to our discussion, for instance, in reports on adaptation to urban stress (Glass & Singer, 1972). Speculations on the "adaptive value" and adaptation in a Darwinian sense will also be avoided.

*Fatigue.* This term will only be used for processes involving effector organs, in particular, the response decrements due to muscle fatigue. It should be quite evident that the response decrement we observed was unrelated to an inability of the endocrine organs or autonomically innervated processes to produce the full response more than once.

*Habituation.* The best understood response attenuation is habituation, which was dealt with in the preceding chapter. To accept a phenomenon as habituation, it is necessary to demonstrate that it is not *adaptation* or *fatigue*. Adaptation is excluded when, for instance, responses are reinstated by changing the pattern of the stimulus or by dishabituating stimuli. This also excludes response decrements due to fatigue.

In physiology and physiological psychology, this nomenclature is now widely accepted. Within this nomenclature the response decrement observed by, for instance, Frankenhaeuser, Sterky, and Järpe (1962) should no longer be referred to as "habituation." They found a response decrement in humans repeatedly exposed to gravitational stress, but there was a period of several days between each trial. The observed phenomenon was probably the effect that we refer to as coping.

*Extinction.* Extinction refers to response decrements due to response contingencies that decrease the probability of a conditioned response to a conditioned stimulus, in particular, when this response decrement is due to the absence of reinforcement. The response decrement we observed does not qualify for this definition. Boudewyns and Levis (1975) observed decreased autonomic reactivity to repeated exposures to anxiety-eliciting stimuli and referred to this as extinction (or habituation). Since this was evident in patients with high ego-strength only, it may be more related to coping.

*Defense.*    The relationship between activation and external stimuli is also influenced by the cognitive defense strategies available to humans. These strategies differ among individuals, and we observed that they did affect the response amplitudes observed in our men. However, the response decrement observed after repeated exposures cannot be accepted as being due to a change in the defense strategies as these are commonly defined. Quite to the contrary, such defense strategies are more to be conceptualized as personality traits, which are far more robust.

*Coping.*    The response decrement we observed was, in our interpretation, due to the gradual development of coping. Coping refers to the processes elicited when a certain stimulus is appraised as a threat (Lazarus & Averill, 1972), threat being defined as anticipation of harm. When the stimulus is appraised as threat, coping processes are elicited to reduce or eliminate the threat. The result of this can again be evaluated by cognitive processes; Lazarus refers to these as *"secondary appraisal."* Within his theoretical framework, our work is related to the development of secondary appraisal.

### Development of Coping with a Threat

Lazarus and Opton (1966) have discussed similar response decrements of "stress" responses induced by stressful motion pictures. When such presentations were repeated, there was a significant reduction in the response. Lazarus and Opton referred to this reduction as "adaptation." They concluded that the problem of "adaptation" to repeated film exposures remained an open research issue. As has been mentioned, "adaptation" is not the best term from a physiological point of view if the underlying process is to be analyzed. In addition, the question of "adaptation" has been raised for other stressors (population, density, noise), but there are no data on possible changes or decrements in the physiological response (see, for instance, Rule & Nesdale, 1976). The "adaptation" that occurs after an initial alarm period in urban stress (Glass & Singer, 1972) is also a phenomenon that must be given a different classification from a physiological point of view. From our definition, it is suggested that such response decrements are also evidence of coping.

### Our Data

According to the definitions given in the proceding paragraphs, the response decrement we observed was due to coping. The initial activation was due to fear, and this fear was gradually reduced. We refer to this process as coping, since the fear reduction was due to the men's actively facing and mastering the situation.

The men experienced fear, or some sort of excitement that they—and we—attributed to fear. In such situations, there are at least two sources of fear; fear of physical damage and fear of failure (Basowitz, Persky, Korchin, & Grinker, 1955). Our multivariate analyses have shown that there are also a host of other factors influencing the activation level reached: Among them, resources, role identification, strategies, and defense mechanisms are important.

The general activation "formula" is perhaps less interesting in this connection, since the complexity in the situation goes beyond such vague and general statements. However, it is possible to account for the observed phenomenon within the model offered. The key issue is the uncertainty involved, which in this case is well defined since we were dealing with a fear situation. The uncertainty has to do with whether the individual dares to jump and whether he will injure himself. His expectancy or set value is to go through with this training. The actual value is that it is still a very open question whether he will be able to do so.

After performing the first jump, the individual has demonstrated to himself that he is able to do it, and he quickly builds up confidence in his ability to master the challenge. Coping, then, is a reduction of a particular type of uncertainty, and the fear reduction is the extinction of the threats both from failure and from injury.

As training proceeds, the relationship between performance and achievement motivation becomes important for the variance of the residual activation (Chapter 15). Again, we obtained a set value/actual value constellation determining activation. For the coping decrement itself, the "fall" (see Chapter 14), no single personality trend was the main predictor; it was a multivariant phenomenon just as the initial rise.

It should be emphasized that performance itself was not the most important factor, but the subjective evaluation of the situation. The jumps were instrumental responses in the sense that they brought relevant feedback to the men: They managed the task and they survived. It did not matter whether the performance was perfect as judged from the performance criteria set by the external world. The important thing was each individual's self-evaluation. The fall in activation, therefore, occurred long before the performance was rated as good according to the standards of the school. If the individual acquired a basic trust in his skills and in his ability to master the situation, then he was coping, even though the school instructors might have been far from satisfied with how well he was stretching his arms and body. In other areas of life, there may be situations in which performance could be excellent, but a coping effect may not be evident until after a very long period of training.

## Why Do Men Cope?

The simplest answer to this question is that it is a silly question. In most situations, we do not have any choice. However, this is not quite so simple for men approaching parachutist training. There is no doubt that parachutist trainees obtain high scores on the Sensation-Seeking Scale (Zuckerman, Bone, Neary, Mangelsdorff, & Brustman, 1972). These men enjoy engaging in this type of activity and in other types of activities that also involve a certain degree of fear. After the first jump, the men reported strong feelings of relief and joy; they had mastered this task. From the subjective reports, it seemed quite clear that the fact that they had mastered such a challenge was strongly reinforcing.

When the jumps became routine, there was less excitement, but the men did not refer to these jumps as boring and still seemed to enjoy them. This is probably true for other potentially dangerous activities: Coping will be established gradually and activation will then be decreased. What, then, maintains this behavior?

The problem seems quite analogous to the problem concerning what maintains avoidance behavior. Two-factor theorists still debate whether the established avoidance is maintained by reduction of residual fear or by positively reinforcing events like "safety signals" (Gray, 1975).

From our data, it seems quite clear that there was a residual activation present, both in rats and in men. In men, activation is task and achievement oriented, as demonstrated in Chapter 15. In rats, Levine *et al.* (1972) have demonstrated that, under established food or water deprivation schedules, rats respond with a clear decrease in corticosterone when they receive food or water at the expected time. Positive reinforcement delivered at an expected moment leads to a very fast reduction in the internal state.

The "smile of joy" is innately activated by any relatively steep reduction in pain, fear, distress, or aggression, according to Izard and Tomkins (1966). However, it remains a puzzle that plain joy, humor, and funny movies also lead to activation, in the same way as unpleasantness and fear (Levi, 1972). It should be remembered that all positively reinforcing brain areas produce activation, and not deactivation, upon stimulation (Glickman & Schiff, 1967). It seems necessary to go one step beyond the simple reduction of fear to explain the strongly motivating effects of mastery.

White (1959) proposed a new drive, "effectance," which is the desire to have an effect on the environment. This leads to the motive of being competent, which is to be able to manipulate the environment to our advantage. Exploration and play, therefore, are motivated in their own right. Previously, Hendrick (1943) had postulated an "instinct" for mastery. Csikszentmihalyi (1975) refers to such activities as "autotelic," activities that maintain themselves. He has compared widely different human activities, such as chess games, rock climbing, surgery, and ballet-dancing. Characteristic of such activities is the strong engagement and high degree of concentration. Particularly in the reports from the rock climbers, it seems clear that the men stress the control aspect. Mastery may be another word for the same phenomenon.

We probably cannot get further at the present time. In the animal experiments, we have not achieved any specification of what "coping" really involves. We do not know whether control or expectancy is more important, even though there is a considerable literature demonstrating that control is an important variable (Frankenhaeuser & Riessler, 1970; Haggard, 1943). The problem is related to the helplessness concept (Mowrer & Viek, 1948; Seligman, 1975). Lack of control and of coping leads to psychosomatic complications (Weiss, 1972).

## PSYCHOSOMATICS

In the early 1960s, the question was whether endocrine responses were affected by psychological processes and, if so, to what extent this really played a role. In contemporary research the question is different; we are not convinced any longer that there is any physical change in the environment that acts on endocrine responses without primarily acting through psychological mechanisms (Mason, 1971). The bodily response to changes in the environment and to threatening stimuli is simply activation. Activation is the normal physiological response to environmental changes and a part of normal physiology necessary to cope with the environment.

There is, however, considerable concern about the possible relationship between this type of response and the development of somatic disorders. Alexander (1950) and Dunbar (1954) suggested that specific emotional factors were involved in several noninfectious degenerative diseases. Individuals suffering from certain emotional factors over a long period of time might develop symptoms of a particular psychosomatic disorder. Repressed rage was believed to lead to hypertension, repressed dependency to peptic ulcers, and repressed chronic anger to migraine headaches. This theory was based on Freud's early "hydraulic" hypothesis of hysteria, a hypothesis Freud himself later abandoned. Still, this theory was regarded as a promise of a breakthrough in psychosomatic research. Unfortunately, this promise was not fulfilled. There is no acceptable evidence of "discharge" of affects through internal organs (Oken, Grinker, Herz, Korchin, Sabshin, & Schwartz, 1962). It now seems clear that many so-called psychosomatic diseases do not have any specific emotional ethology. The specificity is somatic. Both in normal humans and in psychosomatic patients there is an individual response specificity in the autonomic nervous system (Grinker, 1966; Lacey, 1950). This specificity may be related to why a certain organ becomes affected by psychosomatic disease in a particular individual, but even that has not been shown.

It is a commonplace clinical experience that patients with problems in one organ system respond with symptoms and signs from that system during activation (or "stress"). For instance, Wolff (1968) found a clear hyper-reactivity in the affected organ in patients with cardiac problems, vascular headaches, and duodenal ulcers. The most parsimonious explanation is that this disposition is secondary to the organic changes, but there are, of course, obvious but complex interactions with psychological factors. There are many examples of differences in personality between groups of patients with established disease, but this does not prove in any way that there is any causal relationship.

Another important development was the suggestion of Wenger (1966) that a lack of "autonomic balance" was a factor in the development of psychosomatic disease, in particular high blood pressure and heart trouble. Wenger followed 1000 healthy aviation cadets over a 20-year period and found that cadets who had shown "sympathetic" dominance displayed higher incidence of heart trouble and high blood pressure 20 years later. Stoyva and Budzynsky (1974) speculated that frequent stress responses may lead to a loss of ability to shift from a sympathicus activation into "the parasympathetic mode in which bodily recuperation normally occurs." However, arousal is far from an isolated sympathetic event, as shown, for instance, by our data. The parasympathetic system is also involved (Gellhorn & Loofbourrow, 1962).

The establishment of the possibility of instrumental control of autonomically innervated processes (Birk, 1973) may have implications for psychosomatic processes. These have not been elucidated in detail. Most of the attention has been directed toward therapeutic applications of biofeedback (Stoyva & Budzynsky, 1974).

## Coping and Health

The most promising development in psychosomatic theory is the animal model of Weiss (1972), which also is clearly related to our findings. Our model can predict the internal state in coping subjects. Weiss's model is essentially a complementary model, illustrating what happens somatically in noncoping subjects. This model is very well developed from a psychological point of view, but less is known about the pathophysiological mechanisms. For obvious ethical reasons, the Weiss model is not easy to test in humans. Even so, the model is powerful, logical, consistent, and based on an impressive bulk of empirical data from animals.

In many situations in which individuals are unable to control or cope, somatic pathology (in particular, stomach ulcerations) develops. This is an extremely interesting model for psychosomatic disease. Weiss (1972) holds that ulceration is a function of the number of coping attempts the animal makes and the informational feedback it receives from making these attempts. Factors such as predictability and possibilities of avoiding and escaping determine the somatic consequences. The celebrated ulcers appearing in the "executive" monkeys of Brady (1958) may be explained by the same model. In this case, the yoked control managed very well, due to long safe periods, whereas the "executive" received no safety signals and was required to perform in a difficult and unsignaled avoidance task. Arterial hypertension may also be produced in squirrel monkeys on similar demanding tasks, where responses only delay electrical shocks (Herd, Morse, Kelleher, & Jones, 1969).

Ulcerations and hypertension may be provoked in rats and monkeys by emotional states to which there is no solution as well as no coping. These states probably provoke long-lasting demands on the hormonal system, which either breaks down according to a Selye principle or leads to pathological changes by other mechanisms, for instance, by producing changes in the blood vessels (Folkow, 1975). Chronic brain stimulation over months in hypothalamic areas, which increases the adrenocorticotropic hormone level, has been shown to produce pyloric and duodenal ulcers in monkeys (French, Porter, Cavanaugh, & Longmire, 1954). Chronic hypothalamic stimulation produces more severe atherosclerotic changes in rabbits kept on a cholesterol-rich diet (Gunn, Friedman, & Byers, 1960). However, there is no detailed evidence available on the endocrine and pathophysiological mechanisms that are involved.

## Activation—Good for You?

Even though activation is a normal physiological response, there has still been concern about the possibility that it might be pathogenic; this is particularly true when activation is referred to as stress. Perhaps the somatic changes do not have a purpose as suggested by Cannon (1932), who referred to these changes as the "wisdom" of the body. In particular, the "wisdom" of a full somatic response has been questioned when it happens during, for instance, an examination. An important and influential paper was written by Charvat, Dell, and Folkow in 1964 on this topic. The activation changes were assumed to be reasonable and profitable if the organism was to be engaged in fight or flight; even an increased coagulation tendency in the blood could be accepted as part of the "wisdom" if a dramatic fight was to ensue. However, if no muscular use follows and no physical harm is expected, Charvat et al. suggested that the whole process could be maladaptive. Since situations that produce these changes seldom relate to physical damage in civilized men, and seldom relate to muscle use, the defense response is in a way dissociated from the muscular response. Charvat et al. (1964) pointed out that the mobilization of the cardiovascular and metabolic resources, "intended to support a violent physical exertion, will not be utilized in the natural way [p. 130]." They therefore suggested that this dissociation between the defensive responses and the appropriate muscular activity could be harmful to the individual in the long run. No experimental evidence could support this notion at that time, but, in later work, Folkow and his associates (Folkow, 1975) showed that such mechanisms may play an important role in hypertension in genetically predisposed rats. Folkow's findings are compatible with the model we have outlined and constitute an important link in the understanding of why noncoping subjects may develop somatic disease. The phasic type of activation is still puzzling, since it is so resistant to coping (see Table 16.1). Is it possible that the short-lasting phasic effect, present even in coping individuals, may lead to pressor effects that might be damaging to the vascular bed? This cannot be excluded, at least in predisposed individuals. However, Folkow's experiments seem to suggest that this is not the case. Phasic arousal is mainly a withdrawal of vagal tone and an epinephrine release (see Chapters 7 and 9). Hypertension is more related to long-lasting activation and norepinephrine release, and these effects are very sensitive to coping. Therefore, it seems reasonable to shy away from the phylogenetic speculations and comfort people that the body may not be so stupid after all.

## Life Changes, Stress, and Disease

Rahe, Floistad, Bergan, Ringdal, Gerhardt, Gunderson, & Arthur, (1974) have shown that illness is related to "life changes" in large groups of Navy personnel and other groups. However, the correlation levels are generally low (Rabkin & Struening, 1976), and, as Hudgens (1974) has pointed out, most people do not become disabled even if "dreadful things" happen to them. Theorell (1976) found that, in 9097 building construction workers in Sweden, "life change" was only related to subsequent illness or pathological findings when life crises were associated with discord. Social stress caused complications in pregnant women only in the absence of a social support system (Nuckolls, Cassel, & Kaplan, 1972). Again, coping potential and coping mechanisms are decisive for the effects of "stressors" on health. The coping mechanisms involved in dramatic life events have been described in detail by Hamburg, Hamburg, and de Goza (1953).

## Disease, Prevention, and Health Propaganda

The effects on health of "stressors" or environmental factors do not depend on the external situation, but on how each individual experiences the situation. The objective dangers or the strain from a physical point of view are not what elevate the "stress" hormones; psychological variables like defense, expectancy, and trust in the coping abilities of each man determine the response. Therefore, it is not very meaningful to concentrate on the situation itself. This could also influence the experience and expectancies of outcome of such life situations, and this may lead to self-fulfilling prophecies. All evaluations of relationships between the external world and the challenges on health must take into consideration that the conclusions reached may affect the health situation of large populations once they are disseminated through modern mass media. If a population is led to believe that there is a particular relationship between a certain physical state and health, this may become true, not because it was true originally, but because the population was led to expect either health or disease from that particular variable. This is a new principle in health and health care, and much more attention must be paid to this variable. We should approach this problem area with the necessary understanding of the very potent psychological mechanisms that are involved. We believe that the bulk of the data point to the importance of being able to cope with the challenges of everyday life. The stress response is a healthy activation in healthy individuals, and we should not tell anyone that increased heart rate, sweating in the palms of the hands, and an inner feeling of tension and activation are indications of impending death. Such attributions of experiences of peripheral activation may have health consequences. If we convince people that completely normal responses such as increased heart rate and sweating in challenging situations are pathogenic factors, they may indeed become pathogenic. If these everyday experiences are interpreted as normal and healthy responses, they remain so.

If an individual tries to avoid all challenges and "stresses" of everyday life, he may decrease his ability to meet these unavoidable challenges. Challenge and stress may be necessary for fitness, both physically and mentally. The absence of challenge and stress may cause disease, just as overload may produce pathology. The only absolute absence of stress is death (Selye, 1974). The enormous capacity of coping is a remarkable asset for the human species. This does not mean that we should accept all types of environments. We have the right and the duty to define the environment and the life qualities we desire for ourselves and for our fellow men; but we should not found these goals on untenable speculations or unwarranted ideas about the relationship between the environment and our health. The health problem is tied to noncoping, and our attention should be directed to this real source of misery.

## REFERENCES

Alexander, F. Psychosomatic medicine. New York: W. W. Norton, 1950.

Andersen, P., & Andersson, S. A. Physiological basis of the alpha rhythm. New York: Appleton-Century-Crofts, 1968.

Ax, A. F. The physiological differentiation between fear and anger in humans. Psychosomatic Medicine, 1953, 15, 433–442.

Basowitz, H., Persky, H., Korchin, S. J., & Grinker, R. R. Anxiety and stress. An interdisciplinary study of a life situation. New York: McGraw-Hill, 1955.

Berger, H. Über das Elektrenkephalogramm des Menschen. II. Journal für Psychologie und Neurologie, 1930, 40, 160–179.

Berlyne, D. E. Conflict, arousal, and curiosity. New York: McGraw-Hill, 1960.

Birk, L. Biofeedback: Behavioral medicine. New York: Grune and Stratton, 1973.

Bolles, R. C. Reinforcement, expectancy and learning. Psychological Review, 1972, 79, 394–409.

Boudewyns, P. A., & Levis, D. J. Autonomic reactivity of high and low ego-strength subjects to repeated anxiety eliciting scenes. Journal of Abnormal Psychology, 1975, 84, 682–692.

Brady, J. V. Ulcers in "executive" monkeys. Scientific American, 1958, 199, 95–100.

Broadbent, D. E. Decision and stress. London: Academic Press, 1971.

Brodal, A. The reticular formation of the brain stem. Anatomical aspects and functional correlations. Edinburgh: Oliver and Boyd, 1957.

Cannon, J. The wisdom of the body. W. W. Norton: New York, 1932.

Cattell, R. B. Anxiety and motivation: Theory and crucial experiments. In C. D. Spielberger (Ed.), Anxiety and behavior. New York: Academic Press, 1966. Pg. 23–62.

Charvat, J., Dell, P., & Folkow, B. Mental factors and cardiovascular disorders. Cardiologia, 1964, 44, 124–141.

Cofer, C. N., & Appley, M. H. Motivation: Theory and research. New York: Wiley, 1968.

Coover, G. D., Ursin, H., & Levine, S. Plasma-corticosterone levels during active-avoidance learning in rats. Journal of Comparative and Physiological Psychology, 1973, 82, 170–174.

Csikszentmihalyi, M. Beyond boredom and anxiety. San Francisco: Jossey-Bass, 1975.

Duffy, E. Activation. In N. Greenfield & R. Sternback (Eds.), Handbook of psychophysiology. New York: Holt, Rinehart & Winston, 1972. Pp 577–622.

Dunbar, F. Emotions and bodily changes (4th ed.). New York: Columbia University Press, 1954.

Feldman, S. M., & Waller, H. J. Dissociation of electrocortical activation and behavioral arousal. Nature, 1962, 196, 1320–1322.

Fenz, W. D. Strategies for coping with stress. In I. G. Sarason & C. D. Spielberger (Eds.), Stress and anxiety. Vol. 2. New York: Hemisphere (Wiley), 1975.

Folkow, B. Central neurohormonal mechanisms in spontaneously hypertensive rats compared with human essential hypertension. Clinical Science and Molecular Medicine, 1975, 48, 205s–214s.

Frankenhaeuser, M., & Rissler, A. Effects of punishment on catecholamine release and efficiency of performance. *Psychopharmacologia,* 1970, *17,* 378–390.

Frankenhaeuser, M., Sterky, K., & Järpe, G. Psychophysiological relations in habituation to gravitational stress. *Perceptual and Motor Skills,* 1962, *15,* 63–72.

French, J. D., & Magoun, H. W. Effects of chronic lesions in central cephalic brain stem of monkeys. *Archives of Neurology and Psychiatry,* 1952, *68,* 591–604.

French, J. D., Porter, R. W., Cavanaugh, E. B., & Longmire, R. L. Experimental observations on "psychosomatic" mechanisms. I. Gastrointestinal disturbances. *Archives of Neurology and Psychiatry,* 1954, *72,* 267–281.

Gellhorn, E., & Loofbourrow, G. N. *Emotions and emotional disorders.* New York: Hoeber, 1962.

Glass, D. C., & Singer, J. R. *Urban stress.* New York: Academic Press, 1972.

Glickman, S. E., & Schiff, B. B. A biological theory of reinforcement. *Psychological Review,* 1967, *74,* 81–109.

Granit, R., & Kaada, B. R. Influence of stimulation of central nervous structures on muscle spindles in cat. *Acta Physiologica Scandinavica,* 1952, *27,* 130–160.

Gray, J. A. *Elements of a two-process theory of learning.* London: Academic Press, 1975.

Grinker, R. R., Sr. The psychosomatic aspects of anxiety. In C. D. Spielberger (Ed.), *Anxiety and Behavior,* New York: Academic Press, 1966. Pp. 129–142.

Gunn, C. G., Friedman, M., & Byers, S. O. Effect of chronic hypothalamic stimulation upon cholesterol-induced atherosclerosis in the rabbit. *Journal of Clinical Investigation,* 1960, *39,* 1963–1972.

Haggard, E. Some conditions determining adjustment during and readjustment following experimentally induced stress. In S. Tomkins (Ed.), *Contemporary psychopathology,* Cambridge, Mass.: Harvard University Press, 1943. Pp. 529–544.

Halliday, M. S. Exploratory behaviour. In L. Weiskrantz (Ed.), *Analysis of behavioural change.* New York: Harper and Row, 1968. Pp: 107–126.

Hamburg, D. A., Hamburg, B., & deGoza, S. Adaptive problems and mechanisms in severely burned patients. *Psychiatry,* 1953, *16,* 1–20.

Hamilton, V. Socialization anxiety and information processing: A capacity model of anxiety-induced performance deficits. In I.G. Sarason & C. D. Spielberger (Eds.), *Stress and anxiety.* Vol. 2. Washington D.C.: Hemisphere (Wiley), 1975. Pp. 45–68.

Hebb, D. O. Drives and the CNS (Conceptual nervous system). *Psychological Review,* 1955, *62,* 243–254.

Hendrick, I. The discussion of the "instinct to master." *Psychoanalytic Quarterly,* 1943, *12,* 561–565.

Herd, J. A., Morse, W. H., Kelleher, R. T., & Jones, L. G. Arterial hypertension in the squirrel monkey during behavioral experiments. *American Journal of Physiology,* 1969, *217,* 24–29.

Herrick, C. J. *An introduction to neurology* (4th ed.). Philadelphia: Saunders, 1927.

Hudgens, R. Personal catastrophe and depression. In B. S. Dohrenwend & B. P. Dohrenwend (Eds.), *Stressful life events.* New York: Wiley, 1974. Pp. 119–134.

Hunt, J. McV. Motivation inherent in information processing and action. In O. J. Harvey (Ed.), *Cognitive factors in motivation and social organization.* New York: Ronald Press, 1963. Pp. 35–94.

Izard, C. E., & Tomkins, S. S. Affect and behavior: Anxiety as a negative affect. In C. D. Spielberger (Ed.), *Anxiety and behavior.* New York: Academic Press, 1966.

Jasper, H. H. Studies of non-specific effects upon electrical responses in sensory systems. In G. Moruzzi, A. Fessard, & H. H. Jasper (Eds.), *Brain mechanisms. Progress in brain research.* Vol. 1. Amsterdam: Elsevier, 1963. Pp. 272–293.

Jouvet, M. The role of monoamines and acetylcholine-containing neurones in the regulation of the sleep-waking cycle. *Ergebnisse der Physiologie,* 1972, *64,* 166–307.

Kandel, E. R. Nerve cells and behavior. *Scientific American,* 1970, *223* (No. 1), 57–70.

Kierkegaard, S. *Om begrebet Angest.* Copenhagen: Reitzel, 1844. (English translation: *The concept of dread.* Princeton, N.J.: Princeton University Press, 1944.)

Lacey, J. I. Individual differences in somatic response patterns. *Journal of Comparative and Physiological Psychology,* 1950, *43,* 338–350.

Lawrence, G. H. Use of biofeedback for performance enhancement in stress environments. In I. G. Sarason & C. D. Spielberger (Eds.), *Stress and anxiety.* Vol. 3. Washington D.C.: Hemisphere (Wiley), 1976. Pp. 73–83.

Lazarus, R. S., & Averill, J. R. Emotion and cognition: With special reference to anxiety. In C. D. Spielberger (Ed.), *Anxiety: Current trends in theory and research.* Vol. 2. New York: Academic Press, 1972.

Lazarus, R.S., & Opton, E. M., Jr. The study of psychological stress: A summary of theoretical formulations and experimental findings. In C. D. Spielberger (Ed.), *Anxiety and behavior.* New York: Academic Press, 1966.

Levi, L. *Stress and distress in response to psychosocial stimuli.* Stockholm: Almquist & Wiksell, 1972.

Levine, S., Goldman, L., & Coover, G. D. Expectancy and the pituitary-adrenal system. In *Ciba Foundation Symposium: Physiology, emotion and psychosomatic illness.* Amsterdam: Elsevier, 1972, Pp. 281–291.

Lindsley, D. B. Emotion. In S. Stevens (Ed.), *Handbook of experimental psychology,* New York: Wiley, 1951.

Lindsley, D. B., Bowden, J., & Magoun, H. W. Effect upon the EEG of acute injury to the brain stem activation system. *Electroencephalography and Clinical Neurophysiology,* 1949, *1,* 475–486.

Lord, B. J., King, M. G., & Pfeister, H. P. Chemical sympathectomy and two-way escape and avoidance learning in the rat. *Journal of Comparative and Physiological Psychology,* 1976, *90,* 303–316.

Lykken, D. T. Neuropsychology and psychophysiology in personality research. In E.F. Borgatta & W. W. Lambert (Eds.), *Handbook of personality theory and research.* Chicago: Rand McNally, 1968.

Magoun, H. W. *The waking brain.* Springfield, Ill.: C.C. Thomas, 1958.

Malmo, R. B. Studies of anxiety: Some clinical origins of the activation concept. In C. D. Spielberger (Ed.), *Anxiety and Behavior.* New York: Academic Press, 1966. Pp. 157–177.

Mason, J. W. A re-evaluation of the concept of "non-specificity" in stress theory. *Journal of Psychiatric Research,* 1971, *8,* 323–335.

Mirsky, A. F. Neuropsychological bases of schizofrenia. *Annual Review of Psychology,* 1969, *20,* 321–348.

Moruzzi, G., & Magoun, H. W. Brain stem reticular formation and activation of the EEG. *Electroencephalography and Clinical Neurophysiology,* 1949, *1,* 455–473.

Mowrer, O. H., & Viek, P. An experimental analogue of fear from a sense of helplessness. *Journal of Abnormal Social Psychology,* 1948, *43,* 193–200.

Nuckolls, K. B., Cassel, J., & Kaplan, B. H. Psychosocial assets, life crisis and the prognosis of pregnancy. *American Journal of Epidemiology,* 1972, *95,* 431–441.

Nuttin, J.M., Jr. *The illusion of attitude change.* London: Academic Press, 1975.

Oken, D., Grinker, R. R., Heath, H. A., Herz, M., Korchin, S. J., Sabshin, M., & Schwartz, N. B. Relation of physiological response to affect expression. *Archives of General Psychiatry,* 1962, *6,* 336–351.

Rabkin, J. G., & Struening, E. L. Life events, stress, and illness. *Science,* 1976, *194,* 1013–1020.

Rahe, R. H., Flöistad, I., Bergan, T., Ringdal, R., Gerhardt, R., Gunderson, E. K. E., & Arthur, R. J. A model for life changes and illness research. Cross-cultural data from the Norwegian navy. *Archives of General Psychiatry*, 1974, 31, 172–177.

Rule, B. G., & Nesdale, A. R. Environmental stressors, emotional arousal and aggression. In I. G. Sarason & C. D. Spielberger (Eds.), *Stress and anxiety*. Vol. 3. Washington D.C.: Hemisphere (Wiley), 1976. Pp. 87–103.

Russel, P. A. Relationships between exploratory behavior and fear: A review. *British Journal of Psychology*, 1973, 64, 417–433.

Satterfield, J., Cantwell, D., & Satterfield, B. Pathophysiology of the hyperactive child syndrome. *Archives of General Psychiatry*, 1974, 31, 839–844.

Schachter, J. Pain, fear and anger in hypertensives and normotensives. A psychophysiological study. *Psychosomatic Medicine*, 1957, 19, 17–29.

Schachter, S., & Singer, J. E. Cognitive, social and physiological determinants of emotional state. *Psychological Review*, 1962, 69, 379–399.

Segundo, J. P., Arana-Iniquez, R., & French, J. D. Behavioral arousal by stimulation of the brain in the monkey. *Journal of Neurosurgery*, 1955, 12, 601–613.

Seligman, M. E. P. *Helplessness. On depression, development, and death*. San Francisco: W.H. Freeman, 1975.

Selye, H. *Stress without distress*. Philadelphia: Lippincott, 1974.

Sokolov, Y. N. *Perception and the conditioned reflex*. Oxford: Pergamon, 1963.

Spence, J. T., & Spence, K. W. The motivational components of manifest anxiety: Drive and drive stimuli. In C. D. Spielberger (Ed.), *Anxiety and behavior*. New York: Academic Press, 1966. Pp. 291–326.

Spielberger, C. D. The effects of anxiety on complex learning and academic achievement. In C. D. Spielberger (Ed.), *Anxiety and behavior*. New York: Academic Press, 1966. Pp. 361–398.

Sprague, J. M., Chambers, W. W., & Stellar, E. Attentive, affective and adaptive behavior in the cat. *Science*, 1961, 133, 165–173. ·

Sprague, J. M., Schreiner, L. H., Lindsley, D. B., & Magoun, H. W. Reticulo-spinal influences on stretch reflexes. *Journal of Neurophysiology*, 1948, 11, 501–508.

Sterman, M. B., & Clemente, C. D. Forebrain mechanisms for the onset of sleep. In O. Petre-Quadens & J. D. Schlag (Eds.), *Basic sleep mechanisms*. New York: Academic Press, 1974. Pp. 83–93.

Stoyva, J., & Budzynski, T. Cultivated low arousal—an antistress response? In L. V. DiCara (Ed.), *Limbic and autonomic nervous systems research*. New York: Plenum, 1974. Pp. 369–384.

Theorell, T. Selected illnesses and somatic factors in relation to two psychosocial stress indices—a prospective study on middle-aged construction building workers. *Journal of Psychosomatic Research*, 1976, 20, 7–20.

Thompson, R. F., & Spencer, W. A. Habituation: A model phenomenon for the study of neuronal substrates of behavior. *Psychological Review*, 1966, 73, 16–43.

Ursin, H., Wester, K., & Ursin, R. Habituation to electrical stimulation of the brain in unanesthetized cats. *Electroencephalography and Clinical Neurophysiology*, 1967, 23, 41–49.

Weiss, J. M. Influence of psychological variables on stress-induced pathology. In *Ciba Foundation Symposium: Physiology, emotion and psychosomatic illness*. Amsterdam: Elsevier, 1972.

Wenger, M. A. Studies of autonomic balance: A summary. *Psychophysiology*, 1966, 2, 173–179.

White, R. W. Motivation reconsidered: The concept of competence. *Psychological Review*, 1959, 66, 297–333.

Wiener, N. *Cybernetics*. New York: Wiley, 1948.

Wolff, H. G. In S. Wolf & H. Goodell (Eds.), *Stress and disease* (2nd ed.). Springfield, Ill.: C.C. Thomas, 1968.

Woodworth, R. S., & Schlosberg, H. *Experimental psychology.* London: Methuen, 1954.

Zuckerman, M., Bone, R. N., Neary, R., Mangelsdorff, D., & Brustman, B. Personality trait and experience correlates of the sensation-seeking scales. *Journal of Consulting and Clinical Psychology,* 1972, *39,* 308–321.

# Index

A
B
C  8
D  9
E  0
F  1
G  2
H  3
I  4
J  5